My first encounter with Jack M[...]
him with my best friend, Tremper Longman III, after convocation
as first-year seminary students. He was surrounded by a gaggle of
enraptured students. I grabbed Tremper and told him we had to flee
because I knew Jack was dangerous and crazy. After four decades,
Jack still troubles and terrifies me as he invites me to live with the
wild, bold love of Jesus. Michael Graham brilliantly unfolds the
beauty and brokenness of Jack's life with tenderness and scholarly
care. I know Jack far better now, but far more importantly, I know
the Jesus whom Jack followed with even greater joy. If you didn't
know Jack Miller, you are about to meet one of the most amazing
people of the twentieth century.

—**Dan B. Allender**, Professor of Counseling Psychology and
   Founding President, The Seattle School of Theology and
   Psychology

Cheer Up! is honest, comprehensive, and wonderful! Jack Miller was
my friend, and I loved him. My life was changed by knowing Jack—
not because of Jack but because he understood the essence of the
Christian faith and always pointed me to Jesus. I rise up and call
Michael Graham blessed for writing this book, as I do Jack Miller
about whom Michael writes. But I mostly rise up and am overwhelmed by the great Savior whom both of them love. And you will
rise up and call *me* blessed for having commended this book to you.
Read it, be "cheered up," and give it to everyone you know!

—**Steve Brown**, Broadcaster, Teacher, Preacher, Author

Michael Graham has engaged in an epic journey of research into
the historical events and personal experiences of Jack Miller to capture an era of the church, the spirit of the man himself, and the
grace of God that made this jar of clay such a vessel of influence for
the advancement of the glories of the gospel.

—**Bryan Chapell**, Senior Pastor, Grace Presbyterian Church,
   Peoria, Illinois

My wife and I were deeply impacted in a life-changing way by Jack Miller during a Sonship week in 1995. Our strong commitment to the doctrines of grace became a deep experience of the gospel of grace that transformed our marriage and ministry. I personally experienced that transforming grace again in a fresh way as I read *Cheer Up!* Michael Graham has written a profound biography that brings to life the power of the Spirit in the life of a sinner saved by grace who never stopped preaching the gospel to himself. Graham weaves the tapestry of Jack's life together in a way that illuminates the Reformed theological landscape over forty-five years while also showing Miller's significant impact on many leaders and institutions, including the seminary where I have served in various positions for over twenty years. I highly recommend *Cheer Up!* It elaborates Jack's commitment to the inseparable connection of renewal and discipleship with missions and evangelism in a way that makes *Cheer Up!* a valuable resource for personal growth and ministry renewal.

—**Mark Dalbey**, President, Associate Professor of Applied
  Theology, Covenant Theological Seminary

Jack's godly personal love will never be forgotten, but he is also important historically. John Calvin taught us to know God and ourselves, with each knowledge complementing the other. What good is truth without personal application—and the other way around, too? When in the Lutheran world preaching became abstract and impersonal, the Pietists came along. They told us that preachers should spend more time in preparing their sermon applications and that prayer and counsel in small groups were just as important as going to church. Pietism could become "radical," though, and minimize the Word. Regrettably, that's all that many history books remember about it.

Westminster Theological Seminary was founded in a reaction against liberalism in the Presbyterian Church, at a time when religious social interests were crowding out careful attention to the Word. So maintaining God's truth was highest on the seminary's agenda. Its practical theology professor was inaugurated by being told, "Be sure to remember that practical theology is practical theology." Understandably, personal application had become suspect. But Jack had learned the hard way the necessity of grasping the personal love of Jesus—otherwise, how could vital ministry ever be done? He learned that in Europe and in harder places for the gospel than at home. With Jack at our side, we're blessed by being back with Calvin, knowing ourselves and how much we need our Jesus. Westminster's focus on truth will always be foundational, but we grew and grew personally in our faith as Jack helped us to see Jesus in our hearts. Praise the Lord!

—**D. Clair Davis**, Professor Emeritus of Church History, Westminster Theological Seminary

Jack Miller was one of the most unusual personalities I have ever met. He took me into his church as an intern, he and Rose Marie brought me into their living room to discuss life-changing ideas with fellow students, he performed our wedding—in short, he was a tremendous mentor. This biography tells his story, "warts and all," and it is my hope that it will remind God's people of the leaders he has provided for us and our need to emulate them, without either lionizing them or belittling their contributions.

—**William Edgar**, Professor of Apologetics, Westminster Theological Seminary

The writings of Jack Miller have had a profound impact on both my personal spiritual walk and my ministry as a pastor. He's shaped me as a father. Going far beyond strategies for church growth and effective preaching, Jack Miller got at the heart of our calling as believers—to walk as beloved sons and daughters of the King. This book tells the story of Jack's life and ministry, and it's a wonderful read for anyone desiring to dwell in the secret place of the Most High.

—**J.D. Greear**, Pastor, The Summit Church, Durham, North Carolina; 62nd President, Southern Baptist Convention

Michael Graham's *Cheer Up! The Life and Ministry of Jack Miller* is a vivid and accurate portrait of a professor / pastor / evangelist / repentant sinner whose heart was captivated by God's grace in Christ and by the powerful presence of his Spirit. I think of Jack as the humblest, boldest follower of Jesus whom I have ever met. His transparency about himself, and his utter confidence in Jesus, challenged cautious, self-protective Christians (including seminary students like me) to risk admitting (instead of hiding) our weaknesses and to actually "live by faith" in God. I'm glad that, through Pastor Graham's research—especially his interviews with those close to Jack—many others can now meet this extraordinary, controversial trophy and ambassador of divine grace.

—**Dennis E. Johnson**, Professor Emeritus of Practical Theology, Westminster Seminary California

Jack Miller . . . taught me how to preach grace. Whatever the subject and whatever the text, people were being changed by being brought into connection with the work of Jesus Christ on their behalf. He taught me to preach grace no matter what the text. . . . There would never have been a Redeemer Church in New York City without the impact of Jack and Rose Marie Miller on our lives and hearts.

—**Timothy Keller**, Founding Pastor, Redeemer Presbyterian Church, Manhattan; Chairman and Cofounder, Redeemer City to City

From fellow missionaries, whom he deeply influenced, I came to appreciate and admire Jack Miller. Hurray—thanks to Michael Graham's book *Cheer Up!* those of us who didn't know him personally can now get to know him and how God used him. Thank God for enabling Michael Graham to enable us to more deeply know, appreciate, and be strengthened by the Millers and the lives of the Lord's servants whom Jack discipled. Finally we get to know more of the depth of this man I haven't yet met but am looking forward to meeting in our Father's house—and even more so, after taking in Jack's story!

—**Greg Livingstone**, Founder, Frontiers

Spurgeon called tears wept in intercession "liquid prayers." As I read *Cheer Up!* I believe I prayed quite a few "liquid prayers." Michael, with compelling literary force you have portrayed the incisive mind, the expansive insight, the ferocious faith, the relentless repentance, the adoring delight in Jesus, the consuming love for Scripture, and the tireless gospel proclamation that marked Jack Miller. I wept in repentance as I watched over Jack's shoulder once again. You helped me to follow his ministry of dependence on the Holy Spirit for grace, and the holy fear I felt when I was his student came rushing back. His winsome life of love and service, when I sat under his preaching and teaching, unmasked my spiritual mediocrity. Your account of his life unmasked me once again.

Servants of Jesus who welcome truly being made like their Master tend to fascinate the less faithful follower of Jesus with their words and their way—a compelling fascination that is fused to a piercing and convicting godly fear. For both the Savior and one's own sin simply must be faced in the presence of one like Dr. Miller. Such was the case when I was attending New Life Church, and such was the case as I began and finished this book.

I am so thankful to have read this book. Reading it hurt like heaven! Which, to my foolish perception, could seem worse than hell—because heaven wants me to change and hell hopes I never do. The earnest, Christ-centered mirth of the new heaven and the new earth marked the man C. John Miller. It marks this book as well. Thank you. Thank you. Thank you!

—**Joe Novenson**, Pastor of Senior Adults, Lookout Mountain Presbyterian Church, Lookout Mountain, Tennessee

God used Jack Miller to change so many people's lives, including mine. Michael Graham has done an excellent job of capturing what made Jack so special to so many people: Jack believed himself to be someone who was in desperate need of the good news of the gospel and also believed that God was delighted to shower grace on desperate sinners. This emphasis on God's love for broken people spilled over into the way Jack loved others, including those who were still far from knowing Christ. Ultimately, it became the driving force for founding Serge—knowing Christ in order to make Christ known. More than anything else, this dynamic of God's grace renewing our hearts and sending us out to live missionally in a broken world has been Jack's legacy at Serge. It is still the heartbeat of our organization to this day. I'm thankful that Michael has made this story available to a wider audience.

—**Bob Osborne**, Executive Director, Serge (formerly World Harvest Mission)

When people see my wheelchair and ask about my smile, or when they wonder how I'm able to couple a strict orthodoxy with an infectious joy in Jesus, I often parrot a principle I learned years ago from Jack Miller, who said, "Cheer up! The spirit of Jesus is at work in your weakness." Jack helped me to see that you could be a stalwart Calvinist and, at the same time, praise the Lord like a happy Pentecostal . . . even in the middle of pain and quadriplegia. Sound like a strange mix? In this remarkable book by Michael Graham, you'll see how joyful zeal and sturdy doctrine should always reside together. I give this wonderful work on the life and teachings of Jack Miller a double thumbs-up!

—**Joni Eareckson Tada**, Founder, Joni and Friends International Disability Center

An important chronicle of a twentieth-century Christian leader whose spiritual influence far exceeds his name recognition. Michael Graham has given us a solid overview of Jack Miller's personal story and institutional impact.

—**Trevin Wax**, Senior Vice President for Theology and Communications, LifeWay Christian Resources; Visiting Professor, Wheaton College; Author, *Rethink Your Self*, *This Is Our Time*, and *Gospel-Centered Teaching*

CHEER UP!

THE LIFE AND MINISTRY OF
JACK MILLER

MICHAEL A. GRAHAM

P&R
PUBLISHING
P.O. BOX 817 • PHILLIPSBURG • NEW JERSEY 08865-0817

Citations in the book are for published material only. Uncited quotations are taken from unpublished writings and audio recordings, as well as extensive in-person and email interviews by the author. A full bibliography is available on the Jack Miller Project website (www.the jackmillerproject.com), and access to archival material may be requested through the website.

Adapted from Michael A. Graham, "Cheer Up! A Biographical Study of the Life and Ministry of C. John 'Jack' Miller: A Twentieth Century Pioneer of Grace" (PhD diss., The Southeastern Baptist Theological Seminary, 2019).

Printed in the United States of America

Library of Congress Cataloging-in-Publication Data

Names: Graham, Michael A. (Pastor), author.
Title: Cheer up! : the life and ministry of Jack Miller / Michael A.
  Graham.
Description: Phillipsburg, New Jersey : P&R Publishing, 2020. | Includes
  bibliographical references. | Summary: "Drawing on extensive interviews
  with Jack's friends, family, and acquaintances, biographer Michael
  Graham shows how Jack Miller helped to revitalize the contemporary
  church's joy in God's omnipotent grace"-- Provided by publisher.
Identifiers: LCCN 2020032028 | ISBN 9781629957210 (paperback) | ISBN
  9781629957227 (epub) | ISBN 9781629957234 (mobi)
Subjects: LCSH: Miller, C. John. | Presbyterian Church--Clergy--Biography.
Classification: LCC BX9225.M456 G73 2020 | DDC 285/.1092 [B]--dc23
LC record available at https://lccn.loc.gov/2020032028

To my wife,
Victoria T. Graham,
and my four children,
Mary Helen, Michael, Molly, and James.
You have accompanied me on this gospel journey of sonship
that began in 1991.

And to Rose Marie Miller
and the Miller family
for freely sharing the story of your husband and father with me.

CONTENTS

FOREWORD

WE WERE A storytelling family; because, I think, of my dad's pioneer background, our lives were filled with stories of wagon trains, hunting (or being hunted by) mountain lions, and shipwrecks. I was surprised to learn in first grade that not everyone knew about the fearsome one-eyed Cyclops that the Greek warrior Odysseus battled. Dinnertime was story time, and Dad was the lead storyteller. We'd listen intently to Dad, but when he'd take a bite to eat, we'd all rush into the conversation. When Dad finished chewing, he'd say, "You're interrupting me"; we'd fall silent, and the story would begin again.

Dad was an astute observer of the times. On our annual camping vacation in the redwoods, we stopped at Haight-Ashbury in San Francisco in 1966, the year before the famous Summer of Love. This was the year that hippies there were living their vision of love and peace. We spent an afternoon chatting with hippies and just looking. As we crossed the Golden Gate Bridge while traveling north on the coastal highway, Dad said, "From what I know of the human heart, there will be a murder in their community within six months." By the time we got to Eureka, in northern California, there had been a murder among the hippies.

But Dad didn't just critique hippies; he loved them. Partially because of the influence of what he'd seen at L'Abri in Switzerland with Francis Schaefer, he opened up his heart and our home to numerous burned-out hippies and broken people in the early '70s. My future wife Jill was one of them. Jill had grown up in the church, but her heart had become distant, so she'd withdrawn. She didn't want to have anything to do with preachers. She'd become friends with my sister Barbara, who was going through her own rebellion.

When Jill expressed concern to Barb about struggles that her boyfriend was having, Barb suggested that our dad might be able to help him. Jill agreed, but she wasn't about to go into this preacher's house, so she dropped her boyfriend off—and, as she did so, she warned him, "He loves to talk." Waiting outside in her Mustang, Jill grew increasingly impatient. This preacher was taking forever. After an hour, Jill stormed out of the car, ready to extract her boyfriend. When she knocked on the door, Dad greeted her warmly and invited her in. When she was seated, Dad turned to her and asked her, "How are you doing?" Jill burst into tears and said, "I'm not good." In that moment, Jill became a believer. It was that simple.

What happened with Jill came at a time—the early '70s—when the Spirit was breathing new life into the church. While Dad had been on a sabbatical in Spain earlier that same year (1970), God had breathed new life into him as he read Geerhardus Vos's book *The Pauline Eschatology*. Dad came to a new and profound awareness that we live in the age of the Spirit. A constant theme of Dad's preaching that fall was that, since the Spirit has been poured out on us, we can be daring just like the first church in Acts. The Spirit makes dry bones come alive (see Ezek. 37) and pours out rivers of living water (see John 7:37–39). Dad saw vividly that the Spirit makes Christ continually present in our hearts and lives.

I remember sitting in the pew of Mechanicsville Chapel that fall, listening to Dad preach and thinking, *You can't be that excited about Jesus and not have God do something big.* And sure enough, that's what happened. Because of Dad's newfound confidence in the Spirit, he began to take prayer more seriously. Studying the books of Luke and Acts helped him to see the deep connection between prayer and the Spirit's work. For most of the 1980s, Dad hosted a weekly four-hour prayer meeting in his living room in Jenkintown, Pennsylvania. This change in him was as profound as his conversion from atheism had been.

A whole kaleidoscope of new habits and ways of loving people emerged from that time. Jill became just one of countless broken people who were living in our home or just "hanging out." Our home, and later New Life Church, became multicultural—not because Dad set out to make them that way, but simply because he was multi-love. There was Larry, whose mind was burned out by drugs; Babs, who struggled with physical and mental disability; Charlie, who battled alcohol and drug addiction; and Lois, who hung out with a biker gang. What was Dad's secret to connecting with people? Jill reflected, "He enjoyed me for who I was."

Dad had always been bold, but now he became even bolder. He was instrumental in the conversion of my sister Barb (see chapter 5), her future husband Angelo Juliani (see chapter 5), and his other future son-in-law, Bob Heppe (see chapter 3). Remarkably, he led three of his children's spouses to faith. He didn't just "witness" to them; he loved all three into the kingdom.

Interestingly enough, even though Dad's gift was evangelism, his greatest gift was preaching the gospel to those who were already inside the church. He read Romans through the lens of Luke, which made the gospel come alive. Dad was the tax collector in the temple crying out, "Be merciful to me, a sinner"; he was the blind beggar by the side of the road yelling for Jesus. In his preaching, Dad invited the rest of us to join him. So that simple idea, that the gospel is for beggars and that the entrance to the kingdom is down low, permeated his life and preaching. It is behind the single critique he had of his beloved Reformed heritage: "We have created this wonderful castle of grace, but someone forgot to put in a door."

I agree with Michael Graham that my dad is the unsung pioneer behind the "gospel movement" that has been so influential in the Reformed (and wider) church since 1990. Much of his own influence on that movement was indirect and came through people he had inspired, such as the author Jerry Bridges and the pastor and author Tim Keller, but much of it was direct and came through his Sonship course. And while those who are familiar with the Shepherd controversy at Westminster Seminary may be tempted to think that it was a side note in Dad's life, it was actually quite pivotal; because by the early 1980s it had refocused Dad on the doctrine of justification by faith. Rediscovering the present application of justification by faith became the principle cornerstone of the Sonship course.

My father was a great man. He gifted me with his love of the gospel, the church, and the Word, but his singular gift of the reminder that the gospel is for sinners, "of whom I am chief," was his legacy to many of us. I miss him.

We are all indebted to Michael Graham for this labor of love, and for the enormous amount of research he put into this study of Jack, which will bless the church for years to come.

Paul E. Miller

A WORD FROM DANIEL L. AKIN

I HAD NEVER heard of C. John "Jack" Miller until just a few years ago. That was my great loss. To be fair, that lack of knowledge was understandable. Jack was a Presbyterian whose ministry base was in Philadelphia. I am a Southern Baptist who has ministered mostly in the south and southwest. But, in God's gracious providence, our Lord led Michael Graham to come to Southeastern Baptist Theological Seminary in order to pursue his PhD. God's providential hand continued to work when Michael enrolled in a seminar that I was teaching. It was there that I first heard of Jack Miller and saw Michael's love, admiration, and respect for this incredible man. I became intrigued about the possibility of Michael's writing a biographical dissertation on Jack, and he immediately "lit up" at the prospect. The seed was thus planted, and the fruit of that dream you now hold in your hand.

Jack Miller was a remarkable man in so many ways. I deeply regret that I never had the privilege of meeting him. He was a scholar, pastor, preacher, mentor, theologian, evangelist, missionary, and visionary. As you read through this scintillating work, you will be amazed at all that the Lord Jesus accomplished in Jack's life. You will marvel at the lives he touched and the ministries that originated and took inspiration from his influence. Jack was not a perfect man—as this biography makes clear. Of course, none of us is perfect save our King Jesus. However, Jack was a man of God who had been overwhelmed by the Lord's grace and goodness. It was out of this reservoir that he so faithfully and passionately served our Savior until his translation into his presence. My small part in this project was a labor of love. I am so delighted to see its publication. God will be honored. Jesus will be pleased. And, if he is aware of all this, I suspect a humble smile will probably crease the face of Jack Miller, a twentieth-century pioneer of grace.

Read. Enjoy! Cheer up!!! We have a greater and more wonderful Savior than any of us could ever imagine.

Daniel L. Akin

INTRODUCTION

CHEER UP! WHAT HAS HAPPENED TO ALL YOUR JOY?

WHEN DRIVING NORTH from San Francisco to Gold Beach, one clings to the coastal highway as it sharply twists and turns along the shore of the Pacific Ocean. As the motorist veers inland, the scenery changes dramatically. The highway ascends over the Siskiyou Pass and through the mighty redwoods onto southern Oregon's historic Highway 101 before meandering back to the coast. Beautiful views of Haystack Rock, the shoreline, and the rugged sea cliffs compensate for the slow, arduous drive to the small pioneer settlement where C. John "Jack" Miller was born.

Jack's own travels from Gold Beach to San Francisco along these perilous and panoramic coastal highways illustrate the brokenness and the beauty of this young man's journey to faith in Christ and what the sovereign Lord would do through his life and ministry afterward. In every generation, the triune God has been pleased to work through leaders like Jack Miller, who, having discovered the gospel themselves, become God's means of helping others to rediscover the glory of his omnipotent grace. Jack did not *pioneer* grace in the sense of discovering it for the first time in history, but through his teaching and preaching ministry, his writings, and his evangelistic and missionary work, he brought the joy of God's omnipotent grace to the most influential leaders in the church today—Timothy Keller, Jerry Bridges, John Piper, Joni

Eareckson Tada, Dan Allender, and Larry Crabb, among others. In this way, he was truly a pioneer of grace.

Timothy Keller said, "Jack Miller . . . taught me how to preach grace. Whatever the subject and whatever the text, people were being changed by being brought into connection with the work of Jesus Christ on their behalf. He taught me how to preach grace no matter what the text." Likewise, in his book *Him We Proclaim*, Dennis E. Johnson cited Jack Miller and Timothy Keller as prime examples from "contemporary post-Christian and postmodern culture" of preaching that is "Christ centered" and has the effect on the unchurched of "shattering their stereotypes of Christianity and bringing them face to face with Christ."[1]

Cheer Up!

Over the course of his life, teaching, and ministry, Jack challenged Christians to address a key question found in Galatians: "What has happened to all your joy?" (Gal. 4:15 NIV). He explained this question by saying that "I relate to it because many times I have lost my joy. . . . I have forgotten the power of grace, the joy of sonship." In that spirit of gospel joy, Jack memorably declared, "Cheer up! You are far worse than you think" and "Cheer up! God's grace is greater than you've ever dared hope"—connecting pervasive depravity to irresistible grace.[2] "The best news you ever heard," he said, " is that original sin is true. If original sin (the curse) is true, then the grace is true. The love of God is shallow unless there is depth to which it reaches."

Several other "cheer up" statements are equally important to an understanding of Jack Miller: "Cheer up! God's Spirit works in your weakness," "Cheer up! God's Kingdom is more wonderful than you have ever imagined," and "Cheer up! Come on, let's die together! It's a great way to come to life." Together, these statements are a fitting way to understand the whole of Jack's life, teaching, and ministry.

This book fittingly begins with grace. Chapter 1, "Cheer Up! God's Grace Is Greater Than You Ever Dared Hope," introduces readers to Jack Miller's early life through 1949. During this time, Jack discovered that "faith alone" means "faith all the way," in the sovereign preeminent Christ, for the glory of God's omnipotent grace.

Chapter 2, "Cheer Up! You Are Far Worse Than You Think," covers events that took place in the 1950s and 1960s. During this time, as a teacher, church planter, pastor, and scholar, Jack developed a critical theological and cultural apparatus that uniquely qualified him to serve on the faculty at Westminster Theological Seminary (WTS).

Chapters 3, 4, and 5 form the heart of this biography. Chapter 3, "Cheer Up! God's Spirit Works in Your Weakness," focuses on the joy that Jack experienced as God's Spirit worked through his weakness and, as a result of that work, magnified the glory of the Lord Jesus Christ all the more. Chapter 4, "Cheer Up! Justification Is by Faith Alone, Even in the Twentieth Century," shows the theological development that took place within Jack during the controversy that raged from 1974 to 1981 over Norman Shepherd's teaching at WTS regarding the role of works within justification. Chapter 5, "Cheer Up! God's Kingdom Is More Wonderful Than You Ever Imagined," focuses on Jack's rapid expansion of his ministry activities and covers several new mission fields that he opened in the 1980s.

Chapter 6, "Cheer Up! Come On, Let's Die Together; It's a Great Way to Come to Life," ends on the highest note as Jack Miller, a dying man, preached God's amazing grace to dying men.

Why a Critical Biography?

Jack once pastored a church that had a painting of Jesus hanging directly behind the pulpit. When he preached, the congregation saw his face in Jesus's halo. Jack disliked the painting and wanted it removed. Older congregants, who were fond of the painting, resisted. When the church was repainted and the picture taken down, Jack was the last person who was seen with the painting before it disappeared, never to be found again. Though about a small incident, this story illustrates a fact of Jack's life: glorifying Christ, not himself, was his ultimate desire.

Those whom I interviewed in the course of writing this book asserted that Jack would have laughed at the idea of a study on his life and ministry. Thankfully, Jack Miller himself clears the way for a critical biography such as this. He himself enjoyed reading biographies and once wrote, "More than once God has used a stirring example from the life of a more normal Christian leader to arouse me to the truth about my indifference to His glory."³ He also realized that much of discipling is "taught before it is caught," so he often shared personal illustrations of his own weaknesses, failings, and sin in order to help those whom he taught to catch discipleship. "What God wants you to do," he explained, "is to learn faster than me. That is why he has given older Christians to the younger, so you won't have to repeat every mistake."

Christians are often disenchanted with conventional expressions of the church and long for authenticity. However, such authenticity can be a double-edged sword. Preachers have turned pulpits into confessionals in an attempt to imitate Jack's openness in the area of repentance without understanding his vison for its use in evangelism (see chapter 2). Jack was a literature professor and biblical scholar who took words seriously. When he confessed specific and critical sins in his own life and ministry, he was very intentionally leading other sinners to join him in repenting. We should thus neither romanticize repentance nor be shocked and appalled by it.

As Jack's friend Steve Brown has noted, "It is dangerous to have a hero who is still alive. But, frankly, it's dangerous to have a hero who is dead, too. . . . 'Puff' biographies of 'famous' Christians . . . have done Christians a great disservice."⁴ As you read this book, remember that it is a critical biography—and Jack was his own biggest critic. While Jack's sin patterns do not define him, they grew out of real areas of sin that Jack took seriously and often wept over. By taking Jack and his self-criticisms seriously, as he and Rose Marie intended, you will allow this book to accomplish its purpose.

An Unexpected Biography

My wife, Vicki, and I first heard of Jack Miller in 1991. We were experiencing severe marital difficulties and asked our pastor for marriage counseling. He recommended a mentoring course known as Sonship. Begun by Jack Miller in 1982, it was a leadership training program that paired missions and renewal with evangelism and discipleship. Our pastor and his wife had significantly benefited from the course—but at that point, Vicki and I needed counseling rather than the mentoring that Sonship provided. We completed the first three lessons with a Sonship mentor but then dropped out—though the course had already begun to rescue my marriage as it simultaneously discipled and evangelized me. Four years later, when our marriage was stabilized, Vicki and I called our mentor again and completed the course. The sovereign Lord used the gospel teaching in Sonship to convert me and save our marriage.

Over the next several years, we considered whether we were being called to the mission field as we evangelized and discipled other individuals and couples using materials from World Harvest Mission, an organization that had been founded by Jack Miller in 1983 and is now known as Serge. In 1998, we moved our family to St. Louis, Missouri, so that I could attend Covenant Theological Seminary. By that time, the Sonship movement was generating both controversy and revival as it swept the Presbyterian Church in America (PCA). Harsh critiques of Sonship from Jay Adams and others spurred me to further examine Jack Miller as well as the Bible's teaching on the doctrine of adoption. In 2001, we received a call to Mount Juliet, Tennessee, to replant Hickory Grove Presbyterian Church, and we have lived there since.

In 2012, I began formal research and writing at Southeastern Baptist Theological Seminary on the doctrine of adoption and its relationship to union with Christ, justification, and sanctification. While attending PhD seminars, I was surprised that the faculty at Southeastern had assigned a significant number of books written by authors who had been influenced directly or indirectly by the late Jack Miller, including Harvie Conn, Timothy Keller, David Powlison, and Dennis Johnson. I had not expected that in a Southern Baptist doctoral context.

During a seminar on leadership that was taught by Dr. Danny Akin, the president of Southeastern, I commented, "The most important yet unknown leader referenced in this PhD program is a man named Jack Miller"—in response to which Dr. Akin asked, "Who is Jack Miller?" I briefly outlined Jack's life and ministry, noting some important leaders whom Jack had influenced. Dr. Akin immediately replied, "You need to write his biography as a record for the church while so many people Jack influenced are still alive."

Providentially, Dr. Akin took over the supervision of my research and wisely guided the project to its conclusion. On the condition that I not write a hagiography of Jack, the Miller family granted access to his archival material and made themselves available for interviews, in addition to Rose Marie, Paul, and Barbara participating as volunteer outside readers. Along with about thirty others, they reviewed each chapter for accuracy to and consistency with the statements of those I had interviewed. Consequently, after having researched and written from 2012 to 2014 on the relationship of adoption to sonship and union with Christ, in 2015 I committed the cardinal sin for a PhD student and changed my research proposal—instead of writing on the doctrine of adoption as I had planned, I decided to write *Cheer Up! A Biography of the Life, Teaching, and Ministry of Jack Miller.*

While attending the annual conference of the Evangelical Theological Society in November 2017, I met John Hughes— academic project manager for P&R Publishing. Hughes, a former student at WTS, took personal interest in reading a dissertation about his former professor. Later, Hughes introduced Jack's biography to other P&R leaders, who have since worked diligently to transform an academic dissertation into the publication you are now reading.

The Music of the Gospel

The gospel of grace was deep, deep music for Jack. "There should be no need to apologize for . . . lifting up the conquering power of Christ through grace. Here we have on our hands a message about omnipotence moving from eternity into time. And omnipotence—well, we should expect it to do big things. So, do we exaggerate when we say with faith . . . that the gospel has the power to change anyone? I have seen many, many people of all sorts brought to faith just because of the glad elevation of Christ's saving omnipotence." Overwhelmingly, the most lasting impression that Jack had etched on the minds and hearts of people who were interviewed for this study was his delight in the mystery of God's abundant grace. That readers of this book would be left with this same lasting impression is my prayer and hope.

1

CHEER UP! GOD'S GRACE IS FAR GREATER THAN YOU EVER DARED HOPE

Early Life and the Joy of the Gospel

JACK'S EARLY FAMILY life in southwest Oregon forged a pioneering spirit in him that would become an overarching theme that defined his ministry. Both sets of his grandparents, optimistic about their futures, endured great challenges and suffered significant tragedy while pioneering west along the Oregon Trail and over the Northwest Crossing. His parents, too, were brave and resourceful people.

Jack's father, Elmer, the oldest child of Edward and Susie Miller, was born near the Lower Pistol River in Oregon on June 22, 1885. Elmer's father had a gambling habit, and the losses that it incurred created instability in the Miller family as it grew. In 1894, their financial conditions forced the family to move to the Upper Pistol River to a ranch that Susie's parents owned, which was affectionately known as Grasshopper Hill. In 1903, after many losses, Edward's gambling habit finally resulted in his winning a ranch that was located in the more socially vibrant pioneering settlement of Agness. When his parents moved to the new ranch, eighteen-year-old Elmer purchased Grasshopper Hill from his father for ten dollars.

Having learned to hunt at age eight and being intimately familiar with the Siskiyou Mountains, Elmer gained prominence as a predatory game hunter in the state of Oregon. From 1905 to 1910, he caught the attention of both regional newspapers and national magazines as a game hunter, hunting guide, and breeder of champion hunting dogs. In 1910, he was recognized as the most famous citizen in his county.

On July 2, 1893, Jack's mother, Iva Avada Murry, was born in Grants Pass, Oregon. She was the second daughter of Thomas Murry and Sarah "Ellen" Miller—who, when they had married in 1879, had been a mismatch from the start. Thomas was thirty years older than Ellen, and he wasted time drinking in town. Over time, Ellen felt trapped between two dangerous choices: stay with a husband and father who was becoming increasingly abusive or risk exposing herself and her two girls to the dangers of the Wild West. Finally, when Iva was four years old, Ellen and her daughters escaped the drunken wrath of her husband.

For the majority of the time between 1897 to 1910, Iva lived with her mother in the back of a wagon. It was a fatherless and homeless life that involved crisscrossing five thousand miles—taking her as far south as the Sierra Nevada desert and as far north as Seattle. While stopping in southwest Oregon to visit her sister, Ellen agreed to marry Oliver Doolittle and settled there in 1909. Iva, who objected to her mother's choice of husband, joined her older sister in Redding, California, to help with raising the sister's two children and finally to attend school herself. When her sister's husband tried to take advantage of Iva, however, driving her to hit him over the head with a bucket, she returned to settle with her mother and stepfather on the Lower Pistol River.

Elmer had been living a secluded life—hunting, trapping, and ranching on the Upper Pistol River just northeast from Iva's parents on the Lower Pistol River—and he wanted to marry and start a large family. Occasionally he welcomed friends and neighbors to the ranch—people who soon introduced him to the new girl in the small pioneer settlement. Elmer's hunting statistics declined temporarily as he spent more time with Iva than on game hunting.

Elmer Miller and Iva Murry married on May 5, 1912. Leo Miller, their eldest son, was born on the Upper Pistol River in 1913. Then Raymond was born in 1916, followed by Ira in 1918. Three girls followed the three boys: Ella Mae in 1921, Frances in 1923, and Irene in 1925.

Unlike his father, Elmer was an excellent provider for his own family. In 1920, before the girls were born, Iva wanted the boys to be closer to the Swinging Bridge School. In order to accommodate his wife's concerns, Elmer bought a 160-acre homestead that was down the Pistol River and was locally known as the Burn. The Miller boys still encountered wild animals along the way to school, however, and when Ella Mae was old enough to walk there as well, Iva's anxiety about wild animals grew. Elmer rented a small house for the children's safety in Gold Beach, Oregon, in the fall of 1926. The following school year, he bought a house and five lots for his wife on Third Street in the same town. The children were easily able to walk to school, and Iva had access to a twelve-bed hospital in the event that a seventh child were added to their prosperous and happy family.

ELMER AND IVA's optimism peaked with the birth of that seventh and last child. Cecil John "Jack" Miller was born in Gold Beach, Oregon, on December 18, 1928. Married for seventeen years by that time, Elmer and Iva adored each other and delighted in their many children. All the children doted on their baby brother as well. With a bright future ahead, little Jackie crowned a happy, loving, and stable Miller family.

Elmer, who was considered among the greatest game hunters in the West at that time, continued to garner praise as the subject of exposés in newspapers and hunting magazines. The older boys helped their father to maintain Grasshopper Hill ranch and breed his champion hunting dogs. The girls helped their mother at home in Gold Beach and especially enjoyed combing their baby brother's golden curls and watching him learn to walk. In December of 1929,

Elmer retired as Oregon's most celebrated predatory game hunter to accept the newly created position of forest ranger for the United States Forest Service, which he began in January of 1930.

On December 16, 1930, two days before Jack turned two, sudden tragedy devastated the Miller family.

Will Wridge, Elmer's uncle on his mother's side, was visiting from Portland. On December 15, Wridge called and asked Elmer to take him on a bear hunt. With Christmas a few weeks away and Jack's birthday around the corner, Elmer did not want to leave his family. He also generally found it imprudent to hunt without taking another experienced hunter along with him, and his uncle had only limited hunting experience of his own. However, he could find no one either to accompany him and Wridge or to take his uncle hunting for bears in his stead—and Wridge was being persistent. And so, early on the morning of December 16, 1930, against Elmer's better judgment, the acclaimed bear hunter and his uncle left Grasshopper Hill ranch to hunt.

Later that morning, near Pyramid Rock toward the Upper Pistol River, Elmer's dogs cornered a bear. According to Wridge, Elmer moved toward his dogs to pull them away as he yelled for them to stop. Tragically, Wridge thought his nephew was yelling "shoot" rather than "stop." As Elmer was moving downhill toward his dogs and the bear, Wridge fired. His bullet struck Elmer in the hip, ran downward through his leg, and nicked an artery along the way. Wridge left Elmer and ran to get help, only to wander for hours, lost, as his nephew bled to death. The rescue party found Elmer's body sitting on a rock with his pocket watch in one hand and a knuckle clenched between his teeth to try to temper the pain. He had dragged himself two miles to the Low Glades before giving up.

Reporters from as far away as Los Angeles, California, wrote about Elmer's unexpected death, which many considered "the greatest tragedy in [that] part of the country." Some of Elmer's family and friends, unconvinced about the circumstances surrounding his death, questioned whether the shooting had been accidental. Their questions led to an investigation: Why had Wridge been so insistent that his nephew take him hunting? Why had he left Elmer after shooting him? How had he wandered, lost, for seven hours in an area where he had once lived before finding help? What had happened to Elmer's prize hunting dogs? Why would an expert hunter like Elmer have run in front of someone's line of fire? The investigation, however, turned up nothing actionable, and further inquiries were dropped.

Iva suddenly found herself a single mom with seven children from ages seventeen to two. She sufficiently satisfied herself that Elmer's tragic death had been accidental and turned her attention to the survival of her family. Her eldest son, eighteen-year-old Leo, took paternal responsibility for little Jackie.

The juxtaposition of the Millers' lives before and then after December of 1930 would have been difficult for anyone to fathom, much less a two-year old, as they moved from happiness, security, safety, and stability to instant fatherlessness, upheaval, and poverty. While Elmer's success had insulated his family from economic difficulties, the full weight of the Great Depression now collapsed upon the Millers.

The desperate family was suddenly property rich and cash poor. Remote, illiquid real estate that had once promised them long-term prosperity now worsened their freefall, and the work of maintaining the large Grasshopper Hill ranch and the Burn overwhelmed the older boys. Iva's job of raising seven children paid nothing, and government aid was not available for widows and orphans in southern Oregon. Although the neighborly rules that existed among families and communities dictated that pioneers in Oregon always rallied to the aid of a troubled neighbor, everyone was suffering under the weight of the Great Depression. There was not enough food, supplies, or extra money available to meet the ongoing needs of the large Miller family.

Jack's once idyllic family situation only continued to worsen as time went on. Iva's mother and stepfather, Ellen and Oliver Doolittle, sold the store that they owned in Agness and moved to the Upper Pistol River in an attempt to save both the Grasshopper Hill ranch and the Burn. By the end of 1932, however, they too had lost everything that they owned in their attempts to rescue Iva and the ranch; Ellen's health was also broken. By the time Oliver brought his wife to the Lower Pistol River for medical care, it was too late. Loss added to loss and death added to death when Jack's grandmother died a month before his fourth birthday. Unable to afford a funeral for her mother, Iva buried her in a pauper's grave in the Pioneer Cemetery next to the Presbyterian Church in Gold Beach.

IVA'S HAPPY MARRIAGE to Elmer had redeemed much of the suffering she had endured as a young girl, but circumstances were now plunging the thirty-seven-year-old widow into another tragic spiral. At the time of Elmer's death, social security for a young widow in Iva's situation equated to remarriage—but having seven children and few available men severely limited her choice of husbands. Soon, friends were introducing Iva to the few eligible men in Pistol River and Gold Beach.

Finally, on January 24, 1933, two years after Elmer's death, Iva remarried. Andy Allen "Al" Lawrence was a fifty-seven-year-old single man living on his parents' ranch on the Lower Pistol River. After the wedding, he moved into the small Miller house on Third Street in Gold Beach. Iva's eighth child, Andy Allen "Junior" Lawrence, was born in 1934.

None of the Miller children cared for their severe stepfather. The two youngest children, Irene and Jack, had the most traumatic relationship with Lawrence—though it was Jack himself who often took the brunt of his anger. In the words of Jack's cousin Ben Gardner, "Al would beat the hell out of Jack." In an incomplete manuscript, "Book on Love," Jack describes his bullying stepfather as a "victimizer who enjoyed the role of taking pleasure in sucking the joy out of life for me." He writes in another draft of that manuscript, "This powerful man would hit one of our older sisters or me without warning. . . . Challenge him, or even question him in a way he didn't like, and you risked a severe beating."

Soon after Lawrence moved into their home, Jack began to nightly experience a terrifying fear of death. His fears became so strong that they prevented him from sleeping. "I was terrified with the nightly fear that if I fell asleep I would simply disappear into the darkness of death never to return—just as I imagined my dad had done." Sometimes he jolted out of dreams in which his stepfather would strike him without warning or beat him in his rage.

There was little opportunity for Jack's older brothers in Gold Beach or Pistol River, and so, as soon as they were old enough, they enlisted in the military to get away from their stepfather. Before leaving, Leo—Jack's eldest brother and surrogate father—warned Lawrence that if he ever touched Jack again, Leo would kill him.

Jack feared his stepfather's abuse, but he also feared Lawrence for an even deeper reason. While he was a victim of physical abuse, Jack feared that victimhood would become his basic identity. He would later explain that "to make victimhood your basic self-identification is to disconnect yourself from the world of people and ultimately from God. It turns the world into an orphanage and yourself into an orphan numbed by disappointments, betrayals, and broken dreams." The temptation Jack felt at the age of ten to feel sorry for himself threatened to consume him in self-pity, until his older sisters noticed their little brother turning into a "first-rate whiner" and confronted him.

Jack dreaded seeing his stepfather and increasingly isolated himself from his family because of the man's abuse. When he wanted to escape, which he often did, he walked to Gold Beach's library. By the time he had turned ten years old, he had read all the books that were available there, so Iva brought her fourth-grade son to see their lawyer. The attorney took Jack to his private library, reached up to the shelf, and took down a large book by Tobias

Smollett. Over the next several years, Jack read all the books in the attorney's library as well.

As part of Jack's chores, he fed and milked the family's cow and cleaned the barn twice each day. Initially, the chore took Jack an hour in the morning and an hour in the evening. Over time, he came to enjoy the work—and especially the cow's playful affection. Even though Jack cut the work time of each session in half, he continued to spend the full two hours in the barn. Joy, affection, and play abounded freely alongside his work during the time he spent with the cow. As he contemplated his relationship with his stepfather, he realized that his fear had led him to hate his stepfather and to prefer to remain isolated in the barn with the playful cow. Jack had to make a decision: he could keep running from his stepfather, or he could take a stand.

At dinner one evening, Jack sat at the table on the other side of his mother, to ensure that he was out of the reach of his stepfather. Safely walled away, he took courage and tried to talk to the hot-tempered man. Despite the contempt that Lawrence showed for him and his ideas, Jack held his composure and calmly continued to interact with him. Eventually, after enough similar interactions had taken place, Iva and Junior joined Jack in his questioning of Lawrence's attitude and behavior—including his abusive hitting of the children. For the first time in Jack's presence, Lawrence admitted that he was wrong about something. "Till then, I had never heard him admit the slightest flaw in his words or life," Jack wrote later. "I cannot say that I ever loved him the way I loved the rest of my family. But I know I stopped hating him. Eventually I gained compassion for this strange man." Over time, Lawrence's hitting stopped.

Like his mother, Jack bore the deep scars that come from familial brokenness, forced relocations, and devastating loss at an early age. He came to believe that the calamitous death of his biological father, followed by his decade of living with an abusive stepfather, damaged him and would have permanently marred him had it not been for the saving grace of God.

GRACE, HOWEVER, was not something on the minds of many people in southern Oregon at the time. Most of them counted themselves among the virtuous. Oregonians were also pragmatic—more interested in the natural world than in theology and philosophy—a down-to-earth, traditional people who enjoyed hunting and fishing in the mountains and forests of their state. Not long descended from the state's early settlers, they were good neighbors who lived by a moral code that was based on honesty and kindness as well as keeping one's word, doing hard work, and paying the bills. Jack explains, "Some of them went to church, but most did not. But although they were not churchgoers, they had moral standards derived from the teachings of the Bible."[1] When Jack was growing up, the only church in the small coastal community was First Presbyterian Church of Gold Beach, and this was the church that Jack's family attended. Southern Oregonians who did not go to Sunday worship commonly claimed that the big outdoors was their church.

Jack's mother Iva was among the most virtuous people whom he knew. She endured much hardship, and yet Jack never heard her complain or gossip about others. She was kind to neighbors and readily sacrificed for her family. Iva taught her children about the Ten Commandments and emphasized the Lord's second coming as a way to keep them in line when they were erring. Jack later wrote, "None of us wanted to be caught breaking one of the commandments when Jesus reappeared! In fact, I got into the habit of always looking to the east before I did anything wrong."[2] Jack grew up thinking that good people would survive judgment day—though he often wondered if there were much chance of that for him.

Years later, as a seminary professor, Jack spoke to his mother about their family's faith. "You know we all grew up thinking we were Christians, went to church, and all that. But I can't recall anyone ever telling me that I was lost and that I needed Jesus to give me a new life."[3]

"Of course, I always believed that," Iva replied. "[Your father and I] took it for granted."[4]

Jack highly respected his mother, and yet he was troubled that she and his father would take Christ and his love for granted. That his parents had never said anything like "Christ died for our sins, and it means everything to me" puzzled Jack.[5] Were others, like himself, presuming to be Christian just because they attended church?

Sadly, Jack also heard little about Christ's dying for sinners at the church they attended. No one encountered the living Christ there; no one was converted or transformed. The community at Gold Beach considered Sunday morning to be the dullest time of the week. The worship services were boring, and the preaching was moralistic.

In a testament to the ineffectiveness of the Gold Beach church, at one point in the late 1930s, the town's mayor proposed installing slot machines in the sanctuary to take advantage of the church's prime location on the historic Highway 101 and capture tourists who were passing through the pioneer village. The congregants of the church admonished the mayor for his blasphemy—yet Jack acknowledged, later in life, that the mayor had accurately taken the pulse of the lifeless church. Something *should* happen at church, Jack went on to note, but, to the congregation in Gold Beach, exactly what seemed unclear. No one, including the preacher, quite knew what to expect.

When a public schoolteacher whom Jack admired announced that he was an atheist, he gave Jack the language to explain what he himself already believed but had lacked the words to communicate. Atheism seemed to explain the fact that God had seemingly been silent in Jack's life and absent from the First Presbyterian Church of Gold Beach. Jack announced to his family and school that he too was an atheist.

Twelve may seem like a young age for a boy to make such a weighty announcement about an even weightier decision. But, given his long exposure to tragedy and evil, Jack's announcement of atheism was not the facile declaration of a naïve boy. As Jack explains, "I was clear the church did not have a purpose beyond that of comforting people who need religious solace. In my view 'church' was for timid people—not for the tough-minded type[s] like myself who are ready to face the unpleasant truth that God probably did not exist and that worship was a charade designed to conceal that he was permanently absent from worship and the universe."

Life circumstances had made Jack angry and rebellious. As he prepared to leave home in his mid-teens, he completely rejected his family's religion and washed his hands of the church altogether. Good riddance to the God who was not there! He dropped out of school and moved to San Francisco in order to get away from his stepfather and make his own way in life. Jack sums up his spiritual condition at that time: "No one could have started further from God than I did."[6]

DURING WORLD WAR II, San Francisco became the gateway to the Pacific theater. As white American men were enlisting in the military and being shipped off to war, the Navy ramped up for the war effort by recruiting tens of thousands of African American men from around the country to work at the massive Hunters Point Naval Shipyard in San Francisco. It also lowered the age limit for doing so and allowed some teenagers to apprentice. Even so, at age fifteen, Jack was underage when he arrived at San Francisco to earn his machinist's certificate at Hunters Point. Either the Navy or Jack (or both) overlooked or fudged his actual age by a year or more. Although the vast military complex at Hunters Point suffered from notoriously poor and dangerous working conditions, the Navy was still supplying Jack with the means to escape his stepfather. He lived with his sister Ella Mae, completed his last year of high school, earned his machinist certification, and worked at the shipyard.

While this was happening, Ella Mae surrendered her life to Christ; and Jack talked regularly with her about her conversion, the meaning of life, and her new faith. He occasionally went with her when she started attending First Orthodox Presbyterian Church, and he began studying the Bible—initially in order to argue with her and other Christians. Jack both hated for anyone to out-argue him and also thought that these Christians were quoting Scripture without knowing what they were talking about. If they could quote

Romans, then he was determined to know Romans better than they did. While recognizing the irony of his behavior, every morning and afternoon Jack read his Bible on the bus to work, stuffing it in his pocket whenever it drew too much attention. A movie night at the church about modern man's inability to give thanks to God further unsettled him.

Soon, other members of Jack's family became Christians as well. Jack was being exposed to the gospel—and he could not escape the sovereign Christ. And so, in early 1945, he decided that he might as well become a Christian like his sister. "I repented. I thought I believed. I even got down on my knees and wept over my sin. . . . In Oregon you learn how to be . . . tough. . . . The ideal is to be tough and never cry. . . . So I went the whole distance. I did everything. . . . But what was happening were certain modifications in my character taking place which were largely external."

ON MARCH 3, 1945, tragedy struck the Miller family again. Leo had predicted that he would not return from active duty. He died on a mountain ridge in Italy while spotting for artillery—just a few weeks before his scheduled discharge.

Leo had been the closest person to a father whom Jack had known. When Jack received the heartbreaking news at age sixteen that his beloved brother and protector had died in action, he became completely derailed. Despite Ella Mae's protests for him to stay and take classes at San Francisco State College, where he had enrolled for the fall, Jack dropped out and returned to southern Oregon in late August, a few weeks after the war in the Pacific ended.

Although Leo's death sent Jack spiraling, the Lord kept challenging him in unexpected ways. Jack described one such instance: "It was August 1945, and the atomic bomb had just been exploded over Hiroshima. As we commuters boarded our bus, people were shaking their heads and wondering whether this new weapon would destroy the world. A sailor responded quietly: 'No, the world won't ever be destroyed by atomic bombs. Jesus won't let that happen.

He's coming back first.'"[7] That sailor's unquestioning confidence silenced any argument or debate from Jack.

Jack had been too young to work on the coastal highways when he had left Oregon in 1943, but when he returned in 1945, he immediately found a job working as a flagman and laborer and shoveling gravel on those familiar serpentine coastal roads that he had traveled to and from San Francisco. Working outdoors rejuvenated Jack physically, but spiritually he remained a wanderer. When he had decided to become a Christian, he had somehow missed something vital—though he did not know what he had overlooked. "I was always traveling through outer physical space in order to cope with the empty inner space."

Jack thought that witnessing and preaching could resolve his uneasiness. And, certainly, his dedication and apparent growth— the effort to live the Christian life that he described as "a powerful labor"—looked impressive to outside observers. He cleaned up his life in many areas, passionately pursued piety, gave up bad habits and started good ones, and energetically studied Scripture. In fact, when he visited his sister in San Francisco again in April of 1948 and went to First Orthodox Presbyterian Church with her, the church's pastor asked him to speak at their Friendship Night. Jack spoke for the first time about his decision to become a Christian— before he actually became a Christian.

Looking back on the period of his life from 1945 to 1948, Jack described himself as being "half-way converted"—"If I had to introduce [a non-Christian] to what I had [before December of 1948], they were going to be miserable. At least a non-Christian still had some fun. Who wanted to drink the vinegar I had going down me every day?"

ELLA MAE'S CHURCH was part of a small new denomination—the Orthodox Presbyterian Church (OPC)—that had been founded in 1936 by J. Gresham Machen, who had also founded Westminster Theological Seminary (WTS) in 1929. Machen, the OPC, and

WTS would each play a pivotal role in Jack's life—starting with his conversion.

One October day in 1948, Jack picked up a book by Machen called *The Christian View of Man*. Throughout that fall, Jack had been desperately reading Scripture without getting much out of it. Romans and Ephesians had especially drawn his attention, and he was looking for help with understanding them. As he read Machen's book, although he was beginning to fall asleep, he pushed on through it—ever a disciplined reader.

When he read what Machen said about election being the power source for life, his temper flared. Predestination struck Jack as the world's most awful doctrine. He loathed it. When Machen cited Ephesians 1 as his warrant for this teaching, Jack thought it was surely impossible for such hideous doctrine to be in the Bible. He incredulously threw aside Machen's book and opened his Bible to Ephesians 1. There it was—right there in the Bible. Jack writes, "It was like gasoline touched by a lighted match. Almost instantly I was fully awake. What was this incredible stuff?"

Jack was shocked by the revelation. He argued with Machen and God, rhetorically demanding to know what predestination did for his freedom. To lose his ability to choose "seemed somehow to rob me of the most important thing in my life." Who did God think he was?

In response, what seemed to Jack "like a voice," arose from the pages of Scripture to say, "God! And who do you think you are?" The question shocked Jack's soul. There was only one possible answer he could give: he thought *he* was God. For the first time in his life, Jack realized the treasonous nature of the sin that lay underneath all his other sins.

> The starkness of my insane answer shocked me. . . .
>
> My thoughts were in complete upheaval, but one truth cut into me with the force of sharp-edged surgical steel. I had lived only for my glory and not for God's. His plan was for me to live for His

glory and will, and I had never done that for a single moment in my life. In fact, it had seemed to me that I had done Him a considerable favor by believing in Him.

The idea that He was the absolute center of all things glorious had never crossed my mind.

Now exposed, my conscience said to me: what a cagy, selfish, evil person you are! Of all people, you are the most hugely egocentric man who ever lived!

Scripture and the Holy Spirit awakened Jack to the truth about himself and the truth about God. He realized that his mighty self-generated labors over the previous three years had been for his own glory and not for God's. He knew that he had judged other people wrongly before; now he realized that he had judged God wrongly, too. He had been so neurotic about his sins that he had missed the truth that the heart of his sin was directly against God's majesty, against God's glory, and against God's holiness. As shocking as this sudden recognition of God's holiness was to him, another breathtaking revelation staggered him even more.

At that moment I was cut to the heart. I realized the utter impossibility of ever changing myself. . . .

I was hurt so deeply by the law of God I couldn't even cry. I was beyond tears.

All I could say is "God, forgive me. God, I had you all wrong. I will put down my weapons. I will stop fighting you." I could say, "God, I don't know why you would want me, but I am giving myself to you anyway, here."

I wasn't expecting anything, but when I said that, when the pride that ruled my life for the first time was exposed, cut into my heart by the Holy Spirit through the Scripture, I was desperate, and I was astonished by what happened to me then.

Completely unprepared for it, the next moment I knew assurance of total forgiveness.

How could you know like that? I just knew that God had moved me, that he had received me, and my sins were on the cross and Christ carried them away.

I had such peace in my heart; I was so filled with joy over the gospel.

Before, Jack had thought that he was a Christian. Others, too, had presumed the same and even let him teach. But Jack had done nothing more than work at saving himself for more than two years. "When I do anything . . . I do it with my whole heart. And if anyone could have saved himself, I could have." After reading Ephesians 1 that day, Jack was completely stunned by God's omnipotent grace. He was utterly helpless and speechless. "A sense of shame began to come over me that I had misunderstood God and the universe. And that behind it all, I wanted to be saved for my glory. And I wanted to insist that it had been my will that had chosen Christ."

Jack's pride had blinded him to the state of his own heart—to its belief that God should have been grateful that Jack had taken the leap of faith and believed in him despite such little evidence. After all, God had robbed him of his father and substituted for him an abusive stepfather. Then he had robbed Jack of Leo. Now he expected to get the glory for Jack's choice to believe? Was he saying that Jack's faith did not create anything—that even his faith was a gift of God's omnipotent grace?

When Jack finally gave up his right to independent choice—the most precious thing in his life—and surrendered his false idea that he somehow had to save himself, suddenly the music of the gospel sang from Ephesians 1 into his heart and life. He finally settled things with God.

For Jack, becoming a Christian meant choosing to give up his trust in his own wisdom and choices. He later wrote, "A lot of people who pray the Lord's prayer 'Your kingdom come' would be horrified if it happened, because what you really want is 'Lord, I want my agenda.' I want to protect myself, defend myself, make excuses. . . . And God says now, 'I'm going to give you so much love you won't need these other things.'"

Now in union with Christ instead of fighting God's sovereign grace, Jack found the joy and peace of God flooding his heart and mind. He now placed his faith in "a God who is God all the way."

Although Jack had originally feared that a predestining God would squash his freedom, his knowledge of divine election instead produced a continual power source that enabled him to live in joy and freedom. Furthermore, his recognition of God's irresistible grace gave him the courage that was necessary to free him from the fear of people like his stepfather. The oft-misrepresented doctrine of predestination, which Jack had once hated, supplied him with an inexhaustible love that conquered his driven, restless heart. He thought that "it seemed such a shame that there could be anyone in the universe who didn't live for the preeminence of Christ."

Jack Miller had become a new man in Christ. His life, which now had Christ at its center, had new purpose, new coherence, and new direction. After he had learned of Leo's death, Jack had rejected family counsel, dropped out of college, and returned to Oregon for three years. Now, he readied himself to study philosophy and history back at San Francisco State College.

Before he left, Jack shocked his mother and the little Presbyterian church in Gold Beach by asking if they would like him to preach a sermon. His request so astonished the church that they decided to hear what the young man had to say. Once Jack started preaching, they could not turn him off. When he wrote about it later, he could not remember all that he said that Sunday morning, but he did recall one central point that he made: "One thing I'm terribly afraid of is that some of you might think you know Christ, but you are still living for your own glory, and you haven't had the joy of a surrender to God who is God all the way."

When Jack returned to San Francisco in December of 1948, he arrived in a grossly overcrowded city that had been transformed since he was last there during the war years. He had little money and no sustainable job, and, since staying with his sister long-term was no longer practicable, he needed a new place to live from which he could more easily access his church and school. Since his family history and pioneering mindset did not allow him to avoid work, miss a meal, or look for a handout, he picked up a bucket and rag and spent a month offering to wash windows in an urban neighborhood. Though he was inexperienced at both window washing and door-to-door evangelism, he used this opportunity to share his new faith, figuring that if he could ask strangers to wash their windows for money, he could also ask them if they had "heard about Jesus and the joy he brings to those who have him all the way as their Lord and Savior."

After about a month of window washing, Jack found a job working as a breakfast cook for twelve single men in a boarding house on Eddy Street. Boarding houses with low-cost rooms were common in San Francisco—especially in the Tenderloin district, which was considered to be the "black hole"[8] of San Francisco. This particular boarding house was dilapidated on the outside—and even worse on the inside. Despite its conditions, the work offered Jack a place to live, food to eat, a pittance of income, and close proximity to his school and church—which was important in a city that was hard to traverse on foot. Bill, the owner, trained Jack to cook for his rough, blue-collar boarders.

At the boarding house, Jack came to understand that omnipotent grace runs downhill. He was cooking for men who were belligerently irreligious. So he offered to share more than food with these men and talked to them about Christ as he served breakfast. Since he was their cook, they could hardly avoid him. Jack, as a former atheist, knew what it was like to have others preach down at him, and he did not want to force his ideas or religion on anyone. As a college student, he also wanted to speak intelligently. Yet he soon realized that communicating the Christian faith required more than friendliness and intelligence. He had to meet the men where they were.

Among the men who were staying at the boarding house, Jack encountered a revolutionary who despised Christians and the Bible. As a member of the Socialist Party, the man looked forward to the day when enlightened society would line Christians up against the wall and shoot them. Jack decided to treat the man courteously while praying that the Lord would open his heart to the gospel. Although nothing came of his relationship with this angry revolutionary, he remained undeterred.

Another man, a dock worker named Tony, was also bitter toward Christianity—in his case, because he was an atheist. An Oregonian background had taught Jack that men like Tony respected courage, and although he was smaller than Tony, he wanted to reach him for Christ. He agreed to arm wrestle him, praying for the strength to keep his arm unmoved as Tony tried to wrestle him into compliance. Despite Tony's best effort, Jack's arm held up to the man's strength. Within a few days, Jack gained permission to talk to Tony about Christ.

Jack felt the instinct, as a new Christian, to witness to those who were closest to him. As a young man in the rough-and-tumble world of the Tenderloin, he also learned the importance of trusting others, including non-Christians, rather than trying to handle things by himself. Jack wrote later, "Some Christians want to rush in and confront others with the gospel without taking the time to build a relationship of trust. Others . . . [build] relationships, but never . . . lovingly confront their friends with the claims of Christ. I have been guilty of both mistakes. This is when we learn what prayer is all about. As we pray, the Holy Spirit gives us what we need: the right combination of love and boldness as we share with others the words of life."[9]

Jack knew that "the gospel was intended for desperate people."[10] And, especially in the absence of his earthly father and brother, he himself urgently needed to hear the voice of his heavenly Father. He pored over the books of John, Romans, Ephesians, Galatians, and James like a "Bibleholic"[11] until whole chapters fixed themselves in his memory. Another resident at the boarding house, an unemployed drunk named Mel, asked Jack why he read the Bible all the time. "Mel," Jack replied, "it's the only way I'm going to make it."[12] Both men had big needs. Jack's drove him to the Bible; Mel's drove him to the bottle.

Jack's openness about needing the gospel intrigued Mel, but initially Jack did not take Mel's ensuing interest in the Bible seriously. Then, around one o'clock one night, Mel knocked on Jack's door; his knock, however, did not awaken Jack. Determined to read the Bible with him that night, a drunken Mel charged the length of the hallway and rammed his way through Jack's door, tumbling on top of a now fully awake and terrified young man.

Another encounter in the boarding house taught Jack an important lesson about the power of grace in situations when a Christian humbles himself and leads in repentance. Thankless housemates complained about Jack's average cooking or criticized his naive faith. After one of them, Big John, had spewed complaints and criticisms for weeks, Jack finally told him off in front of everyone. The man stopped complaining, but Jack's conscience troubled him so much that he finally approached Big John to apologize for being a rotten example. As Jack spoke, Big John's expression changed. "Please, please, don't apologize. I think you are right . . . I'm not thankful for anything. I'm so ashamed."[13]

Jack honestly received John's apology and forgave him. As little Jack and Big John talked about the work Christ had done on the cross, Big John humbled himself, kneeled in his bedroom, and prayed to receive Christ. Jack and his most vocal breakfast critic became friends—and, more importantly, brothers in Christ. God was demonstrating the power of his gospel to hard-case sinners, who, like Jack, were also discovering that God's grace is far greater than they could have ever dared hope.

Jack did not fully realize at the time that he was "learning more about sharing Christ by living in this boarding house and cooking breakfast than [he] ever could have learned from a systematic course of instruction."[14] He would go on to advise others, "Wherever you 'cook breakfast,' there is your classroom for learning to share your faith. The people you encounter daily are the ones Jesus wants you to share the gospel with. But make sure that you are understanding and loving the gospel more each day yourself or you will not be able to love and understand the friends at your 'breakfast table.'"[15] As Jack publicly displayed his faith through life encounters that he had with these men across the table, he recognized how much he himself continued to need the gospel if he was going to be able to love others.

The relationship between Jack and another of the boarders—Gus, an atheist who was studying biology at San Francisco State—started poorly. A month after Jack arrived at the boarding house, the two men, who both deeply cared about the truth, engaged in an intense argument about science, evolution, and Christianity. On New Year's Eve, Jack invited Gus to a young people's gathering at First Orthodox Presbyterian Church. Gus agreed to attend but planned to leave before midnight in order to make it to some New Year's festivities. When the group started talking about what Jesus meant to them, Gus remained fixed in his seat. On their leisurely walk home, Gus astonished Jack by saying, "I don't see how anyone could be here tonight and come away an atheist."[16] Arguing about the truth had not changed Gus. Instead, he had been won over by seeing the love that believers had for one another in their community of faith.

The boarding-house owner, Bill, believed that truth was a matter of preference—that it was different things for different people—rather than an unalterable reality. He had a weak moral center and had made lying and questionable business practices into a way of life. For some time, he used a naive Jack to carry his illegal bets to his bookie. Bill laughed at Jack and dismissed his frustration when he found out what he had been doing for Bill. Displaying no indication of remorse, Bill figured that he would find another unsuspecting person to carry his illegal bets for him.

By the end of May 1949, deteriorating personal health, combined with the disrepair of the boarding house, forced Bill to close it. Overlooking his unscrupulous behavior, Jack and Gus took care of Bill and closed his business—not because he deserved for them to continue to care for him in this way, after everyone else had left, but because the young men loved their unloving boss for Christ's sake. All three of them needed the gospel. Whether or not Bill would receive God's grace was not primarily Jack's burden but ultimately, like his own salvation, a work of the sovereign God.

DESPITE THE TRAGEDY and abuse that had occurred during Jack's childhood, he remained proud of his pioneering heritage and loved the untamed, pristine beauty of southwest Oregon. During the summer of 1949, Jack worked for the National Forest Service by spotting fires in the Siskiyou Mountains. He boarded in the Snow Camp Lookout, which was located above the Upper Pistol River and the Grasshopper Hill ranch that had once been owned by his father, Elmer.

In San Francisco, the city lights had obscured the majesty of the stars. Now, as he looked at the concentrated glory of God's creation—at the stars that were amassed above the great shafts of the mighty redwoods and Douglass firs—Jack thanked the Lord for everything that had happened to him.

2

CHEER UP! YOU ARE FAR WORSE THAN YOU THINK

Unmasking the Divides in Theological Education and Practical Ministry

JACK FIRST MET Rose Marie, his future wife, at First Orthodox Presbyterian Church early in 1949, after he had returned to San Francisco following his conversion in Oregon. He began teaching a class of young people at the church at the same time that Rose Marie was teaching a class of her own there. She caught Jack's attention at once, and he decided that the best way to start a conversation with this attractive young woman would be to help her to better examine her dispensational theology.

In an interview, Rose Marie laughed when she recalled letters that she received from Jack that first summer while he was working at the lookout in southern Oregon. They were all about doctrine—good doctrine, of course, but still doctrine. For example, Jack once wrote to her, "Dear Rose Marie, isn't it wonderful! Christ died for us. The God 'who formed the heavens in patterns of awe'—He died for us! How incredible, and I know I could not believe Christ died for us unless all nature witnessed to it. That is, if nature failed to bear out what the Bible says about creation, I would reject it. Yet the Bible gives the only rational explanation concerning the world, the only competition being pantheism. But any other system than Reformed catholicism breaks down at the first hurdle." The letter continued for several more pages—Jack never did anything half-heartedly. In view of these theology-laden letters, it is a wonder of God's sovereign mercy that Rose Marie said yes to Jack's marriage proposal the following year.

After Jack returned to school for the fall semester of 1949, his relationship with Rose Marie grew more serious, and he worked up the courage to ask her on a date in October after saving enough money to take her to a restaurant in Chinatown.

ROSE MARIE'S FAMILY background was very different from Jack's. Her parents, Lorenz and Annemarie Carlsen, had emigrated from northern Germany to settle in Daly City, just ten miles southeast of San Francisco. Lorenz came from a long line of Lutheran ministers, and Annemarie similarly had an aristocratic Lutheran upbringing. The Carlsens labored to recreate a comfortable and orderly German life for Rose Marie and Barbara, her younger sister, who had been born with developmental disabilities. Lorenz owned a busy automobile garage and some real-estate investments in Daly City. Annemarie cleaned houses for affluent San Franciscans to supplement the family income.

Growing up, Rose Marie "studied German, went to the opera, took ballet, learned to waltz and dance the polka, and acted the role of a gracious cultured hostess." Like her father, who taught her to swim at an early age, she excelled in athletics and joined the swimming team at the University of California in Berkeley. She never saw her parents argue or heard them raise their voices at each other. She also never talked with them about spiritual matters. As she recalls, "It was a world of human goodness and careful morality."

But her world was not what it seemed. Lorenz had invested the family savings before the market crash in 1929 and then concealed the resulting failed investment from his wife. Annemarie had lived frugally, sacrificed, and saved in order to recreate their stable

German life in the United States. When she discovered Lorenz's deception, she could not bear the betrayal of her trust in him or the loss of financial stability that had resulted, and she experienced a serious breakdown.

Rose Marie's orderly childhood crumbled. At thirteen years old, she prevented her mother from committing suicide. By the time she was sixteen, her mother had completely withdrawn affection from her husband, who in turn avoided family conflict by plunging into his work at the auto garage. Lorenz's flight from his wife's worsening condition multiplied the burden that his elder daughter carried. She assumed the role of caregiver for the Carlsen household and looked after her mother and Barbara while working with her father to try to keep her mother from taking her own life.

Annemarie's fragile mental health led her to become paranoid, which increasingly isolated the family. When she accused other guests at restaurants of spying on her, the family quit going out in public. When she accused house guests of spying as well, friends eventually stopped visiting their home. When Rose Marie was seventeen, Annemarie made several more suicide attempts.

During these incredibly difficult years, Rose Marie and her father began to take their spiritual situation more seriously. At a church service, they both committed their lives to Christ. Even so, Lorenz still did not talk to her about any of these matters. She wrote later that "I believed in God . . . but I wasn't sure he was particularly concerned about our problems. I believed that Jesus came to die for sinners, but since I didn't see myself as much of a sinner, that didn't have much of an effect on me."[1]

When she graduated high school, she enrolled in Cal-Berkeley's nursing program. The university's proximity to Daly City enabled her to continue to help with caring for her mother and sister. Two years later, wanting to learn more about her new faith, Rose Marie transferred to Biola, an evangelical university in Los Angeles.

During the fall semester of her final year at Biola, when she was twenty-three years old, a young man proposed to her, and she accepted. However, while he did want to marry her, he had expressed concerns that marrying Rose Marie would also mean marrying her family. And she knew he had to be even *more* concerned that she might end up like her mother.

After prayerfully considering her fiancé's reservations, Rose Marie decided to call off the engagement. She recalled that "it was over, all of a sudden—and you know how God speaks. He presses his will on your will, and you don't know how but you know it's God saying, 'It's over. Take off the ring.' Just like that, I went upstairs, took the ring off, put it away, and wrote him." She finished the fall semester and returned home. In the spring, she resumed her studies at Cal-Berkeley so that she could again assist her father with caring for her mother and sister. It was soon after that she met Jack at church.

WHEN JACK HIMSELF proposed marriage to Rose Marie in October of 1949, he gave up his approach of wooing her with theology and opted instead for romantic poetry. Always the avid reader, he recited Lord Byron's "She Walks in Beauty" on the night of the proposal.

> She walks in beauty, like the night
> Of cloudless climes and starry skies;
> And all that's best of dark and bright
> Meet in her aspect and her eyes;
> Thus mellowed to that tender light
> Which heaven to gaudy day denies.

Rose Marie remained hesitant, asking, "Why do you want to marry me?" She wanted Jack to acknowledge that, by marrying her, he would be taking on the obligations that she had to her family.

Rose Marie's responsibilities led two pastors at First OPC to caution Jack against marrying her. He had shown great promise in the area of ministry, and his pastors were encouraging him to consider attending Westminster Theological Seminary (WTS) in

Pennsylvania before he married anyone. Jack, however, did not see attending WTS and marrying Rose Marie as being mutually exclusive. He believed that God had called him to marry Rose Marie, and he believed that God would ensure that he attended WTS at some point.

With this being the case, and once Rose Marie had been reassured that Jack would support the role she had as a caregiver to her mother and sister, the two were married on January 29, 1950. Rose Marie's mother refused to attend the wedding if it were held at First OPC, so it was moved to the Carlsen home. Jack's friend Gus, whom he had met at Bill's now-closed boarding house, served as his best man.

Jack and Rose Marie began their married life with several concrete goals. Jack's express desire, which Rose Marie fully supported, was to teach philosophy as a college professor. Since he was still a sophomore at San Francisco State College (SFSC), he would first finish his education there. Then he hoped to learn under the Dutch Calvinist philosopher Cornelius Van Til at WTS—although, while he was considering attending that seminary, his plan did not initially include pastoral ministry or teaching in a seminary himself. Rose Marie, for her part, after completing her final semester at Cal-Berkeley, would not work outside the home. Jack would take financial responsibility for both of them, and they would not incur debt or borrow money from friends or family. Finally, they both addressed the weighty issue of birth control, deciding to leave the timing of their children to God.

Since they had little money, their family budget was straightforward. Jack earned a hundred dollars a month working at his college's cafeteria, and twenty of those dollars went to a bedroom in a boarding house where Jack and Rose Marie now lived together. The remaining money paid for necessities such as food and transportation. Their financial constraints, along with the schedules of the classes they were both taking, postponed the newlyweds' honeymoon.

WHILE JACK TOOK on a second job working part-time for the post office, both of his jobs ended once the semester ended. He planned to go to Oregon for the summer, so that he could work for the National Forest Service and spot fires on the Upper Pistol River, and to bring along Rose Marie, who had become pregnant three months into their marriage. Unfortunately, however, the young couple had no money left to purchase bus fare for the trip. Then, just in time, a few days before the semester ended, a friend hired Jack to deliver an automobile to its new buyers in Oregon, who just happened to live three blocks from Jack's mother.

Before leaving for Oregon, Jack wrote to Cornelius Van Til, the professor of apologetics at WTS. For his summer self-study, the college sophomore wanted Van Til to recommend a good textbook on logic, another on the history of philosophy, and one on the history of the Christian church. He also asked Van Til to send him his classroom syllabi, and the professor obliged.

The Millers' postponed, summerlong honeymoon was worth the wait. Alone with his new wife atop Snow Camp Mountain, Jack instructed her in the topics of the Bible, theology, and logic. They also studied Shakespeare together, and Jack taught her to love all sorts of literature. Rose Marie said later, "Jack taught me more in one summer than I learned in four years at the university."

The summer job gave the Millers free housing, in a one-room lookout where Jack watched for fires, plus enough money to pay for their food. Rose Marie, a city girl, learned to cook on a wood-burning stove and to clean using water that was carried from a nearby mountain stream. Many mice scampered through the cracks in the walls, and when Rose Marie started to wonder what else might squeeze through the gaps, Jack taught her to shoot a .22 caliber rifle.

When they returned to San Francisco in the fall, Jack became shift manager for the cafeteria. The new position helped him to earn a little more money and, in turn, to upgrade their lodgings from a room in a boarding house to a one-room apartment that cost thirty dollars per month and included a small kitchen. Still, their money was tight. Rose Marie wanted to deliver their first child at the hospital where she had worked during her nursing program, but they could not afford the eighty-dollar hospital bill this would involve. The young couple scrimped and saved to be able to prepay twenty dollars a month for four months.

Roseann was born in January of 1951. It was a difficult delivery—Rose Marie lost a lot of blood and took several months to recover. It was typical at the time for husbands to be excluded from delivery rooms; Jack drove Rose Marie to the hospital, dropped her off, and went home to finish his term paper. He would not find out that he had a daughter until the next morning.

The young family spent that next summer at a different lookout in southern Oregon. Jack again informally enrolled himself in his self-study educational program for becoming a philosophy professor. The lookout this time was so small that the family slept in a tent, placing Roseann in a banana crate that they used for carrying groceries up the mountain.

When Jack, Rose Marie (who was now pregnant once more), and their daughter returned to San Francisco again, they discovered that a friend at church had a beautiful seven-bedroom home that was tied up by the city's rent-control ordinances. For as long as the city mandated a rent that was no higher than twenty-five dollars a week, the friend let the growing family live comfortably in the large house as Jack continued his studies in philosophy and history. The Millers' second daughter, Ruth, was born in March of 1952, and just before Jack's final college exams in May of 1953, Rose Marie gave birth to Paul—their only son. Around the same time, the property owner at long last settled the house's rent-control issues. The Millers, who were unable to pay a higher rate, now had to find a new place to live, pack, and move—all within a month.

Again God provided for the Miller family. Another friend from church offered them a short-term lease on a three-bedroom apartment for thirty dollars per week. While this was all going on,

Jack completed his undergraduate education at SFSC, earning a degree in philosophy with a minor in history. The previous winter, he had applied to the master's program at Cal-Berkeley and received his acceptance letter. He planned to start classes there in the fall semester.

DURING JACK'S TENURE at SFSC, he studied under Alfred Fisk—a professor of philosophy and religion who was known as "the lion of San Francisco State."[2] On more than one occasion, Jack watched silently as Fisk, a liberal theologian, destroyed the faith of young, naive conservative Christians. He dreaded the day that Fisk would subject him to one of his notorious attacks.

Eventually Fisk challenged Jack in front of his classmates, asking him, "How can you believe in miracles that break the laws of an orderly universe?" and going on to make an argument that Jack summarized as "God cannot break his own laws and be trustworthy; therefore there is no place for miracles if God is dependable."[3]

Jack's fear faded as the Lord came to his rescue. Quoting from Scripture and citing Machen's *A Christian View of Man*, he questioned his professor's presupposition that they both mutually agreed about the "laws of nature" and the "plan of God."[4] Jack explained that God sovereignly exercises wise control over both the miraculous and the ordinary—over every part of life, not only miracles. Fisk recognized the influence of Machen—his former Princeton professor—in Jack's answer. Instead of engaging him further, he moved on to another student.

Emboldened by his classroom encounter with this professor, Jack decided that there was no reason to fear the lion of SFSC. Thinking of the warning in Matthew 18:6 for those who cause little ones to stumble, he scheduled a meeting with Fisk during his office hours a few weeks later. During their meeting, Jack explained the conversion he had undergone from an atheistic background and the fact that reading Machen had originally made him furious—an explanation that he later summarized this way: "I couldn't understand—and didn't like—the idea of God being in charge of every part of my life. . . . If there was one thing I had learned from my family, it was the importance of self-reliance. Until I met Christ, this [self-reliance] had been my religion."[5]

Jack momentarily forgot that he was talking to the lion of SFSC as he said, "God showed me my ugly egocentricity, and this knowledge of my deep sinfulness drove me to trust in Christ's work on the cross for me. My surrender to Jesus has given me a joy that I can't find words to express."[6] He then came to the reason that he had scheduled the meeting with Fisk: he was concerned about what Fisk had done to another student. "He came to your class a believer and will leave it deeply confused. He is a simple person and untaught. I don't think what you did to him was right."[7]

Fisk astonished Jack by opening his life to him. On his journey to liberalism, Fisk had written to Machen, in hopes that his Princeton professor could give him guidance before he threw off his Calvinist upbringing. He wanted someone to help him to sort through his growing doubts about Christianity and the fundamentals of the faith. "Machen wrote only a brief note to acknowledge my long letter. He did not say much more than that 'I would understand when I became older.'"[8] Fisk felt that Machen had dismissed him—and he did not want to dismiss Jack in the same way.

Filled with compassion, Jack said, "Dr. Fisk . . . come to faith. There is no other hope for a sinner like me except Jesus and his blood, and that hope can be yours."[9] That his professor refused to trust in Christ deeply saddened Jack.

Jack's encounter with Fisk profoundly challenged and stimulated his thinking. He realized that Fisk, and those like him, "were believing [in themselves] when they should be skeptical. [Fisk] had his faith entirely in the wrong place. He was trusting reason as his final authority, making his human mind into his Bible."[10] Doubts were not Fisk's primary problem—instead it was that he was not doubting *himself* enough! Jack wanted Fisk to "doubt [his] doubts"[11]—to doubt his self-reliant reasoning and his humanistic understanding of natural laws, on which he had constructed his dismissal of the sovereign God and of his providence over both nature and miracles. Jack left his professor's office resolved to become God's skeptic to modern skeptics—a resolve that shaped his life and ministry in the long term and altered his study program in the short term.

JACK'S ENCOUNTER WITH Fisk had gone better than he had expected, but it had also exposed a significant divide between theological education and real-world experience. Even though Jack had withstood liberal theology up to then, he began to realize what sorts of assaults on his faith might come from the philosophy faculty at Cal-Berkeley. In the end, he decided that he needed to study under WTS professor Cornelius Van Til in Philadelphia before pursuing advanced studies in philosophy at Cal-Berkeley.

Rose Marie's father's business was doing well enough for him to afford to employ additional help who could care for his wife and for Barbara, which freed Rose Marie and the children to join Jack as his short-term educational plans changed. First OPC in San Francisco financially supported the Millers' move to Pennsylvania by sending them money monthly for food. Jack Julien, an elder at First OPC, paid for their airline tickets to Philadelphia. The family lived in a cramped four-room apartment on the second floor of a row house in Germantown. Roseann slept in the front room; Ruth slept in the second room; Paul was in the kitchen; and Barbara, who was born in Philadelphia, slept in the hallway.

WTS charged no tuition at that time, and support from First OPC paid for a few of the family's expenses. To cover the rest, Jack worked at a nearby milk factory in the early mornings. His days were long, however—the morning shift at the milk factory began at 4:30 a.m.—and after the gentle climate of San Francisco, he found the cold Philadelphia winters extremely difficult. Because the family had no transportation of their own, Jack waited outside for the bus on blistering cold, wintry mornings—until eventually Bob

DeMoss, a fellow student at WTS, helped him by giving him a lift to and from school. Jack and Rose Marie both became sick during those cold winters, and Jack in particular suffered from debilitating sinus infections.

Jack enjoyed sitting under the esteemed faculty during the two years he spent at WTS, and he especially enjoyed John Murray's teaching on union with Christ. He excelled in his classes—until his exhaustion and recurring sickness began to prohibit him from working, which overwhelmed the struggling family with financial problems. After experiencing a particularly difficult second winter, the Millers decided to return to California—despite pleas from professors at WTS, and from OPC church leaders, for Jack to complete his final year at the seminary. To make the most of his remaining time there, Jack quit his job in order to take as many extra classes as the seminary allowed.

As Jack RETURNED to California in 1955, Van Til recommended him to his friend Dr. Gilbert den Dulk, a physician in a small Dutch community in the town of Ripon. Ripon Christian School (RCS), which was associated with the Christian Reformed Church (CRC), had a teaching vacancy in English. Even though Jack preferred to teach philosophy, he gladly accepted the available position. The one source of frustration, for both Jack and leaders in the OPC, was the CRC's requirement for Jack to transfer his officer ordination as deacon from the OPC to the CRC in order for him to teach at RCS.

When the Millers arrived in Ripon, they had no savings, no phone, no car, no bank account, no insurance, and no credit. Jack worked in local peach orchards until school started, and then, from September of 1955 to May of 1961, he taught English and church history to RCS high school students.

After their move to Ripon, Rose Marie began to experience a growing discontent with Jack and with their living situation for the first time in their marriage. RCS paid Jack $285 per month—just enough for the family to afford food and rent. The Millers, who now had four children who were all under the age of five, squeezed into a small two-bedroom house near Ripon's one-bed jail. Feeling out of place in the closed Dutch community, in a house that was on the opposite side of town from the school and the nicer neighborhoods, Rose Marie thought it would be reasonable to find a new house that would move them a little farther from the jail and would have one additional bedroom. In addition, while her and Jack's own health had improved since they had left Philadelphia, Roseann now had a heart problem. Rose Marie felt defeated—anger with God and with Jack, as well as guilt over feeling that anger, began to replace her faith.

While Rose Marie struggled with her discontent, Jack busied himself teaching school. As a student of Van Til, he was particularly drawn to the thought Van Til's fellow Dutch Calvinist philosopher Herman Dooyeweerd, who was first published in English in 1953. Those who were in their Amsterdam school of philosophy took presuppositions about the truth of the Bible, God's sovereignty, and the gospel and then used common language to apply them in practical ways to different fields of study: Dooyeweerd to science, Van Til to apologetics and philosophy, and Rousas Rushdoony—an OPC pastor and theologian—to government and law. Jack saw that this Dooyeweerdian approach could be applied to literature as well, and he started writing a text outlining his original ideas for doing so. His high school students responded positively, but the leaders of the school pushed back. They wanted Jack to teach English and church history rather than pursue his own new ideas.

Summer breaks gave him further opportunity to study, research, and write. He sent a two-part essay on John Milton and John Bunyan to his OPC colleague Rushdoony and published an article titled "Love and Sentiment" in *Torch and Trumpet*, a periodical that was published within the CRC. Van Til would come to visit his friend den Dulk in the summers and would freely tutor Jack while he was in town. Jack looked forward every year to his arrival and was always ready with a list of discussion points for him. When Van Til would come to Ripon, Jack would disappear with his philosophy mentor for hours, leaving Rose Marie to tend to meals, the children, and the house.

In order to earn additional income, Jack worked part-time raising awareness and support in central California for WTS. He also started a Bible study in Modesto, California, twelve miles south of Ripon, after visiting homes as part of support-raising travels that he performed in November of 1956 and meeting numerous families who invited him back. Other families joined the growing study, and by the end of 1957, the group began having discussions with the OPC's presbytery about organizing morning and evening worship services. Though the church that resulted credits Jack to this day with laying its foundation, to him it "appear[ed] to be one of [God's] spontaneous products, a grass-roots development."[12]

Seeing the success that Jack was having at generating interest in WTS, Robert Marsden, executive secretary of the OPC, pressed him to extend his support-raising work full-time and to travel around California raising support for the seminary during the summer of 1957. Jack was open to working for Marsden over the summer, but when he proposed that he bring his family on the road with him, Marsden rejected the suggestion. Although Marsden offered to pay him eighteen dollars per day—far more money than he could earn in the peach orchard or at the lookout—if he would travel for the summer by himself, Jack turned down the offer.

Marsden had had even higher hopes for Jack than just wanting him to raise support over the summer. The OPC desperately needed qualified pastors, and he believed that the success Jack had experienced with the Modesto Bible study suggested that he had "all the gifts necessary for pastoral work"—a work that Marsden considered to be a more important calling than that of teaching in a Christian school. He wanted Jack to complete his own seminary training in Philadelphia and thought that Jack should leave his family out west during that time as well, saying that "there are very few fellows who are able to get through seminary when they have several children for distractions."

Jack had no intention of leaving his family behind—but he was torn between his love for Christian education and his love for the work of ministry. Although he was committed to follow the educational track that would lead him toward becoming a philosophy professor, he was becoming more open to the idea of teaching in a seminary such as WTS. Nonetheless, in letters that he wrote to Marsden, he explained a specific task that God had given him: "I am trying to write a text in the field of literature. I think I have some original ideas about interpreting literature from a Christian point of view. . . . My scholarship needs to be sharpened considerably before I can accomplish this task. This is the main reason I am not rushing into the ministry. God has given me a task to complete in this field, and I must see it through. I am afraid there would not be time for it in the ministry."

Jack and his family spent the summer of 1957 at the lookout in southern Oregon. Jack rested, studied, and enjoyed time with his wife and children. Then, fortified by the training he had received at WTS, for the second time he applied for and was accepted into the master's program at Cal-Berkeley, where he was scheduled to start classes in September of 1958.

Even as Jack continued to teach in Ripon, the Presbytery of California recruited him to plant an OPC mission in Stockton, California—a city of more than a hundred thousand people. Stockton had a core group that was gathering for a Bible study, and the presbytery had been looking for a church planter there. Jack already knew several of the Stockton Bible study members through the Modesto Bible study and RCS. He accepted the presbytery appointment—and once he did, things moved rapidly. In January of 1959, the session of an OPC church in Sunnyvale ordained Jack as an elder and appointed him and another elder to the Stockton mission. In early April, the presbytery received the church plant, which had been newly named Bethany OPC, and licensed Jack to preach there. Bethany OPC issued a call to Jack at the presbytery's September 24 meeting that year. The presbytery ordained Jack as an evangelist on October 9 at an adjourned meeting, while noting his call as an "irregular call"—since he had not yet completed seminary or filled in all the gaps of his education with self-study. (In the words of WTS professor Clair Davis, Jack's future colleague, "Irregular means [that] it's so hard to do it right you end up doing the best you can."[13]) Rousas Rushdoony moderated Jack's installation service while Henry Coray preached a sermon from Joshua 4:6 titled "What Mean Ye By These Stones?" The Miller family moved to Stockton in late 1959, and Keren, the last of the Miller children, was born in Stockton the following April.

In Stockton, Rose Marie became deeply discouraged. She had believed that she and Jack were in partnership with God. Now, both God and Jack were beginning to feel more like her enemies. She did not want to be a pastor's wife—all their plans, for so long, had been for Jack to become a professor of philosophy. Now the church took up Jack's time and attention, which left Rose Marie to try to take care of the children without as much support as she'd had before. Anger, self-pity, and bitterness toward God and Jack joined her growing list of disappointments.

It was not just Rose Marie who became discouraged in Stockton—Jack also lost his joy there. The church plant was the most difficult ministry experience he had undergone to date. The Stockton group of diehard Calvinists differed dramatically from the Modesto group that Jack had started from scratch with people who were hungry for the gospel. The church was stable financially, growing slowly (after having managed to purchase a building in February of 1961), and sound theologically (in its own estimation), but it had little joy. To address the problem, Jack taught a series from Jonathan Edwards on glorified joy—a joy that he himself was not experiencing in his own life. He started a prayer meeting, recognizing that true joy comes as a result of God's presence. When no one showed up to the meeting, including God, Jack's joylessness deepened as he started to believe that he had killed the prayer meeting and was on his way to killing his joyless church as well. Rose Marie described Jack's first pastorate succinctly: "It was a mess."

Teaching at RCS while simultaneously serving the church plant in Stockton made for a hard and busy life for Jack during the school year. When he was given the opportunity to begin his doctoral studies at the University of the Pacific in September of 1961, he did so rather than returning to teach at Ripon and beginning his classes at Cal-Berkeley. Though Pacific was less distinguished than Cal-Berkeley was, it had the notable history of being the oldest chartered university in California and a good reputation for training professors and teachers. Pacific gave Jack a full tuition scholarship and a $1,750 stipend to teach undergraduate-level courses in literature and English comprehension. He consequently ended his employment as a high school teacher at RCS in May of that year.

Jack also resigned as pastor of Bethany OPC when a prominent conservative libertarian think tank hired him as a research consultant in January of 1963. Bethany OPC called Gerald Latal to succeed Jack that November. Although Jack led prayer at Latal's installation, the session refused to allow him to preach at the service. The refusal surprised Jack, who thought he had left them on good terms. When he inquired further, he learned that he had offended an elder's wife the year before. His attempts to reconcile with the elder and his wife would not succeed until a decade later.

DURING A PIVOTAL time for the formation of the religious right in the United States, Jack would sharpen his scholarship as a consultant at the highly regarded think tank that had hired him.

The organization had originally started as the William Volker Fund (WVF), a charitable trust that was named after the business magnate and Christian philanthropist who founded it in 1932. At first, WVF focused on local philanthropy. However, when Volker's nephew, Harold Luhnow, was entrusted with the fund in 1944, he began to use it to shape American opinion and national politics.

WVF funded the Intercollegiate Society of Individualists and the Foundation for Economic Education (FEE), as well as FEE's flagship publication, *The Freeman* magazine; supported conservative libertarian scholars and intellectuals such as Milton Friedman, Friedrich Hayek, and Ludwig von Mises; and supplied significant financial and intellectual resources to Barry Goldwater's 1964 presidential campaign.

At first, WVF worked indiscriminately with atheists, secularists, Roman Catholics, nationalists, Protestants, and Calvinists as long as they were libertarian and conservative. Then, in the summer of 1962, Luhnow announced that the conservative libertarian movement should merge its economic and social conservatism with Christianity. He changed the fund's name from WVF to the Center for American Studies (CAS). In addition, he called for the removal of irreligious staff and directed the remaining leadership to wind down financial support for non-Christian scholars. Then he hired promising scholars to join the leadership team and directed leaders to further recruit scholars who were not only conservative and libertarian but also committed Christians whom CAS could support in their research. With Luhnow's approval, CAS hired three leaders to key positions: Rousas Rushdoony, who was made responsible for formally integrating Christianity into CAS; editor-in-chief of the University of Chicago Press William Terry Couch, who focused on publishing; and nationalist Harvard historian David Hoggan, who actively recruited academic scholars.

Seeing an opportunity to bring Van Tilian presuppositionalism to shape CAS, Rushdoony immediately hired Jack as a research consultant for the fund at $9,000 per year—far more than Jack and Rose Marie had ever earned. The Miller family moved to Redwood City in January of 1963 with the help of a $500 loan from Luhnow. But, while Rushdoony and Jack agreed in part about Calvinism and Van Tilian apologetics, their approach to them differed. Jack's was winsome and gospel-centered, while Rushdoony would aggressively push his Calvinism onto non-Calvinist intellectuals who were just as entrenched in their beliefs as he was—leading CAS to terminate his management contract in September of 1963.

Although Jack feared for his own job, he survived his association with Rushdoony. The same leaders at CAS who had resented and unequivocally rejected Rushdoony's wrathful brand of Calvinism seemed pleased with Jack's winsome approach to apologetics. Jack used the language and apparatus of culture to expose non-Christian presuppositions and then rearticulate them on a Christian foundation. Had he watered down his Calvinist commitments in order to accommodate the CAS leadership? Jack did not think he had done so—at least not in a way that undermined his beliefs. In a letter, he wrote, "I have been plain-spoken in questioning the vagueness of the Center's aims."

CAS paid Jack primarily to focus on his doctoral research and writing—a job description that he heartily embraced, as he went on to read widely in areas and subjects of interdisciplinary studies that few have ever had opportunity to pursue so diligently. He saw his time at CAS as an "opportunity to meditate and mature for further service," and he appreciated the chance to gather "varied contacts"— some wealthy and influential—whom he believed would "eventually turn to the benefit of God's Kingdom." He became academically conversant in a wide range of subjects that lay under the general heading of intellectual history. WTS professor William Edgar said, "He knew about the rise of the middle class in the eighteenth century, and he knew about the secularization of the American novel in the nineteenth century, and he was very conversant in politics. . . . You know he'd read everything, and he could comment on anything. We could ask him about eschatology, and we could ask him about his views of the church; we could ask him about trends in the world or trends in America; we could ask him about the arts. I mean, he was just un-stumpable."

For his doctoral dissertation, Jack brought a Dutch Calvinistic approach to the field of literary analysis. Writing on the last five novels of the nineteenth-century author James Fenimore Cooper, he applied Dooyeweerdian thought to literary analysis in the way that Dooyeweerd himself had applied it to science and Van Til had applied his Dutch Calvinism to philosophy and apologetics. Secular humanists had dismissed Cooper's last five novels as being made up of religious pessimism and rants against society. Jack argued, in a thesis that he would eventually defend successfully in front of a secular faculty, that Cooper's optimistic Christian realism involved trusting divine providence and sovereign grace to continue moving history onward, not downward—despite the magnitude of human pride and the depth of social decay that the author saw in the United States.

During his eighteen months at CAS, Jack rapidly wrote a comprehensive, three-volume work on the history of public education in the United States, which was titled *Man in Modern Education*. The work took a Van Tilian presuppositional approach, and its thesis asserted that "modern education is without a coherent anthropology." Highly regarded scholars reviewed the comprehensive history, and CAS hired former *Time-Life* editor Herbert Kay to serve as its editor. Jack described Kay as "a well-known rationalist who has become a zealous Romanist convert," and he was relieved when circumstances prevented Kay from working on the project.

WHEN JACK TOOK the research consultant job, CAS had been in discussions with the Hoover Institution at Stanford University about becoming a permanent, self-funded conservative think tank under the university's umbrella. They also were discussing the formation of a Christian college. Both possibilities gave Jack reason to hope that his consultancy with CAS would lead to a full-time professorship.

The reality turned out to be far different, however. This towering international fusion of academics and intellectuals collapsed as CAS's focus shifted and conservative libertarians, many of whose influential leaders were not professing Christians, scattered into groups and subgroups across the United States. Then Luhnow had a severe stroke in January of 1964, which ended his discussions with

Stanford. In February, CAS renewed Jack's contract for a second year as *Man in Modern Education* moved toward publication. However, Jack was concerned about the direction of the organization's leadership and about Luhnow's deteriorating health. According to Edgar, whom he confided in later, Jack also thought that "the Theonomy people [at the think tank] verged on prejudice. The theme of anticommunism had been overdone, and he just worried that it was a kind of strange version of Christian America that he just couldn't entirely buy into."

Meanwhile, Edmund Clowney, head of the WTS practical theology department, was hiring faculty members to join the department. In March, he recruited Jack to return to WTS, finish his seminary training, and then join the faculty after also completing his PhD. Jack traveled to Philadelphia that month to map out this plan with Clowney. Soon after, Hoggan, the Harvard historian at CAS, made international headlines when it surfaced that he was a Nazi sympathizer, supported Hitler, and denied most accounts of the Holocaust. Without Luhnow's leadership, CAS collapsed under the intense, unanswered criticism that arose over this Hoggan debacle. Luhnow shut the organization down in September of 1964, and *Man in Modern Education* was never published.

PRIOR TO MOVING EAST, Jack needed to complete his qualifying exams at Pacific, find employment in Philadelphia, and rent a large home that would be sufficient for five children as well as Rose Marie's side of the family, who were now planning to join them. He passed his comprehensive exams in March of 1964; the OPC's Committee on Christian Education hired him, at thirty hours a week, to help to publish *The Mark Magazine*; and he and Rose Marie rented a large house on Walnut Street in Jenkintown, Pennsylvania, from Robert den Dulk—a son of the Californian den Dulks and a recent graduate of the seminary. Rose Marie's father had sold his auto business, so he, his wife, and Barbara were able to move to the in-law suite of the Millers' Jenkintown home six months later.

When Jack and his family began visiting OPC churches in the area, the churches struck Jack as being ingrown—turned in on themselves and their own needs—rather than being outward-facing, and he was concerned about how that attitude might impact the spiritual well-being of his children. He decided that assuming a part-time pastorate would best serve his family's needs as well as his personal goals for teaching at WTS. In its April 1965 meeting, the presbytery of the West Coast approved Jack's request to transfer his ministerial credentials to the presbytery of Philadelphia. He started serving Mechanicsville Chapel (MC) as stated pulpit supply that summer, was enrolled as a regular member of the presbytery of Philadelphia in September, and was called as the pastor of MC by November.

When Jack came to MC, it was barely surviving as a church. Remotely located in Bucks County twenty-five miles north of WTS, the small independent church had gone without a pastor for years. A devoted remnant of older members had one foot in the church and one in the church's cemetery. Jack was essentially free to do what he wanted with the church, and so he turned it into a preaching station—a practical theology laboratory for WTS students to work out what they were learning in the classroom.

Enthusiasm for the direction that MC was taking grew at once among the handful of its remaining members, and, as an outworking of the church's renewed sense of mission, new converts to Christianity started attending weekly gatherings. Connections among the faculty of WTS, and with students who were hungry for practical ministry experience, gave Jack access to gifted teachers and future church leaders whom he could recruit for ministry. He enlisted Edward J. Young, professor emeritus of Old Testament at WTS, to teach on Isaiah. He also started an unofficial internship program for WTS students and targeted several Harvard graduates who had recently enrolled at WTS for inclusion in it.

God blessed the Millers in Philadelphia. Jack completed his seminary training at WTS in 1965 and became a professor there the following year. He also successfully defended his dissertation in 1968. His interdisciplinary studies in theology, philosophy, education, literature, culture, and politics—combined with his college and high-school teaching, church planting, and pastoral ministry—had uniquely equipped and prepared him for this next phase of his life and ministry.

Jack served in WTS's practical theology department from 1966 through 1982. Because of his catalytic leadership, he is inevitably brought up in debates about the high point of the seminary and used to demonstrate either the confessional strength or weakness that it evidenced during that period.

As of the year 2020, the seminary's history is typically divided into three generations: early Westminster (1929–1969), middle Westminster (1969–2009), and late Westminster (2009–). Several of Princeton Seminary's faculty, led by J. Gresham Machen, founded WTS in 1929 after Princeton turned away from historic Reformed Calvinism. The days of early Westminster ended with the seminary's fortieth anniversary, and Edmund Clowney, who was then president of WTS, stood at the transition.

In a special edition of the *Presbyterian Guardian*, Clowney published an article on behalf of the faculty that was titled "Moulded by the Gospel." In it, he publicly set forth an agenda for how the second generation of the seminary's faculty would build on the responsibility they had inherited to preserve the Reformed heritage in the United States. The same edition contained articles from Cornelius Van Til and Henry Coray—Van Til's looking back to the founding of WTS and its early faculty and Coray's looking forward to the threat that WTS would face should it forsake its own heritage.

Clowney explained the discontinuity between early and middle WTS with a changing of signs: a clenched fist signified the posture that early WTS had taken in its relentless battle with theological liberalism, while a bowed head signified middle WTS in its equally intense multifaceted struggles. In his use of these signs to mark the seminary's change, Clowney was suggesting neither prayerlessness within early WTS nor conflict avoidance within middle WTS. He wrote, "Westminster in years to come must be increasingly moulded by the gospel of Christ.... That means active, renewed subjection to the gospel.... There is an ever-present danger that we will take ourselves seriously instead of taking the gospel seriously. An academic community is particularly vulnerable to traditionalism and pride."[14]

An interest in biblical theology, which was a clear distinctive of WTS, unified its faculty's approach to the study of the Bible. Clowney noted the positive impact that biblical theology produced on different disciplines such as systematic theology, practical theology, Christian apologetics, and Christian philosophy. He traced this emphasis on biblical theology back to the founders and faculty of early WTS and to WTS supporters such as Princeton's Geerhardus Vos. Clowney also described, in that same article, a "new appreciation at Westminster for the infallible authority of Scripture" and emphasized the connection between piety and learning: "The teacher of theology must be a spiritual leader. The repetition of unappropriated truth is a peril to the soul of teacher and student alike."[15] This joining of piety with learning required the renewing power of the Holy Spirit in order to lead the teacher to deeper penitence, more urgent trust, and more faithful obedience to Christ. Ultimately, Clowney wrote, "we will be brought to fresh and immediate application of the gospel to our times. Our task is to present the message of the gospel, to prepare the messenger of the gospel, and to do so in the contemporary world."[16]

Jack, perhaps more than any other member of the WTS faculty, embodied the wholeness of this middle-WTS vision that Clowney had articulated—his content was biblical, he combined piety with learning, and he brought a gospel perspective to his times. He could express a bold clenched-fistedness when needed; more often, however, colleagues and students associated him with the sign of a bowed head. In addition, his emphasis on evangelism at middle

WTS maintained continuity with Van Til's emphasis on evangelism during both early and middle WTS. For years, Van Til had charged seminary graduates to engage in evangelism—a charge that was built into the heart of his complex apologetic thought. Jack's WTS classmate Bill Krispin recalled that "Van Til had a natural affinity toward evangelism. He believed you could trust God to use his Word according to his purposes." Consequently, Jack and Van Til would go street preaching together in the 1960s and 1970s.

Faculty and students of both middle WTS and late WTS have claimed that they are the heirs to the legacy of Machen and early WTS. Many former middle-WTS faculty consider their generation to be the high point of the seminary, while late WTS, to some lesser degree, considers the faculty of middle WTS to have moved away from the earlier "confessional" history of the school toward a more "broadly evangelical" or even liberal WTS.

The retiring faculty members of early WTS, however, did not think that middle WTS was breaking with the WTS of Machen. Van Til, who had been Machen's colleague and a founding faculty member of the school, wrote, "There is now still at Westminster a band of men who are resolved that, though they have little strength, they will use all strength to keep [God's] word and not to deny his name so that through that name the world may be saved. . . . Our faculty and our board are in entire agreement on the nature of our task in this situation. We would do what Machen tried to do, what Kuyper and Bavinck, Warfield and Vos tried to do, namely, take the flag with the name of Jesus to the top of the highest mountain."[17] In contrast, Rousas Rushdoony accused Clowney of being a liberal who "regretted the OPC's middle-class white Protestant look."[18]

Krispin, in an interview, expressed his belief that "Clowney was leading the revolution [at WTS] from the institutional side. He brought in Jack . . . as a specialist in evangelism. Jay Adams [whom Clowney also recruited] was there as a specialist in counseling and preaching." Bob Strimple, former academic dean at WTS, described Jack, Clowney, and Adams as three remarkable professors of practical theology: "It would be difficult to put together another team, all Reformed and sincerely subscribing to the Westminster Standards, and yet so distinctively different in their approach to preaching. In my role as VP for Academic Affairs, I would have students coming to my office to complain about [their] classes . . . all three prof[essors] had students who found their teaching not to their liking at some point. And my advice to these students was always the same: 'Take advantage of learning from the very best each has to offer while you are here.'"

Clowney recruited new students from around the United States, and the student body grew rapidly. In 1968, sixty-seven students in total were enrolled at WTS. By the early 1970s, student enrollment had nearly quadrupled to over seventy-five students per class. WTS would eventually boast a student body that was drawn from forty different countries and eighty different denominations. Since its inception, WTS has, in the words of the school's former professor John Frame, "supplied the theological leadership for the conservative evangelical Reformed Christians in the United States."[19] Seminaries, denominations, networks of churches, and parachurches across the United States and around the world have thus felt the impact of middle WTS—and of Jack.

OVER THE DECADES since the founding OF WTS, a gulf between education and ministry had begun to widen—while some seminaries and institutions emphasized practical theology in their courses, WTS emphasized theological education. To many minds at WTS, an emphasis on practical theology would threaten to open a door to liberalism—this was, after all, what they had seen happen at Princeton in the 1930s. Robert Godfrey, former president of Westminster Seminary California, explained.

There was this rather intense feeling that we [Westminster Seminary] are the academic successors of Princeton, we are the continuation of true American Presbyterianism, we have this burden to provide the best academic defense of Reformed Christianity. And I think there is still a kind of spirit that our main responsibility is an academic defense [against] the attack of the liberals on Christian truth. I think it was Jack who began to raise the question "Are we doing this at the expense of vital Christianity? Are we allowing our concern about an academic response to undermine an outreaching, evangelistic church life?"

WTS had carried over the theological rigor of Princeton without the theological liberalism, and, as a result, the seminary had an "extreme academic character," as former student Bill Krispin put it. Professors at WTS tended to busy themselves with their academic research, writing, and preparation for class lectures or with the special speaking engagements that are often requested of theological experts. Weekly Saturday faculty meetings followed Robert's Rules precisely. After the three-hour faculty meetings, a few professors, who had formed an amateur investment club, would remain behind to discuss their portfolios. Jay Adams temporarily succeeded in organizing the professors to eat lunch together, but soon the growth of the student body and the resulting academic pressures on the professors displaced his well-intentioned lunch gathering. In the classroom, professors would "exegete the passage in hopes that you'd see the principles they'd use," according to Krispin—and many would not allow questions during class.

When Jack joined the WTS faculty as a lecturer in practical theology, Van Til, who was aware of Jack's catalytic personality, cautioned his former student not to force any changes during his first year. Following Van Til's advice, Jack kept somewhat quiet for two years. Nonetheless, the lack of practical ministry opportunities for students appalled him.

Jack believed, as John Newton had said, that "Calvinism [is] one of the worst systems preached theoretically, but one of the best preached practically."[20] While other professors taught practical theology, Jack *did* practical theology side-by-side with his students.

He had a practical theology classroom at WTS, a preaching station at MC, and laboratories in the form of indoor and outdoor ministries all over the Philadelphia area. He maintained an open home and office in order to give students access to him; at times, he even threw his arms in welcome around students who came to speak with him. Hungry for ministry experience, students eagerly followed Jack wherever lost people lived and worked.

When WTS went on to appoint him as assistant professor of practical theology in 1968, Clowney expected him to do what other full-time faculty had done and resign his pastorate at MC— but the church wanted Jack to remain as their pastor. When he refused to resign, Clowney pressed him—in part because the seminary separated itself constitutionally from the church in order to avoid the complications that had been caused by the union of the Presbyterian Church in the United States of America with Princeton Seminary. However, as he saw the fruit that resulted from the connection between WTS and MC, he stopped pressuring Jack to resign his pastorate and continued to support the approach Jack was taking to practical theology by bringing together seminary education and ministry practice.

Krispin, who was a student himself at the time, recalled a growing frustration on campus—much of which was inspired by Jack's concerns: "There was a lot of ferment going on in the seminary. . . . We had something of a student revolution in 1968 where a group of us went to the faculty with a list of changes in the curriculum," such as adding a hermeneutics course. According to Krispin, when student representatives met with faculty, history professor Paul Woolley responded, "In order to have discussions in class, you have to have thoughts to think, and we give you the thoughts to think in class." "You mean we don't start thinking until we come to your class?" the student leaders asked. Woolley's comment came at a time when Harvard and Bob Jones were competing for first-place honors for the highest number of their own graduates who went on to attend the seminary—which made the insinuation that the students didn't already know how to think seem particularly unfounded. Eventually some students even began to boycott classes.

Campus speakers who focused on practical ministry caused further friction at the school. Van Til objected to Francis Schaeffer's coming to speak at WTS, so the seminary would not officially invite him; but then Clowney overrode his objection by giving students permission to invite Schaeffer instead—students who had interned with Jack at MC. The students also invited D. James Kennedy, founder of Evangelism Explosion, in the early days of his ministry. Since WTS was a faculty-run institution, it rubbed many of the faculty the wrong way when students brought visiting instructors to the campus without formal faculty permission—but with the support of Clowney and Jack.

Despite good developments in ministry practice at the seminary, Jack's first three years at WTS proved difficult. Years later, Adams described the tensions: "[Jack's] strong emphasis on evangelism, which was one of his most attractive qualities so far as I am concerned, often led him in different directions from others who were more academically inclined. . . . He often had little time for the sorts of concerns that were the prime interests of other members of the Westminster faculty."[21] Clowney had articulated the vision for middle WTS, and Jack catalyzed that vision on campus and at MC, which took some pressure off Clowney—but not without cost to himself, his wife, his children, and others. While some among the faculty and student body gravitated toward Jack, others avoided him.

JACK HAD RECOGNIZED at WTS a troubling divide between theological education and ministry practice, yet he was blind to a corresponding dualism within himself: a divide between the way he was practically working out his Reformed theology and the truth laid out in God's divine Word. "My entire theology had a big hole in it . . ." he confessed later. "I was stuck having to work out my salvation in my own effort, and I felt that was Reformed theology." He had missed something vital.

Jack's basic alienation from God left him insecure. He started seriously questioning his preaching, even though people who heard it found it to be more engaging and life-giving than most preaching. He found himself dealing with the same sense of nervous driven-ness that had marked his life before he became a Christian. Since his childhood, he had struggled with a hunger for acceptance and a deep insecurity—and now, in a seminary and ministry context, he had a much greater reputation to lose.

Rose Marie would later tell Jack that his ministries were "the source of [his] deepest joy and greatest fears"—she and his children could not compete with them for his attention, and they knew it. As a result of this, the Millers' eldest daughter, Roseann, struggled with suppressed anger as a teenager and believed that, in her words, "being a [husband] was far better than being a wife." Meanwhile, her younger sister Barbara drifted away from the Lord unnoticed.

Nonetheless, from 1968 through 1970, Jack received over-whelmingly positive responses from students and auditors who attended his assorted literary and theological courses: European Theological Novel, Christian Poets, Man in Contemporary Culture, Contemporary Culture and Evangelism, Gospel Communication, Calvinism in American Literature, and Group Evangelism. When WTS opened courses to the public, Jack's class filled the largest room at the seminary, then moved across the street to the sanctuary of Calvary OPC. The number of people who were auditing Jack's classes led WTS to charge auditing fees.

Work piled on top of work. Although he already had little time for his family, Jack took on even more responsibility by agreeing to edit a series of books in connection with the fortieth anniversary of WTS. He taught classes during the day, at night, and on week-ends in addition to going with Clowney to speak at conferences and churches from Pennsylvania to Florida to California as well as places in between. Meanwhile, he also took part in presbytery and served on presbytery committees as well as teaching evange-lism seminars at presbytery and at other churches. He accepted a presbytery appointment to the Standing Committee on Christian Education, was elected to the Committee on Home and Foreign Missions, and served on the Committee on Chaplaincy for In-State Institutions. At MC, he committed to pray one hour per day, preached, took students street preaching, and brought them to the hospital and on in-home visits. He even officiated the marriage of Broadway star Zoe Caldwell and producer Robert Whitehead. Throughout all this, an exhausted Jack continued to smile—earning him the reputation of being "the nice pastor in town."

As his reputation as an evangelist grew, however, so did his critical spirit. Pride that he felt in his ministry led him to be angry with others—an anger that the devil used as a foothold to fill Jack's impenitent heart with self-pity and bitterness. He judged others, saying that "it was plain to me that it [was] dangerously easy to play academic games in seminary and religious games in church," without seeing the ways that he too was playing academic and religious games. When he did not get his way, he fell into what Rose Marie called "Presbyterian minister's sin": "a tone of mild annoyance . . . expressed from the standpoint of moral and personal superiority."

Jack was not above receiving criticism—that is, if he could control the criticism. He did so by offering self-criticism and also by inviting critical feedback. As an example of the latter, he asked Schaeffer and D. James Kennedy for input about how to make his ministry effective and sought counsel from Martyn Lloyd-Jones, who was then a visiting lecturer at WTS. In June of 1968, he traveled to Fuller Seminary to ask Professor Donald McGavran, a highly esteemed leader in the Church Growth Movement, to critically assess Calvinists. Yet, even though Jack invited criticism from others, he had few people who were positioned to speak freely and critically into his life. Too many of his student acolytes overly adored him, and at times he did not respond well when he was questioned.

Insecure, Jack turned to research to improve his preaching. From his conversations with Schaeffer, Kennedy, Lloyd-Jones, McGavran,

Albert N. Martin, and many others, he distilled four common features that distinguished fruitful ministry leaders from those who were less effective: they (1) labored to make the gospel clear and relevant, (2) made themselves available to people and communicated the gospel where people lived and worked, (3) took risks and put themselves in vulnerable positions, and (4) demonstrated an unusual commitment to and effectiveness in prayer. By 1970, he had integrated the first three of these into his own ministry with a modicum of success—at least outwardly speaking. However, the significant hole in his theology and practice had taken a particular shape: prayerlessness. He simply could not produce in himself a life of committed, effective prayer—it eluded his techniques, models, methods, and resolve. Jack followed up with the leaders he had studied but was frustrated by their responses. Rather than giving him concrete things to do, these leaders spoke to him about how poorly they, too, prayed.

In 1966, Jack had been elected to the Committee on Church Extension and Home Missions of the OPC. When the committee approved a ministry three years later that would be based in the little town of New Hope, forty-five miles from Philadelphia, and would be modeled after Schaeffer's ministry L'Abri, Jack recruited William Edgar, one of the WTS interns from Harvard, to lead this initiative. Edgar had graduated from WTS that same year and moved to Connecticut with his wife. Now he returned to Pennsylvania, became a home missionary for the OPC, and was assigned to live in New Hope and reach out to the local community.

Edgar described New Hope as "an artsy community. It had art galleries and all kinds of alternative people. This is, you know, the 1960s, and there were a lot of . . . hippies and just people who would have been a good caricature of the '60s." The New Hope work started out with great enthusiasm. Jack and Edgar taught a lecture series in a local art gallery, and a Bible study started in the area as well.

Within six months, however, the ministry collapsed. Edgar felt that his gifts had been overestimated by Jack, and his L'Abri background translated poorly to New Hope. Not only did the Edgars need to raise their support from outside sources, but they also had a new baby during this time. With no regular paycheck or organization behind their work, money was tight for them; and Jack could not always help them, either, since he was often busy with all his other work commitments.

As the New Hope work began to fail, Jack grew suspicious of Edgar. He expressed concern that Edgar was spending too much time and energy at MC rather than in the nearby New Hope community. He also thought that Edgar might be asking people from MC for additional financial support—going back on an agreement that he had made to raise his support elsewhere. Jack sent another minister to investigate Edgar, then made unfounded accusations against him. Edgar, deeply hurt by his mentor, resented Jack's false witness against him. When he expressed his hurt and frustration, Jack responded in anger and required Edgar to attend counseling. The ministry came to a grinding halt, and the Edgars returned to Connecticut.

When New Hope failed, it took Jack's own hope with it. As he would later write, he could see "no future for the Christian church" and was "soured by [his] own failure as an instrument of change."[22] The state of the church distressed him: "I had been a pastor for more than a decade and an instructor at Westminster Theological Seminary in Philadelphia for four years. I had given it all my best shot. But as a change agent I had bombed out. I was awash with cynicism about the prospects of the Christian church and went around with continual sorrow in my heart over the state of the churches around me."[23]

WTS's classes would end in May of 1970. Jack had completed his two-year term there. He had not yet confirmed his acceptance of a new three-year appointment that was to start in July of that year. "In a mood of dark despair,"[24] he told Clowney and MC that he was resigning from both the seminary and the church, having already put together pulpit supply for MC for the next several months. Then he came home and broke the news to Rose Marie: "Honey, we don't have a job anymore." The announcement did not surprise Rose Marie; she had already known that her husband could not continue as things were.

Jack finally had time in his busy schedule to listen to and talk with God. He spent his first unemployed weeks in May thinking, praying, crying, and praying some more. As he prayed, he realized how much he "had been crippled by [his] liking to be liked."[25] He had entered into what Richard Lovelace called "an unconscious conspiracy" between this desire of his to be liked and applauded and the desire of his congregation to remain comfortable and undisturbed. In such a scenario, Lovelace said, "pastors are permitted to become ministerial superstars. Their pride is fed . . . and their congregations are permitted to remain herds of sheep in which each has cheerfully turned to his own way."[26]

Jack had been frustrated by the lack of change he had seen in the people around him, but he was, as he later confessed, "expecting [my church members and students] to have a life of repentance and faith that I didn't have myself. . . . I was a proud church leader who did not want to get hurt by his fellow Christians. I was expecting others to change in ways that I had not."[27] As a result, he had been "unable to deal with the lack of zeal for Christ that [he] constantly encountered among [his] fellow Christians."[28]

As he wept, Jack began to confront himself through a series of questions: "Why are you weeping?" "Do you see yourself primarily as a victim?" "Are you blaming others when the basic fault may be yours?"[29]

The demise of New Hope gave face to Jack's idolatrous need for approval. He had wounded Edgar and, in so doing, had sinned against Edgar's wife and newborn child—people whom he loved and who had trusted him. He had failed. He had made a fool of himself and lost his temper. Now the Spirit cut all the way into his heart, confirming his deepest suspicion and fear. Jack was far, far worse than he had ever imagined he could be. Without realizing what he had been doing, he had been abandoning the gospel—supposedly while doing gospel ministry—in order to build a record of his own righteousness and achievement. Now, naked before the Lord, he saw the sheer ugliness of his controlling desire for others to like him. He saw all his perceived good works come crashing down—in front of his family, MC, WTS, and the OPC.

As he realized that he and his need for approval were the problem, Jack repented before God and others of his "pride, timidity, and love of peer approval."[30] The faculty of WTS and leadership at MC urged Jack to rescind his resignations, which he, chastened as he was, gladly did soon after.

It was many years before he could express to Edgar the fullness of his repentance, since he would not see him again for nearly two decades. After WTS hired Edgar as a professor of apologetics in 1989, Jack immediately worked to fully repair the relationship. He invited the Edgars to his home and gave Edgar a letter containing his apology, which was too long and personal to be spoken. In an interview, Edgar described Jack's repentance as being "more than anyone could ask for. It was sincere and articulate. . . . It was wonderful."

Late 1969 through April of 1970 had been one of the bleakest periods of Jack's ministry. Coming out of it, however, he had learned that "[the Word of God] does not change men in the abstract, apart from application. A hammer suspended in the air never broke a rock, a fire must burn something, a sword must cut, and food must be eaten." In the summer of 1970, the hammer of God's Word would break the rock, the fire would burn, the sword would cut, and a starving Jack Miller would, as he often memorably put it, "eat the promises of God like a pig."

3

CHEER UP! GOD'S SPIRIT WORKS IN YOUR WEAKNESS

The Advantage of Weakness in Prayer,
Evangelism, Repentance, and Discipleship

ALTHOUGH ROSE MARIE was glad that Jack had taken back his resignations from WTS and MC, she knew that her husband had to leave Philadelphia for the summer or else his catalytic personality would keep him from getting any rest. Besides, this had been his crisis, not hers—and she wanted to go swimming. She made arrangements for friends to care for her parents and sister and contacted a Spanish acquaintance who offered the Millers a place to stay in Barcelona for two weeks. Their plans for the rest of the summer would have to fall into place later.

Rose Marie, along with the three youngest Miller children—Roseann and Ruth having moved away from home by this time—scrambled to earn money for the trip, and she and Jack applied for credit at a local bank to be able to purchase tickets for a flight to Luxembourg. Not only would this cost less money than a direct flight to Spain would, but flying to, and then ultimately back out of, Luxembourg also meant that they could stay with the Schaeffers at L'Abri while traveling to and from Barcelona. But even with the money that this saved them, Rose Marie would go on to work part-time as a teacher at a special-needs school until 1974 to help to pay off debt from their travels.

As he spent time with the Schaeffers, Jack saw that they prayed constantly. They dedicated whole days to prayer and seemed to pray before and after everything they did. Jack had previously thought that the reason he couldn't pray was that he was discouraged and depressed; now, however, as he watched the Schaeffers, he realized that he'd really been unable to pray because he was proud and unbe-lieving. His prayers had been hindered by his sin and weakness, and his ministry had nearly collapsed as a result.

Now, Jack began to see his weakness as an advantage—as the *occasion* for prayer rather than as a hindrance to prayer. "The whole idea of prayer is that we call on the name of the invisible God. To come in prayer is to abandon everything, to claim God's promises, and to know God."[1]

Once the Millers arrived in Barcelona, they had only two weeks in which they could stay at their acquaintance's second home before they would need to move to other housing. Acting on what they had seen at L'Abri, they prayed, asking God to provide them with a place for the summer that they could afford. On the beach, Rose Marie providentially met a woman from Germany. As she befriended the woman using the German that she remembered from her childhood, she learned that the woman and her husband were planning to return to Germany for the summer. The couple graciously allowed the Millers to housesit for them while they were away from Barcelona.

WHILE ROSE MARIE and the children enjoyed the Mediterranean, Jack, in Rose Marie's words, "did nothing but study." As he did so, he began to see that prayer is the means of laying hold of God's promises and realized that those promises God gives us in Scrip-ture are not an abstraction—instead, practically speaking, "each promise is a hook for pulling our faith into the heavens. There we catch God's missionary vision of a world filled with His praise."[2] He began to diligently chart these promises of God throughout the pages of Scripture.

In his studies that summer, Jack saw that the Old Testament prophet Isaiah drew a contrast between two distinct ages: the former age—which Jack himself also referred to as the old age—and the new age, or the last days. Isaiah compared the desert that had been central to the old age with the divine promise of a watered garden that would come in the new age. God promised that in the new age there would be an outpouring of water—which signified his Spirit—on those who were thirsty and that streams of water would flow on the dry ground (see Isa. 35:6–7; 41:17–20). Where there had once been only withering and desolation, he promised a new age of abundant fruitfulness—an age that would even include the Gentiles. Whereas the Lord had left only a very small remnant during the old age (see Isa. 1:9), he promised that in the new age his righteous servant would justify many by the knowledge of God (see Isa. 53:11). After the Lord's house would be cleansed by a spirit of judgment and burning in Isaiah's age, his glorious presence would cover the whole of Mount Zion and her assemblies (see Isa. 4:4–5). All the nations would flow to the mountain of the house of the Lord (see Isa. 2:2), and he would make a feast of rich food for all peoples (see Isa. 25:6–8). These Old Testament prophecies applied to the new age that has begun with the coming of the Messiah and the outpouring of the Holy Spirit at Pentecost and will continue to the new heavens and new earth.

As he studied these promises, Jack reached several conclusions that radically differed from those that are commonly held by Reformed people. Many Reformed Christians tend to believe that they live in an era of increasing apostasy and expect only a small number of people to be saved. Under this assumption, an embattled Reformed church construes its primary role as one of defending the truth. One pastor summed it up when he said, "Apostasy has reduced us to a remnant. We should really rejoice that ours is the privilege of purifying and strengthening these few."[3]

But Jack rejected this assumption: "Today we have the banquet of abundant grace! We must open the eyes of faith to the wonder of God's saving purpose, reaching out . . . to embrace the nations."[4] Though a remnant-minded church might view it this way, evangelism could not be secondary; it was, Jack said, "God's first priority for His Word and His Church."[5] He concluded, "In the new age, the state of life and power is normal for the church. . . . Rather than only a few people saved during an age of apostasy, Scripture itself characterizes the New Testament as fields white for harvest and the gathering in of large numbers of people." Jack argued that *many* will be saved, rather than just a few—that we live in the age of abundant life. In view of what happened at Pentecost, Reformed people must "abandon the idea of a Calvinist remnant."

Jack next abandoned another misguided notion: the idea that "Arminians are bound to be more successful evangelists" than the Reformed are. He was glad that Arminians took evangelism seriously; nonetheless, he believed that if God's promises in Scripture are true, then Reformed people should be the greatest evangelists of all. The absolute sovereignty of God and the lordship of Jesus Christ provide believers with the greatest possible motivation and confidence for evangelism.

Finally, Jack questioned a view that was common among Reformed people regarding prayer and evangelism. Calvinists tend to agree that prayer changes the one who is praying. They also agree that prayer is important for missionary work and has been commanded by God. But Jack argued that many Calvinists had the idea that "[because] God is sovereign . . . nothing much is going to happen in prayer"—leaving them unsure how or why prayer was important and thus also leaving them with little motivation to pray.

In contrast, he concluded that the sovereign Lord had ordained prayer as the means for Christians to activate the fulfillment of God's *missionary promises*. He explained,

Christians . . . have missed the exciting link between prayer and God's purposes in the world. It is, simply, that *prayer starts the promises of God on their way to fulfillment!* In prayer, God allows us to lay hold of His purposes as these are expressed in His promises. . . . By claiming God's promises as we petition Him in prayer, we set God's work in motion (Luke 10:1–3, Acts 4:23–31). Unbelievable as it may seem, the omnipotent God permits our requests to activate the fulfillment of His mighty promises in history (Rev. 8:1–5). As the laborers pray, He begins to ripen the harvest for reaping (Acts 13:1–4).[6]

"When I pray and do evangelism, I have laid hold of God's own . . . method [of salvation],"[7] Jack wrote. Therefore, he concluded elsewhere, "we must get down to knee-work."

THE MILLERS REMAINED in Spain through late August. The trip was a highlight of the children's adolescence—and the prelude to a revolutionary period of Jack's life and ministry. On the way back to Luxembourg, the family stopped at L'Abri once more. Jack disappeared with Schaeffer so that the two Reformed leaders could discuss what he had learned. The most important breakthrough, however, still remained weeks away.

When the Millers arrived back in Philadelphia after the trip was over, the children returned to school and Jack returned to his teaching responsibilities at WTS and his preaching at MC. Outwardly, things appeared normal. However, a thoroughgoing change was taking place in Jack's heart. Sensing that he was nearing a breakthrough, he continued studying God's promises into the fall.

As Jack read the gospel of John, he noticed a grammatical feature throughout the book that he had somehow overlooked. "I was astonished to see how many of [the promises in John in particular], possibly all of them, especially the thirsting and drinking ones, were in the present tense." When Jesus spoke, for instance, of the Isaianic promise of water in John 7:37–39, he used the present tense.

Moreover, he linked the fulfillment of this Old Testament promise with *himself*, and the apostle John then immediately connected its fulfillment to the promised Holy Spirit. Seeing how Jesus had spoken about these promises shook the former English professor. His use of the present tense indicated that the coming of the Holy Spirit inaugurated a whole new age.

Jack pulled out his Greek grammar and confirmed that the present tense of the language ordinarily includes a present linear sense. Thus, the Greek present tense involves the idea of continuation: "he goes" carries the meaning "he is going" or "he keeps going." Jack now saw that the English present-tense verbs "come," "drink," and "believes" in John 7:37–38 should be read as including that same idea of continuation: "come and keep coming," "drink and keep drinking," and "believes and keeps believing." Additional support for this conclusion appears in verse 39, in which the apostle John ties the nowness of the gospel promise to Pentecost: "Now this he said about the Spirit, whom those who believed in him were to receive, for as yet the Spirit had not been given, because Jesus was not yet glorified."

This exegetical insight struck a personal chord with Jack. He had looked to the past and seen a partial fulfillment of God's promises at Pentecost, then looked forward to their consummation at the second coming. Similarly, God's people in the Old Testament had looked backward and seen a partial fulfillment of the promises that had been made to Abraham and then looked forward to their consummation at the Messiah's coming. Jack noticed that, at the same time, he was also experiencing the same dryness and prayerlessness in his own life that the Old Testament people of God had commonly experienced. Rather than depending on the ongoing partnership of the Holy Spirit, he been trying to live his Christian life on his own strength—and thus, without realizing it, he had uncritically imported an overemphasis on covenant continuity between the Old Testament and New Testament. In so doing, he had failed to account for the stated *discontinuity* between the two that Jesus himself had identified.

By applying the Old Testament promises to both himself and the Spirit, Jesus was indicating a major change that had taken place within the new age. As the crucified Christ is glorified, he becomes the Lord of the Spirit—hence, the apostle Paul refers to the ascended Christ as now being the life-giving spirit (see 1 Cor. 15:45) and the Holy Spirit as being the Spirit of God's Son (see Gal. 4:6).

As conscientious biblical scholars do, Jack remained cautious about this possible new exegetical insight. He turned to other theologians—John Calvin, John Owen, and important Dutch Calvinist theologians such as Abraham Kuyper, Herman Bavinck, and Geerhardus Vos—and corroborated his findings with theirs.

Looking back years later, Jack wrote, "That was the crucial turning point in my life and ministry. Not just that I studied the promises, but I decided to become a Trinitarian. I believed in the Sovereignty of God, the greatness of the Father, the efficacy of the atonement, the riches of grace, the Son of God. But it all short-circuited because I had left the Holy Spirit out. . . . The Reformed insistence on the priority of the Spirit had drifted out of my life. It wasn't there." If he had not already been a Trinitarian at *all*, Jack could not have been ordained in the OPC or joined the faculty of WTS—what he was saying was that he became a *functioning* biblical Trinitarian in a way that closed the hole of prayerlessness in his theology.

He explained, "[Pastors] go month after month and they do not ask for the Holy Spirit to come to them. . . . They may even be suspicious [of being too] Pentecostal. Of course, it's Pentecostal, it comes straight from Pentecost." He did not believe that every event within the book of Acts would recur later in the history of the church—Pentecost itself would only happen once. However, "the book of Acts is not to be approached as a divine museum. . . . No, at Pentecost the resurrection life of Jesus Christ was imparted to the church by the Father as permanent and ongoing."

From that point onward, Jack fully embraced the role that both Christ and the Holy Spirit play in the gospel. He had come to see that, just as we have an advocate with the Father in heaven, so also we—both the church and individuals—have the Holy Spirit in us as the advocate of Jesus to effectually apply the gospel within the hearts of the elect. He delights to exalt the Lord Jesus Christ; to convict the world of sin, righteousness and judgment; and then to pour out the love God has shown in Christ into the hearts of those who believe—and keep on believing.

Jack credited Edmund Clowney for playing an instrumental role in helping him to work out the implications of this new biblical understanding of partnership with the Spirit. Clowney spent an evening with Jack and Rose Marie at the Miller home, during which he expounded the redemptive-historical significance of the promised Holy Spirit in Luke 11. The word *bread* appears frequently in the first thirteen verses of the chapter. Jesus taught God's children in verse 3 to ask for their daily bread when they are praying to their heavenly Father, and in verse 5 someone begs his friend to supply bread so that he can welcome another friend who is traveling. However, rather than using the word *bread* in verse 13, as one might expect, Jesus refers to the Holy Spirit instead: "If you then, who are evil, know how to give good gifts to your children, how much more will the heavenly Father give the *Holy Spirit* to those who ask him!" What was true about the present-tense verbs in the gospel of John is true about those in Luke as well—Clowney concluded, "If we are going to see God bless us in our time, we are going to have to keep asking for the Holy Spirit."

As Jack sharpened his focus on the way that we claim the promises of Scripture through prayer, he began to see that Christians have an important role within God's kingdom—not because of ourselves, in any egocentric way, but through our partnership with the Spirit. The triune God has chosen to work through sinners who are saved by grace in this—and every—generation.

Jack saw from Scripture that the promised Messiah and the promised outpouring of the Spirit had become one glorious promise that had been fulfilled through the person and work of the Lord Jesus Christ—a glorious promise in which all the other promises of God found their resounding "Yes!" in Christ. "To have the Holy Spirit in you is to have more of Christ in you, to be more like Christ and to bear the fruit of the Spirit which comes through faith in Christ and His merits (Gal. 5:22–23)."[8] Whereas Jack had earlier lived a fractured life, the *nowness* of the gospel brought a new harmony to both his life and his ministry. He saw that, theologically and practically, prayer, faith, repentance, and evangelism came together in a Trinitarian gospel harmony. He wrote, "Believing in Christ— the committal of the soul to the Lord in a faith-surrender—involves a deep humbling. . . . Repentant believers have the power to perform the deeds of repentance because they are in life-union with the resurrected Christ. They are full of the Holy Spirit and through earnest prayer seek and receive more of the fullness of God from the Father."[9]

Jack would often laugh as he joyfully declared, "Cheer up! You are far worse than you think you are"—which he always quickly followed with "Cheer up! God's grace is far greater than you ever imagined." And, while he is known for these two crucial statements, his 1970 breakthrough made it clear to him that they cannot stand apart from a third and equally important one: "Cheer up! God's Spirit works in your weakness." As he began to take small steps of obedience and trust that he was in partnership with the Lord, "bigger things began to unfold. As bigger things began to unfold, [he] began to realize, increasingly, [his] helplessness and inability." The more Jack saw his helplessness and inability, the more he prayed; the more he prayed, the more open he became to God's promises and the more he relied on the Holy Spirit's wisdom and strength to enable him to stand and move forward on the sure foundation that he had in Christ.

When Christian leaders would come to Jack for help after 1970, he would listen to them and ask questions. He saw how these leaders were as hopelessly stuck between the promise of Pentecost and the fulfillment of the second coming as he had been. After making little headway with some of the more stubborn ones, he would laugh with self-recognition as he asked, "Why did you come to me? I see you don't believe in the Holy Spirit. Have you ever thought about becoming a Trinitarian? Let God have a chance. Have you ever met God?"

WHEN JACK BECAME a biblically functioning Trinitarian, what impressed him the most was the divine power of the gospel. Before 1970, he had learned to communicate the basic content of the gospel message effectively (compared to most Reformed leaders), even though he had a bad conscience and an unravelling ministry.

After his spiritual revolution, Jack began to see the ongoing need that he had, as a Christian, for the gospel. He began to realize that if God was able to save him and his ministry from his self-trusting pride and unbelief, then no one was beyond the reach of God's omnipotent grace: "The love of God is shallow unless there is a depth to which it reaches, compelled by God's own justice and holiness in the gift of His Son." When he saw people who were trapped in unbelief, he was no longer angered or shocked by their sin. Instead, he was far more impressed with the omnipotent grace of God, who had poured out his love into people's hearts through the Holy Spirit. He wrote, "[When you meet human depravity,] it's like somebody throwing ice water in your face—utterly unexpected. You're shocked to see the evil in the human heart, and you suddenly realize what you knew theoretically—that only God saves people."

His knowledge that only God could save meant that Jack did not have to be afraid of the sin that was in the hearts of Christians and non-Christians alike. Instead, as someone whose own sin had been unmasked by the Holy Spirit, he could partner with the Holy Spirit in turn to unmask the sin of others and then call them to join him at the foot of the cross. He called this approach "Lordship evangelism" and referred to it elsewhere as "New Life evangelism" and "God-centered evangelism."

While the church had replaced the gospel's command for all men to repent with a polite suggestion that becoming a Christian would be a good choice, Jack's Lordship evangelism had a confrontational aspect: "You haven't really evangelized until you stand before the heart's door of the sinner and boldly knock." In order to evangelize effectively, Jack wrote, "we must be determined to get the message into the heart as well as into the ears. Our love must enable us to get past the man's prejudices and misconceptions so that the lost man hears the gospel as it really is." God's role, however, is essential: "God must use the words we speak to bring the sinner to the place where he is deeply ashamed of his sins, and God must teach his heart to trust in the Lord Jesus as Savior."

Jack's Lordship evangelism was influenced by J. H. Bavinck's discussion of *elenctics*—a term that comes from the Greek word *elegxei*, which means to convince, convict, or rebuke. Bavinck defined elenctics as "the science which is concerned with the conviction of sin,"[10] and Jesus shows in John 16:8 how important elenctics is to the sharing of the gospel when he says, "When [the Holy Spirit] comes, he will *convict* the world concerning sin and righteousness and judgment." In Bavinck's words, elenctics similarly "unmasks to heathendom all false religions as sin against God, and it calls heathendom to a knowledge of the only true God."[11]

Although elenctics often keeps company with the study of apologetics and philosophy, Bavinck argued that it properly belongs under missions. His insights impressed Jack, who developed his approach to Lordship evangelism by building up the elenctical aspect of Bavinck's thought in his own teaching and writings. The Lord had brought Jack down from his ministry pedestal to a place of shame and failure in order to rebuild him on the foundation of omnipotent grace. As a result, Jack learned how to confront people boldly and humbly with their sin by welcoming them as fellow sinners and inviting them to join him at the foot of the cross. In the vein of the basic concern of elenctics, which is to ask a person, "What have you done with God?," Jack would often ask questions such as "What have you done with the Lord Jesus Christ? What have you started doing or stopped doing because you love Jesus Christ?"

The part of elenctics that Christians often miss is their own personal unmasking—something that Bavinck warned against.

> The sharpest weapons must in the first place be turned against ourselves. . . . To be really able to convict anyone else of sin, a person must know himself, and the hidden corners of his heart very well. There is no more humbling work in the world than to engage in elenctics. For at each moment the person knows that the weapons which he turns against another have wounded himself. The Holy Spirit first convicts us, and then through us he convicts the world.[12]

When it is not combined with God's grace, the unmasking of sin is dangerous and cruel. To see the utter sinfulness of sin exceeds human ability. Therefore, the Holy Spirit is the only one who is truly qualified to convict the world of sin. He has sovereignly chosen to use unmasked sinners who are saved by grace as his instruments for doing this. Bavinck concluded that "elenctics is possible only on the basis of a veritable self-knowledge, which is kindled in our hearts by the Holy Spirit,"[13] and Jack himself agreed: "The essence of elenctics, the bringing of sinners to shame for their playing God, depends upon ourselves having been first brought to shame." He wished that Bavinck had spent more than one paragraph, out of hundreds of pages on elenctics, on this important point.

As Jack prayed for God to search his own heart, he realized that his basic alienation from God was a "root sin" that was feeding an organic network of "branch sins" that were appearing in his life as the works of the flesh. He had a problem with deeply seated pride and unbelief; and, while he had superficially struggled with this and repented of it, he had not really accounted for the inglorious nature of sinful unbelief and how deeply it contrasts with the splendor of God's majesty. He began to see that an ongoing struggle with unbelieving pride and self-importance was the central temptation for leaders in ministry—that "unbelief is the supreme transgression of the world."[14] While writing to a colleague, he confessed, "I would like to tell you . . . that I have solved this problem once and for all, but this is a struggle that is intense, like tearing the flesh off your bones."[15]

He could not have taken his sins of pride and unbelief seriously without having apprehended—or, better yet, having been apprehended by—the mercy of God. "Unbelief as the supreme sin is covered over by [Jesus'] sacrifice on Calvary as the supreme gift of the Father's mercy. . . . Repentance for the worst of sins is freely given to believers on the basis of the greatest gifts."[16]

When he confessed his pride and unbelief to his seminary colleagues, he naturally asked them how they were handling their own. Rose Marie said that Cornelius Van Til was among the few who joined Jack in his repentance, and she quoted him as confessing that "I struggle [with my pride] every day." When Jack asked people whom he discipled what they had repented of recently, he discovered that most Christians had stopped repenting after their conversion.

As he continued to be stretched spiritually, he wrote an informal essay on repentance in order to sharpen his understanding of the truths that God was teaching him. In the essay, he connected nearness to God with faith and repentance, which themselves then led to evangelism and discipleship. "Without sincere repentance," he wrote, "there can be no face-to-face fellowship with the Father of lights. For an unrepentant heart is self-satisfied, proud, cold." When others, seeing the change in Jack, would ask him for help, he would give the essay to them as "a single letter from [his] heart to [theirs]."[17]

Jack wanted non-Christians and Christians alike to discover the joy of coming clean with God. He strongly encouraged his WTS students to lead their churches in repentance. As he said in his book *Repentance*, the gospel should be preached to "both new believers and long-time Christians"—because the same danger faced both: "the temptation to think of the first conversion as everything and to forget that repentance and faith include a continuing, radical reorientation of the life toward God."[18] The Reformers and Puritans had described a life of repentance as a putting to death of the flesh. Jack, referencing Vos while giving a lecture, described ongoing repentance as a return to sanity—a coming back to God as the center of life.

Although many people found Jack's emphasis on repentance to be disarming and attractive, his leadership in this area could make others deeply uncomfortable. No one had witnessed another WTS leader confessing his sins, struggles, and weaknesses or inquiring so boldly about the sin of others. Some thought that he talked too much about repentance. Responding to this criticism, Jack said, "Jesus is not calling us to the great cover-up of all time in salvation. He's calling us to the great uncovering. That is what Judgment Day is going to be about; everything is being uncovered. So make sure you are confessing a lot of your sins now. If anyone complains about it just tell them you are getting ready; a lot more is going to come out."

Bill Krispin described what it was like to watch Jack "develop the whole idea of the pastor as the chief repenter":

> He couldn't give a talk without repentance. He would tell you what he was struggling with. He had a way of making you feel uncomfortable by asking, "What are you struggling with?" I'll tell you, I struggled with Jack for a long time. . . . It took me a long time to see this was genuine with Jack. He really meant this; he is really serious about this. I struggled. I had never heard anyone like that.
>
> I began to watch him more closely. Okay, he says this, but how does he follow through on this and how genuine is this? And I discovered over time that he was extremely genuine, and that was who he was. . . . He said, "We've got to begin our day prostrate before God, for God to examine our hearts and expose our sin and to humble us." Well, I didn't like the humbling part.

Jack did not set out to offend people, but the spiritually probing questions that he asked had that effect. The local church, he saw, wants "unrelieved blandness: a 'nice pastor' preaching 'nice sermons' about a 'nice Jesus' delivered in a 'nice tone' of voice. What is twisted about all this is that 'niceness' is being substituted for Christ's holy love, a heroic quality that might not in some circumstances prove to be nice at all. What we really want is to be comfortable and undisturbed. 'Nice' is just another way of being safe."[19] Thus his elenctical approach to leading the way in the area of repentance called for Christian leaders to have courage: "It will not be easy to tell those outside of Christ that their lives are built on presumption and pretense. And it will not be easy to tell confessing Christians that they too have taken for granted God's blessings upon their lives."[20]

Some students and colleagues tried their best to avoid Jack's spiritual probing. Joe Novenson, senior pastor at Lookout Mountain Presbyterian Church, writes, "There were times when I avoided the door of the church because I knew that he might challenge me again. Yet I never avoided him because I doubted his love. . . . I don't know that any pastor ever pressed me to see my sin while simultaneously pressing me to see my Savior with greater wisdom and faithfulness in my life."

WHEN JACK RETURNED to his teaching and pastoral responsibilities at WTS and MC, he was determined to act on faith rather than his feelings. Previously he had been immobilized by any weaknesses that he found in himself, because they challenged his self-reliance. Now his sin, failings, and inadequacies became occasions for him to ask God for more grace. In his teaching, he "focused on Christ's willingness to give the Holy Spirit on an ongoing basis to us now, as we in our weakness claimed the promises in prayer."[21] He had been freed from his crippling desire to be accepted and approved and liked, and no longer did he fear the judgment of his congregation. Instead, he wrote, "I had a new heart concern for them to enter into a life of faith, conditioned by the freedom of daily surrender to Christ and reliance on His Spirit."[22]

God's grace freed Jack to share his faith boldly with others as a sinner who was in need of grace himself. The Spirit filled his heart with the love of Christ, which he rejoiced to be able to share with others. This changed the way that he looked at people—"Instead of seeing the people I was teaching and ministering to as enemies, I began to see that they were as thirsty for living water as I was. I saw that as we drank of God's promises together, we would begin to change. What I didn't know was how contagious it would be when 'good' people began to repent of their superficial goodness and their underlying pride, greed, and arrogance."[23]

Biblical counselor Edward Welch, who would later sit under Jack's preaching, wrote, "I like Jack in the heat of battle, [especially] when he is preaching—when he is obsessed with the desire to communicate Jesus." Bill Stump, a WTS student in the early 1970s, described the first time that he heard Jack preach: "It was like a bright light lit up the room. Because he is so—I'm kind of paraphrasing . . . people who say they had heard Jesus—it was like he spoke as other men didn't speak. And there was something about him, a gentleness but firmness, and a love for Christ and love for people and love for the Word that oozed out of him in a way that I had never heard from any other faculty. . . . And I said, I've got to hear more from this guy."

As Jack and those who were around him embraced God's promises, they thought of unique ways that they could engage others with the gospel, through both open-air and indoor ministries. A friend who owned a restaurant called the New Hope Diner allowed Jack and some of his students to use it as a teaching venue, so they spoke there about relevant subjects such as drugs and the occult, literature, philosophy, art, and culture. They also taught at art studios, bookstores, and vacation resorts. Jack essentially moved his seminary classroom onto the streets and into the marketplaces of Philadelphia. When he preached outdoors, he would bring groups of people along to pray and to worship the living God together with him, as a demonstration of the harmony that Lordship evangelism emphasized between worship and missions. He also encouraged MC to hold Sunday evening worship services in front of the courthouse in Doylestown. When he would hear students expressing the gospel harshly, condescendingly, legalistically, cheaply, or dispassionately, he would teach them instead to preach by faith in a way that did justice to God's missionary love for a world that was under condemnation. This led, as a result, to an increase in conversions.

Jack occasionally engaged in door-to-door evangelism, but he preferred visiting malls, coffee shops, and restaurants in his neighborhood and asking God for someone he could speak to about Christ. He would introduce himself to people, listen to and converse with them, and trust the Lord to give him a natural opportunity to share the gospel with them. The most loving thing that he could do, he knew, was to ask people what they had done with the Lord Jesus Christ.

ONE DAY, when Jack was speaking on evangelism at a Philadelphia church, a pastor challenged his assertion that the gospel can change anyone. The pastor argued that "only the medical experts can help people who are psychologically damaged—like the people who want to commit suicide."[24] Jack later learned that a woman in the pastor's church had recently killed herself despite the pastor's attempts to help her.

Over tea that evening with Rose Marie and a WTS student, Jack sat quietly and thought about the pastor's objection. He asked himself, "Do you really believe that Christ's gospel can change anyone who believes it—or was that just talk on your part?"[25]

After praying, he talked with his wife, and the two of them committed to operating on the principle that "the Gospel would change anyone who will take it to heart." The Millers decided to open their home to *all* who might come to them in need of assistance—anyone, at any time. If anyone showed up at dinnertime, the family shifted around to make room for them. And, while Rose Marie's mother and sister were living with them on the second floor following her father's death, the basement and third floor were available for additional people who needed a place to stay. Although the Millers did not have much money, they made do.

Roseann, the Millers' eldest child, married James Trott, a Harvard graduate and soldier, in 1971. Soon afterward, she returned to live with her parents for a few weeks while her husband attended basic training. Although the ministry Jack and Rose Marie were doing was fundamentally the same as before she had left, it now had a vitality and excitement that she had not seen in it when she had lived with them prior to Jack's 1970 transformation.

At the time that she returned to live with them, an Irish girl with developmental disabilities was also living with Jack and Rose Marie, whom they had taken into their home in an attempt to help her before she could be given a lobotomy—her last proposed treatment. They gave her simple chores, such as setting the table, which she found impossible to do. She could not even pour water, because her hand shook so much. Jack and Rose Marie told her that not setting the table was sin—and that Jesus had died for sinners.

"I suppose this would be considered psychiatric malpractice today," Roseann said later, "and it might have been except for the startling fact that it worked. I saw her change before my eyes. She could set the table and function in the home. Talk of lobotomy faded. The gospel was alive and well under that mop of reddish hair."

Seeing the change in this girl made Roseann begin to wonder if God could change her, too. "I prayed and prayed, begging God to change me. Begging him to help my marriage. Nothing happened. One night at an outdoor youth group in Bucks County when the stars had come out and it was time for questions, under the cover of darkness I said, 'I keep repenting and repenting and nothing is happening.' And Dad said, 'Unless you turn to Christ, repenting is just turning in circles.'" God used her father's response to her question to help her to stop turning repentance into a new form of works-righteousness.

By the end of 1971, MC was growing so rapidly that the elders began pushing Jack to resign from WTS so that he could dedicate his time to pastoring the church. The twenty-five-mile commute to MC from home and WTS was also becoming increasingly difficult for him. When Rose Marie began experiencing a series of health problems in December, Jack knew that it was time for him to make a choice between the seminary and the church. Over Christmas break, he and Rose Marie looked for housing options in the Mechanicsville area. After the new year, still unsure about what to do, he traveled to New York to seek counsel from Francis Schaeffer. Recognizing the influence that Jack had on the generation of leaders he was training, Schaeffer advised him to remain at WTS. Thus, Jack informed the leaders of MC, to their disappointment, that he had decided to resign as their pastor.

Rose Marie's illness forced Jack to confront a new fear that he might lose his wife just as he had lost his dad. Despite periods of discouragement and strain they had experienced, their twenty-two-year friendship had been Jack's one stable point of reference throughout his life, and he depended on her more than on anyone else. On occasion he even became jealous of those who competed with him for her time and attention—including their children. Rose Marie often told him, "Jack, you can handle any conflict as long as you and I are secure in our relationship." She ended up requiring major surgery in February of 1972—and thankfully it went well.

Ministry success for Jack again collided with problems in his family during the summer of 1972. A group of his students at WTS worked during that summer at the Boardwalk Chapel in Wildwood, New Jersey. Over forty people trusted Christ during that summer, and several of them started auditing Jack's evening classes at WTS. But in July, while he was speaking at a missionary conference in Mexico, his daughter Barbara announced that she was rejecting the Christian faith. As she prepared to start college, she wanted no more to do with the rules and restraints of Christianity or with her parents' way of life.

In the heat of the moment, Jack and Rose Marie argued with Barbara. Jack recognized afterward, however, that he needed to understand God's love in a deeper way before he could help her.

He knew that only God can change sinners and that he himself could not. And since he could not, all that he could do was learn to depend on his heavenly Father.

Jack studied Scripture and expanded his personal essay on repentance that August. Three years later, Christian Literature Crusade published the expanded essay as what would be Jack's first book: *Repentance and Twentieth Century Man*. He had not written it about a theological abstraction; rather, as Rose Marie explained, "[Jack] wrote *Repentance* to remind himself and me that we were no different than Barbara—just helpless sinners who needed to turn from our sins and toward our heavenly Father who welcomes us for Jesus' sake."[26]

In November of 1972, Jack started a prayer meeting in his home for Barbara. At these meetings, houseguests who were living with the Millers shared their personal testimonies of the new life they had received in Christ, which set a tone of joy and expectancy. As those who attended prayed with one mind, they focused on the greatness of Christ's work on the cross, his resurrection, and the promise of the Spirit. During the first month, eight people were attending these prayer meetings. By the end of January, two attendees who had been unbelievers had surrendered their lives to Christ, and twenty-five people were packing themselves into the Millers' living room on Wednesday evenings.

During these meetings, the group began praying about a different kind of ministry that would be aimed at reaching non-Christians as well as people like Barbara who had left the church. They began asking Jack to consider planting a new church for this purpose, even though the OPC already had a presence in the Philadelphia area through several other churches. As they prayed, the group asked the Lord to bring about conversions and to raise up leaders as a way of giving a sign that he was at work to establish a new church. "Our aim was pretty clear," Jack wrote. "We wanted to reach people that ordinarily don't go to church."

Soon the presbytery of Philadelphia approved a church plant

for this purpose and appointed Jack to oversee it, along with Hugh Whitted and D. Clair Davis—elders from a local OPC church. In January of 1973, Jack taught a winter-term intensive course at WTS, "Evangelism and the Local Church," in which students met with him three hours a day, five days a week, for a month. The class led to a long-term ministry and mentoring relationship that developed between Jack and WTS students such as Bill Stump and Ronald Lutz. It also helped to establish the new church plant, since Jack organized an evangelism team that the students could take part in as one of the practicum options for the course. The team canvassed the neighborhood around his home and the seminary in order to gauge interest in the church plant and to invite people to its first worship service.

Finally, in February of 1973, forty-eight people packed themselves into the Miller home for the first official meeting of New Life Church (NLC). They began the worship service on Sunday afternoons at 4:30 p.m. as part of their aim to reach unchurched and de-churched people. "We discovered that there were an awful lot of people that would come to church if they could come just as they wanted to," Jack wrote. "They didn't mind the way I came, and I told them I didn't mind the way [they] came. . . . These people felt really at home."

NLC saw right away that they needed a larger meeting space. Jack assigned Stump and another WTS student, Steve Hohenberger, to find a suitable location. They found space in the Jenkintown Library, which was closed on Sundays and was grateful for the much-needed rental income that NLC was offering. At full capacity, the library accommodated 115 people. A Sunday morning service was added alongside the afternoon service in late 1973 to accommodate the church's growing attendance. Yet, even after dividing into two services, NLC had outgrown the library by July of 1974. The church moved across the street into the gymnasium of the Abington YMCA in August of 1974, where they remained until 1981.

For a church to meet at 4:30 p.m. in a library or gym is more acceptable today than it was in the mid-1970s—especially among conservative Presbyterians. NLC's decision to do so was, however, most effective. As space and available seating ran out, first in the library and then in the gymnasium, people brought blankets and sat on the floor for services—which could last for two hours or more, depending on the number of testimonies they contained and the length of Jack's sermons. And, because of the length of some of those sermons, some people brought snacks as well.

NLC formally petitioned the presbytery of Philadelphia in January of 1974 to become an established church in the denomination and was recognized by the presbytery as a particular church of the OPC on April 21, 1974. By early 1975, the average attendance of each service at NLC was well over two hundred people, and it was nearly three hundred people by 1976 and over four hundred by the end of 1977—which made NLC the largest church in the presbytery of Philadelphia. It grew by drawing in primarily new converts and people who no longer attended any church—when Christians from local churches would express an interest in transferring to NLC, elders would encourage them to return to their former churches instead. And eventually, so many WTS students—an estimated 10 to 15 percent of the student body—started attending NLC as well that the church was forced to ask them to find other churches in the area.

Jack explained, "A big factor in the growth of [NLC] . . . was commitments by leaders not to gossip again. And you know, you are surrendering some of the best pleasures in life when you stop gossiping. You have all this time on your hands, and what are you going to do? Well, you can pray. We would have revival, instant revival in America if all the church leaders and church followers stop gossiping and use that blank space for prayer."

Although Jack leaned toward the traditional when it came to music, he gave up his personal preferences in order to love the lost. William Viss, an elder at NLC and a classically trained musician, recruited gifted and trained musicians to lead worship with him. He typically selected songs from *The Trinity Hymnal* and his *Scripture Song Book* to serve as a source of biblical lyrics while giving the skilled musicians some freedom to adapt the songs' music style. The result was music that was lively, joyful, and familiar to new people who were attending church for the first time.

Jack's son-in-law Bob Heppe described what had struck him when he had first started coming to NLC. Although, at the time, he had been an "unbeliever hippie kind of guy" who "thought religion, Christianity, was passé, hypocritical, old fashioned, fuddy-duddy, unreal, and not authentic," NLC had impressed him.

> It was not extremely liturgical, but personal, and it was participatory. It wasn't just a leader who spoke to a congregation. . . . There was a time for interactive prayer, people raised their hands and asked for prayer, and people gave testimonies on a regular basis. There was structure to the church and there was freedom as well. . . . That impressed me. . . . There were older hymns . . . but they were played on a guitar with a piano and drums and musical instruments that I identified with. . . . And the teaching of the Bible was personal as well. Not just doctrine . . . not just knowledge about the Bible or faith, but you were hearing Jack and others speak about how the truth was touching them: their failures, their sin, their repentance, their discovery of grace. I don't think that was happening in other churches that much.

Some people ascribed the label "Wild Life" to the welcoming church rather than "New Life"; many people who attended it had never gone to church before, and some of them behaved in ways that made some Presbyterians uncomfortable—by, for instance, dancing at the back of the gym during the music. The discomfiting behavior even spread to some of the people who were *not* new to church—in one memorable instance, a seminary student picked up a basketball and started shooting hoops during a worship service. But, as abnormal as it was for these activities to be occurring during a worship service, the fact that they were coming from people who were generally unfamiliar with church as a whole served as a positive sign that the growing church was reaching the demographic it had hoped to—and its leadership quickly addressed any worship practices that were contrary to Scripture.

Some unbalanced social activism in the earliest stages of the church also attempted to overshadow the proclamation of the gospel in favor of social justice. As these types of issues arose, the leadership addressed them as well. The session regularly and consistently practiced biblical church discipline, regardless of the status or wealth of the person who required it or the complexity of situations that were involved—even if doing so came at a high personal cost to the church or to Jack himself. Some people left the church as a result.

From the start, "prayer was not an emphasis at New Life Church, it *was* New Life Church." Dave Miller, an elder of the church during the 1970s, wrote, "New Life was founded on prayer. . . . It wasn't just prayer for its own sake, it was prayer that was full of an awareness of the Presence of our Holy God. It was prayer that was full of adoration and joy in Christ. The prayer meetings went on for three hours and no one was bored! . . . New Life never had to say 'we are a praying church'—it just was." Wednesday night prayer meetings that the church held lasted for several hours. Its leaders also gathered to pray together on Sunday mornings from 6 to 9 a.m., although that morning prayer time narrowed to an hour and a half as the church continued to grow and add more services.

New Life Church did not hold evangelistic meetings. People simply shared their faith and invited non-Christians to church services and prayer meetings. Jack often said, "A prayer meeting where God's people are really engaged in and focusing on the Lord and worshipping Him was the best place for unbelievers to be converted because they saw folks honest before God. They could sense the Lord's presence and so were often led to confess 'God is truly among you' (1 Cor. 14:25)."

Roseann and her husband, James Trott, returned to the Philadelphia area after he completed his tour of duty with the military. When they returned, NLC was exploding. If Roseann had been surprised by what she had witnessed several years earlier when she had been living with her parents, she was now amazed to see homosexuals, drug addicts, demon-possessed people, and many others being saved.

John Julien, a student of Jack's at WTS who lived for a short time with his professor, characterized his own experience at the Miller house as that of an ongoing prayer meeting. When he would come downstairs to get his morning coffee, he would inevitably find Jack praying with a group of people in the living room. Occasionally, the half-awake Julien would try to tiptoe his way through the prayer meeting to get to the kitchen, but Jack would catch him and drag him into the group. Julien discovered that if he went out the back door and walked around the house to the kitchen, he could at least get his coffee before his mentor caught him.

The revival that was underway at NLC happened at the same time that a new Bible translation—the New International Version (NIV)—was hitting the shelves of bookstores. Edmund Clowney, president of WTS, served on the NIV translation committee for a short time, and a number of Reformed scholars and leaders who were directly associated with WTS also served the project in various scholarly capacities. Decisions about how to translate texts, passages, or pericopes of the NIV were thus the source of significant discussions among the faculty and students of WTS. Of particular interest to both WTS and NLC was the NIV's translation of Ephesians 4:11–12—the passage that stressed the clergy's responsibility for equipping the saints to do the work of ministry. Instead of saying, as the KJV did, that God had given apostles, prophets, evangelists, pastors, and teachers to perfect the saints, do the work of ministry, and edify the church, the 1973 NIV said that apostles, prophets, evangelists, pastors, and teachers had been given "to equip [God's] people for works of service, so that the body of Christ may be built up" (Eph. 4:12).

This NIV translation of Ephesians 4:11–12 completely changed the way that pastors and church leaders began to be trained throughout seminaries and across the church. It also fit Jack's approach to evangelism, which regarded it as the foundation of discipleship. Jack wanted every person at NLC, not just church leaders, to learn how to share their faith with one another as well as with those outside the church. He recruited Dan Herron, a WTS student, and his son-in-law James Trott, who had been elected as a deacon at NLC, to form the church into small-group teams—a relatively new phenomenon in churches. He also enlisted Karl Cooper, a seminary student who was attending NLC, to develop the church's small-group ministry—a ministry in which the church's leadership funneled new attendees and members into discipleship groups that were committed to evangelism. Members of these small groups that gathered could pray and preach the gospel to one another in preparation for sharing their faith.

To give these small groups a starting point for their preparation to do so, Jack wrote a booklet called *A New Life*, which helped to disciple the people of his church in evangelism. In it, he affirmed three essential components of the message of the cross, which he summarized in a personal overview of the booklet:

- "The facts—that is, the intellectual content of the gospel message that human beings need in order to find salvation."
- "The assurance of God's personal love—that is, the gospel as the cause of faith through the promise of God to the undeserving."
- "The saving power—that is, the power of the message of the gospel to change the standing of the person with God and change the inward life."

Importantly, Jack also realized a fourth essential component: that "the gospel is a preached message—a word of grace designed to be presented with persuasion, gentleness, and the authority of faith."

He explained that "preaching the message of the cross by faith (both in formal and informal settings) is the divinely appointed means for bringing human beings to Christ." While it had no cause for being insensitive, pushy, manipulative, or harsh, this preaching did require boldness—"a keen believing awareness of the saving power of Christ combined with an extraordinary indifference to human opinion."

"How do you get the faith to present the gospel like this?" Jack asked. "Can you find this faith inside of yourself?" He knew, from his own experience, what *not* to do: the more he looked for faith inside himself, the less of it he would find. No—the answer was this: "I must preach the gospel to myself as the instrument for believing, for 'faith comes by hearing, and hearing by the [preached] word of Christ' (Rom. 10:17)."

The phrase "preach the gospel to yourself" is commonly identified with Jack and has been criticized by men such as Jay Adams. It is, however, a concept with ample biblical and historical warrant. Drawing from the example of the psalmists, Martyn Lloyd-Jones writes, "You have to take yourself in hand, you have to address yourself, preach to yourself, question yourself."[27] Preaching the gospel to oneself is also another way of doing what the Puritans referred to as claiming the promises of God. Jack was not using this phrase to encourage morbid introspection, nor did he want Christians to confuse preaching the gospel to themselves with the fruit of gospel transformation. Instead, his intention was for a thirsty sinner to preach the gospel to himself so that, as a chief repenter, he could then proceed to share God's gospel with other Christians and non-Christians.

IN JACK'S MIND, the home was key to evangelism. There, hospitality and friendship could be united to a living faith in Christ. He noted that "witness through diaconal ministry, Bible studies, culture, and public ministries from door-to-door evangelism and on the street wonderfully harmonize with the home as the vital heart of the evangelistic enterprise." The relationship between hospitality and evangelism was not *always* harmonious—but even when human weakness and messiness introduced their inherent tensions, it could be beautiful and powerful.

Gwen was among the first guests to live in the Miller home after the founding of NLC. The young woman had been deeply involved in the occult, drugs, and motorcycle gangs when she arrived in 1974. A darkness was growing inside Gwen even as she received the Millers' care, hospitality, and friendship, and she began planning to murder her host family. As the gospel touched her life, however, she was overcome with guilt. Jack was surprised, as he describes in his *Outgrowing the Ingrown Church*, when she blurted out, "I've been planning to kill you and Mrs. Miller!" As he recovered from the shock, he told her, "Gwen, before anything else happens, I want you to know I forgive you. I forgive you for planning to murder us."[28]

Gwen was now the one who was stunned into silence. Soon she began to weep. "You are the only people who have ever loved me, and I have been wanting to kill you! I am so sick!"[29] She took the gospel to heart, surrendered to Christ, and experienced a marked change in her life over the following months.

On another occasion, the Millers picked up a hitchhiking teenager in order to give him a ride to his home. Jack proceeded to talk with the captive hitchhiker about the gospel for half an hour. Ironically, the young man—who was himself an addict—thought that Jack and Rose Marie were high on drugs because they had so much peace. For the next several weeks after the car ride, he called the Miller home and asked their daughter Keren, who was then thirteen, unsettling questions about Dr. Miller and his ministry.

One day Jack asked Gwen to arrange for him to meet with the Warlocks Motorcycle Club—an eastern version of Hell's Angels that was operating in the Philadelphia area. He had seen a motorcycle gang gather at the Jack Frost's Drive-In near his house, had heard about the Warlocks in the news, and wanted to reach this marginalized group with the gospel. Gwen was horrified by the idea—telling him, "They will kill you!"—and suggested a somewhat less dangerous alternative: the Pagan's Motorcycle Gang, which was the motorcycle gang Jack had actually seen.

He recruited some people to pray for him and asked others to go with him to share the gospel with the gang. Everyone was willing to pray, but no one was willing to go. When Jack asked his son, Paul quickly responded, "Dad, thanks for the invitation, but I think my gift is more along the line of praying." Don Ritsman, a WTS student and NLC intern who was being funded by the church's presbytery, could not so easily say no to his professor's request.

When Jack and Ritsman arrived, they found more than fifty wild-looking young people, who ranged in age from their mid-teens to their mid-twenties, gathered around automobiles. Jack pulled his car up, stepped out, and said, "Hi, I'm Reverend Miller, and I'm looking for the Pagan's Motorcycle Gang. Do you know where I can find them?"

The group, who were all under the influence of alcohol, drugs, or both, reacted to Jack with jeers, foul language, and threats. The more he tried to talk, the wilder and louder the crowd became. One of the young men started screaming at him like a madman and threatening physical harm. Certain that he was doomed, Jack started praying for help.

As the man pulled his arm back to strike Jack, another member of the group forced his way through the crowd and subdued the assailant. Thanking the Lord for this saving intervention, Jack introduced himself to his rescuer—who reacted with surprise. "Not John Miller? Don't you remember me? I've been trying to call your house."

It was the hitchhiker. Jack asked him why he had called his house and frightened his daughter.

"I wanted to find out if you were for real," the young man said. With that, Bob Heppe reintroduced himself to his future father-in-law. He then formed the gang into two groups—one to listen to Jack and the other to listen to Ritsman.

For the next four months, Jack returned to Jack Frost's to share the gospel with whomever was there—finding, whenever he did, that Heppe was always present. When he visited Heppe's house the following November, he found that the teenager was neither drunk nor high. "Have you become a Christian?" Jack asked, and Heppe answered with a grin, "I think so. I've been sober since you left [Jack Frost's] ten days ago, and I can't remember when that last happened." Jack enlisted Rick Buddemeier, a seminary student who lived with the Millers, to disciple Heppe. Heppe bought a large new Bible and took it to his high school to read during lunch. Soon, the natural leader had attracted other people who also wanted to read the Bible.

As JACK's OWN confidence in the gospel was growing, Rose Marie was experiencing a spiritual midlife crisis. At the same time, she was frustrated and discouraged by her inability to communicate with Jack; she had watched him listen to others and love them well but could not get him to understand how she herself felt. One day, Jack asked her, "If you could change one thing about me, what would you change?" She replied without hesitation: "Jack, you don't listen."

God gave Jack the grace to hear and receive his wife's criticism—at least on a surface level. On his day off each Wednesday, he committed himself to listening closely to Rose Marie as she shared her struggles, frustrations, and complaints with him. He worked for ten months on improving his listening skills. Then, ready to turn his attention to another area of his personal sanctification, he again asked, "Rose Marie, if you could change one thing about me, what would you change?" To his utter astonishment, she told him, "Jack, you don't listen."

Considering all the time and effort that he had invested into listening to his wife, Jack was deeply shaken to hear the same criticism. Although he had some mental idea of what she meant by saying that he didn't listen, emotionally he was deeply confused. "Rose Marie," he blurted, "please, no more. I can't handle it. Just be quiet."

He could not understand how he had succeeded at listening patiently to others whenever he communicated God's grace to them but had failed miserably at listening to his own wife. He was realizing again, in a most intense and practical way, that his sin problem was far deeper than he had originally reckoned. At the same time, Rose Marie herself was expecting him to act in the role of the Holy Spirit—to solve all her problems, rescue their wayward daughter, cause the people who lived with them to be holy, and make her happy, all at the same time. A new dimension came to her anxiety when the wayward Barbara got married while she was in college—a marriage that then ended up on the rocks.

In the summer of 1974, Jack and Rose Marie combined a teaching trip with a long overdue vacation in the mountains of east Tennessee. Walking beside a lake, Rose Marie finally poured out to Jack the frustrations that were damming up her heart and life: "I feel like I am walking under a dark cloud. God seems far away, and I don't even know if I believe he exists."[30]

Jack knew well the pain that comes from isolation and loneliness; at times he too had closed his heart out of self-reliance when Christ had stood ready to provide him with an inexhaustible fount of living water. At last God enabled him to truly hear the cry of his wife. Rose Marie's honesty broke through to Jack, and he could finally listen to her the way that she needed him to listen—as a lover, not as a teacher interacting with a student.

The kind of listening that Rose Marie wanted from her husband required him to be supernaturally humbled. Jack later explained, "My constant tendency as a church leader is to fall into arrogant dependence upon my own gifts and strength. I feel that I am the one who holds the ministry together. People depend upon me, and they give me strokes by telling me so. When this happens, I unconsciously—if I am not very careful—feel superior to other people." He had not been listening to his wife in the way that she needed because his unconscious attitude toward her had been one of tolerant, indulgent superiority. He confessed, "In my heart of hearts, I didn't feel I needed to listen to her if it meant I had to change. After all, I was the teacher of the church whose job was to change others—not to be changed by them." Once he was able to identify this mindset within himself, "[that] superior attitude looked silly, cheap, and disgusting." Although Jack was becoming more aware of his pride, Rose Marie continued to struggle spiritually.

As TIME WENT ON, the Millers welcomed all sorts of people into their home: troubled college students, students from the seminary, Ugandan refugees, felons, people who were mentally ill, and many others. Along with the constant flow of people into their home, increased demands on Jack from WTS and NLC took a heavy toll on the family. In the fall of 1974, to take some of the burden off him and Rose Marie, NLC bought a house in their neighborhood to be used for hospitality ministry, and Dan Herron and his wife Betty became its first houseparents. This house, which NLC called Hillside House, reached capacity simply by transferring in houseguests from the Miller home—in fact, when a destitute family showed up unexpectedly at Hillside, there was no room left for them there, and they moved into the Miller home instead.

When a financially needy stranger showed up at the Miller home one afternoon, Jack gave him all the money that he had—which included Rose Marie's food money for the month. He had forgotten that five additional guests were coming to their home for dinner the following week; now there was no more money to spare for them. Jack asked Rose Marie to join him in an experiment—he wanted her to give God a couple of days to supply the food she would have purchased with the money he had given away. They confessed their weakness and poverty to the Lord and asked him to open the windows of heaven. The following day, an anonymous donor left a load of fresh vegetables on their back porch. Two days later, another person brought triple the amount of vegetables that they had already received, along with a large supply of canned goods. Jack rushed around the neighborhood giving away some of the food, because they now had too much. Two years later, the Millers were still eating some of the canned goods.

Jack wrote, "Through the struggles with strangers in our own home and those of Hillside House, we learned a great deal about human corruption. Along with the Herrons, we learned to endure as a daily sacrifice the depressions, the laziness, the ingratitude, and sometimes the slander of those we welcomed into our lives. But in the conflict I found that I grew as a pastor in an amazing way, partly because my own heart was often revealed in all its ugliness and insincerity."[31]

God was at work at NLC, at WTS, and in the lives of several of Jack's family members. Jim Correnti, a Baptist seminary student and talented musician, had visited the Miller home to speak with Jack about pastoring and theology; while there, he had met their daughter Ruth, whom he went on to marry. Paul, himself, had married a godly woman named Jill. Rose Marie's sister, Barbara, loved the children at NLC and had a powerful prayer ministry. "If I ask her to pray for my sermon," Jack said, ". . . she is going to pray, and she expects her prayers to help because God answers her prayers."

Rose Marie's spiritual crisis was continuing, however; and Jack was uncertain how to help her through it beyond praying for her, listening to her patiently, and answering her honest questions— such as "Is God ever angry at the Christian? What is his attitude toward you when you don't do your duty? When your conscience condemns you, does that mean that God condemns you, too?"[32] Five years after returning from Spain, the family needed time away from all the activity that surrounded their ministry. NLC and WTS granted Jack a sabbatical.

In September of 1975, Jack, Rose Marie, Keren, and her friend went caravanning in Ireland. The trip rekindled a missionary passion Jack had felt for the land of St. Patrick since 1949—although the family was unprepared for the change of weather they experienced as they went from Philadelphia's 90-degree sunny days to the consistently cold rain of Ireland. The sabbatical also took them to England, where Jack visited Martyn Lloyd-Jones and Elizabeth Braund, the founder of the urban youth club Providence House. From England, the Millers traveled to Amsterdam and then ended their sabbatical in Switzerland, where Jack spoke to thirty Americans at a conference in Chateau D'Eaux. Since the conference center was less than an hour from L'Abri, he and Rose Marie took the time to visit the Schaeffers as well. By the time the sabbatical ended in March of 1976, Jack had written the pamphlets *Witnessing to the Dying* and *The Word of God in the Life of the Church* and started an essay for the WTS faculty about the relationship between works and justification.

Rose Marie was carrying with her a sense that she needed to live a moral life of self-reliance that would result in approval from others—a mentality that Jack identified as a form of acting like an orphan. In Switzerland, the heavenly Father assured Rose Marie of his love as Jack preached about the rights that God's children have as his sons and daughters. As a daughter of God who had been adopted through the Spirit of Christ, she was learning that Christ still needed to convert her natural self-trust into daily reliance on him.

WHEN THE MILLERS returned from their sabbatical in Europe, NLC's growth had accelerated further. With its growing attendance came growing spiritual needs and ministry expenses, which required a growing leadership team and budget.

Ron Lutz was one of three WTS student interns who had been hired by NLC in 1974, and he was then called as an associate pastor in March of 1976. In 1977, during a time when every area of the church was experiencing rapid growth, the Lord providentially provided Dick Kaufmann, another exceptional leader, who served as an elder at NLC. In 1979, as Jack's influence expanded nationally and globally, NLC called D. Clair Davis to help in a part-time capacity with presbytery responsibilities, seminary relations, and some of Jack's teaching and preaching responsibilities.

Kaufmann and Lutz complemented one another, and together they balanced Jack's strengths and weaknesses. Lutz was a steady, dependable, detail-oriented pastor-leader. Kaufmann had been a partner in a certified public accountant firm, was president of an insurance agency, and had started, managed, and sold a successful banking business prior to committing to the ministry and moving to Philadelphia in order to study at WTS. Initially, he and his wife Elizabeth decided against attending NLC because the new church plant did not yet have a ministry for children and youth. The Kaufmanns, however, were attracted to Jack and Rose Marie's approach to hospitality evangelism; they too had opened their home and hearts to strangers in need before they had moved to the Philadelphia area. Eventually, they gravitated back to NLC and addressed the lack of a youth ministry by organizing one.

In an interview, D. Clair Davis described a typical session meeting that NLC held during the late 1970s:

> We're having a session meeting at 7:30 p.m., [and there is an] enormous docket. [The session meeting] has to end at 10 p.m. because Jack has to go to bed. I'm looking at it pragmatically, . . . and I said, "Well, we have really got to work tonight," and Jack [looks at the same docket and] says we have really got to pray. There we are praying from 7:30 to 8:30, looking at this enormous docket. . . . Things go so smoothly, we understand each other, zip through this enormous docket. But then about three minutes before 10:00 p.m. there's still a bunch of stuff left. And Dick Kaufmann says, "I move we refer this to staff."

By saying so, Kaufmann was proposing that he and Lutz take care of the remaining docketed items. Davis sums it up: "Jack was not always organized—that is for sure. But when you put Jack and Kaufman together with Lutz on a leadership team, you have really got something."

Plenty of difficulties attended these positive developments that were taking place at NLC. Practicing hospitality evangelism was costly and difficult. In 1977, Dan and Betty Herron stopped being the house parents of Hillside House in order to move to Kenya and work among Ugandan refugees. By 1980, Hillside had fallen into disrepair and its student managers were not getting along. High interest rates on debt, as well as maintenance costs, left the difficult-to-manage house with budgetary imbalances that NLC's other, more fruitful ministry activities did not have.

The church was reminded that hospitality evangelism could be dangerous as well. One evening, Kaufmann returned to his house to find his houseguest, a recently released felon, beating his wife. Kaufmann, a former wrestling champion, wrestled the assailant to the ground and removed him from their home. Thankfully, Elizabeth Kaufmann was not seriously hurt. Following this, however, NLC leaders decided that they needed to have a better handle on the organization of the hospitality ministry.

Despite these difficulties, Jack still considered what he learned from opening his home to strangers who were in need of the gospel to be among the best training he had received for pastoral ministry. He explained, "What gives vital strength to a ministry to the weak and rejected is a willingness to be weak and rejected ourselves—to confront sin in others with love, and to keep right on forgiving when we are wronged."[33] He recognized, however, that living by grace was not easy. David Powlison, an elder at the church, recalled,

> I was over at a prayer meeting [at Jack's house] one morning . . . and he must have noticed I seemed stressed or burdened, and as I was leaving the room, he made a comment I've never forgotten. He said, "Grace means courage."
>
> It was just one of those things that just went in there, the seed God planted, and it has borne fruit for thirty-five years. "Grace means courage." . . . There's actually nothing to be afraid of in a world that's very precarious. Lots of things can go wrong. There's lots of troubles, toils and snares. But "grace means courage."

Many people had surrendered their lives to Christ because the Millers, Kaufmanns, and others at NLC had opened their lives and homes to people in need—according to Davis, over seventy people placed their trust in Christ as a result of the Kaufmanns' ministry alone.

Gifted students and professors were joining and helping with the extraordinary movement of grace that God had brought to Philadelphia. They helped Jack to plant churches, accompanied him on evangelism outings and missions trips throughout the region of Philadelphia and around the world, and joined him in all-night prayer meetings. Some of them were even more gifted than their leader and mentor was—but Jack continued to be the one to set the pace for radical hospitality, evangelism that was tied closely to discipleship, and radical corporate prayer.

Jack's impact extended further after several leaders in Presbyterian Evangelistic Fellowship (PEF), an evangelism-training ministry that was connected with the Presbyterian Church in America (PCA), heard him speak on evangelism and invited him to join their organization. PEF scheduled speaking engagements for Jack at PCA churches and also invited him to be a keynote speaker at its regional and annual pastors' conference. Through the intersection of WTS and PEF, Jack became a major point of connection between these conservative Reformed institutions. However, he would soon find himself at the center of one of the most significant theological controversies of the twentieth century—a controversy that would shake WTS and the OPC and would demonstrate Jack's claim that grace means courage.

4

CHEER UP! JUSTIFICATION IS BY FAITH ALONE, EVEN IN THE TWENTIETH CENTURY

The Shepherd Controversy over Works in Justification

THE REVIVAL THAT was taking place within Jack's ministry at Westminster Theological Seminary and New Life Church was unprecedented in the Orthodox Presbyterian Church (OPC). Yet, while many people concluded that God was using him as an instrument of renewal in the Philadelphia area, skeptics were convinced that Jack and New Life Church (NLC) had to be somehow compromising the truth of the Reformed faith. Otherwise, they reasoned, how could a church be growing so rapidly while other churches around it remained stagnant? Concerned Reformed leaders in the OPC cast further suspicion on NLC when they passed on unsubstantiated rumors about the activities that took place during its worship. Some professors and students at Westminster Theological Seminary (WTS) referred derisively to those who were attached to Jack and NLC as "Jenkintown pietists" or "David's band of malcontents"—a reference to the unhappy people who flocked to David in 1 Samuel 22. Some also criticized Jack's *A New Life* booklet, along with other evangelistic pamphlets of the time, such as those from Evangelism Explosion and Campus Crusade.[1]

Meanwhile, Norman Shepherd, associate professor of systematic theology at WTS, was concerned that teaching from men such as Jack and D. James Kennedy was, according to scholar Donald MacLeod, "creating instant believers" who had a "[minimal] concept of discipleship."[2] It seemed to Shepherd that "superficial faith encounters" and easy-believism within the Protestant church had become the means by which professing Christians avoided "the rigorous and demanding path of discipleship and faith."[3] Accordingly, Shepherd sought to revise Martin Luther's formulation of justification by faith alone and to recover what he saw as the Bible's whole teaching on justification by faith. He did this by introducing a theological framework of multiple justifications: initial justification (in which believers are justified by faith alone), a state of continuing justification (in which believers are justified by their faith and works throughout their lifetime—a principle of ongoing *covenant obedience*), and final justification (in which believers are justified by their faith and works at the final judgment). Beginning in the fall of 1974, he began to teach this novel explanation of the relationship between faith and works with regard to justification in a seminary class, which raised concerns among his students.

Shepherd adapted the teaching of others—from former WTS professor John Murray on the covenants, from Geerhardus Vos on biblical theology, and from Herman Ridderbos on *historia salutis* (the history of salvation)—to support an emphasis that he placed on covenant *continuity*. Rather than the two-covenant structure that was found within Scripture and the Westminster Confession (which consists of the covenant of grace and the covenant of works), Shepherd seemed to teach what Jack called "essentially a one-covenant structure." Jack would eventually describe the essence of his colleague's thought in this way:

[Shepherd's] idea is that we today stand essentially in the same relationship to the law and gospel as the people of God in the Old Testament. To be sure, we have a great measure of grace poured out upon us because Christ has come in all His fullness, but

fundamentally our legal standing is pretty much that of the Israel-
ites as they received the contents of the book of Deuteronomy. The
governing principle of this continuity is defined by the requirement
of covenant obedience on the part of those who already belong to
God by virtue of their inclusion in the covenant (Deut. 7:6ff.). This
requirement for obedience is summed up in the words of Leviticus
18:5: "You shall therefore keep my statutes and my ordinances, by
doing which a man shall live: I am the Lord."

What is omitted, or at least moved into the background, is
the actual passage in redemptive history from law to gospel, from
wrath to grace. There is little place for the fundamental change
in the nature of the divine administration as treated in the Pauline epistles, the book of Hebrews, and the Gospel of John. On
the individual level, what counts most in Old and New Testament saints is not a conversion experience but faithful use of
the external signs of the covenant and faithful obedience to its
requirements. Thus, there is little focus on the radical change in
redemptive history brought in by the gospel replacing the Mosaic
ministry of condemnation and death, or the related radical change
of conversion.

Shepherd's one-covenant structure emphasized the role of covenant
obedience in justification in a way that undermined the biblical and
confessional foundations of the assurance of salvation that believers
found in justification by faith alone.

STUDENT CONCERNS ABOUT Shepherd's teaching on works and justification began to surface in the fall of 1974 as the result of his
class on the doctrine of the Holy Spirit and the application of
redemption. Before the following fall semester, the presbytery
of Philadelphia's Committee on Candidates and Credentials, of
which Jack was a member, had begun to receive complaints from
parallel committees in other OPC presbyteries about Shepherd's
teaching. In one instance, a former WTS student had failed his

ordination exam in another presbytery due to Shepherd's teaching on justification and, in response, had prepared charges to file against Shepherd.

Although WTS and the OPC were separated constitutionally, a number of WTS faculty were associated with the denomination in general and the presbytery of Philadelphia in particular: Norman Shepherd, Richard Gaffin, and Robert Strimple were WTS professors who were also members of the presbytery; Arthur Kuschke had been the librarian at WTS since 1942 and was the head of the presbytery's Committee on Candidates and Credentials; and Edmund Clowney, the president of the school, had served as the pastor of an OPC church. This interconnectedness of the denomination and the seminary impacted the outworking of the controversy almost at once. When Strimple heard about the pending charges within the denomination, he persuaded the former student to delay filing them so that the WTS faculty could begin discussions about Shepherd's teaching on works and justification. This interception by the seminary of the complaint to the presbytery created a conflict of interests for Jack and Kuschke, since they as well as other OPC presbyters on the WTS faculty were members of the presbytery's Candidates and Credentials Committee.

The faculty of the school met to discuss Shepherd's teaching for the first time on August 14, 1975. Jack left for a sabbatical in Europe a few weeks later, where he worked on an essay concerning the relationship of justification and good works. Meanwhile, at a second WTS faculty meeting that took place in February of 1976, Kuschke pushed for a more formal inquiry into Shepherd's teaching. The following month, Jack returned from his sabbatical. He and Kuschke, both of whom were seeing little progress at the seminary, submitted a paper titled "The Relationship of Justification and Good Works" to both the faculty and the WTS board of trustees in an effort to alert the board to the problem with Shepherd's teaching as well as to the gridlock that had resulted in faculty discussions about it.

In response, Shepherd formally submitted a study paper to the faculty that sought to explain and clarify his views, and he included with it the important and controversial restriction that it could "not be used for any purpose other than to serve as a basis for discussion within the faculty of Westminster Theological Seminary on October 1 and 2, 1976." His decision to restrict the paper to WTS faculty alone limited further involvement from the WTS board of trustees in the difficult theological discussions. This, along with the faculty's inability to quickly resolve their disagreements over the biblical and confessional legitimacy of Shepherd's teaching about works and justification, further delayed the presbytery from addressing the original complaint that Shepherd's former student had submitted.

Jack concurred with several of the concerns Shepherd had been expressing: he agreed that "some fundamentalists [had] unwittingly presented the faith involved in justification as mere mental assent or as content-less feelings about Christ" and that "some Reformed pastors had presented justification as something . . . dead and inert and having no relationship to our new standing as living disciples of Jesus Christ." However, such anecdotal observations about so-called fundamentalists cheapening God's grace should not lead to the conclusion, Jack would go on to argue, that "there is an inherent tension between justification and discipleship."

Jack also thought Shepherd erred in the way that he related good works and obedience to justification. Shepherd failed to highlight the scriptural imperative to believers that their faith must rest on Christ alone as the exclusive grounds of their salvation. He tried to avoid what Jack called the "obvious dangers of legalism inherent" in the addition of works to justification by "underscoring that in the covenant union [with Christ] all obedience as well as faith comes to man as a gift from God through Christ." This would mean that the good works of believers could not merit their justification. However, Jack believed that Shepherd's emphasis on what Shepherd called "obedient faith" almost immediately blurred the primacy that faith itself had in justification.

AS DISCUSSIONS AMONG the faculty concerning this topic of justification continued into the following year, Jack wondered whether Shepherd were not the only faculty member who was advancing what appeared to him to be a "new Reformed theology." He explained his growing concern about this in a letter to Clowney: "Somehow this [overemphasis on covenant continuity] seems to come across to Westminster students as Reformed orthodoxy—that which is identified with the faculty as a whole and not with Norman [Shepherd] alone." Since the breakthrough he had experienced in 1970, Jack had been emphasizing the "newness of the new covenant . . . not only the dichotomy between law and grace but also the gift of the Spirit who internalizes the law in the believer's heart and liberates him for a life of prayer, zeal for God's name, and boldness in witness." Jack wondered if others at the seminary had "[blurred] the difference between what happens at Sinai and Mt. Zion" and concluded that he saw Shepherd "as simply an unusually able thinker who has done more than the others to work out the consequences of 'covenant continuity' as a position."

Jack elaborated on this position in another letter to Clowney, in which he pointed out "a foundational difference between Mr. Shepherd's theology and [his] own." He wrote,

> My brother sees much more covenant continuity than I do and much less of a radical transition from law to grace in the history of redemption.
>
> As I perceive his comprehensive approach, Norman is underscoring the law as a guide to the covenant people . . . and as having pretty much the same relationship to them in the new covenant as in the Mosaic covenant.
>
> By contrast, I read the covenant at Sinai as bringing condemnation and death to God's people not because the law is not good and holy but because they are unholy and depraved in heart. And I also see the great event in redemptive history to effect a radical transition for sinners from wrath to grace. Or to speak more

precisely, for me redemptive history is marked by a change from a covenant of law and its accompanying curse to a new covenant of grace and life. . . .

. . . I must conclude that the heart of our problem lies right here. It strikes me that the history of redemption presents us with a dichotomy between law and grace and not to recognize that this is Pauline teaching is to blunt the force of Romans, Galatians, II Corinthians 3–4, and 1 Timothy 1. Furthermore, my understanding of Paul's argumentation on the giving of the law is that he is saying that Israel's experience with the law as a ministry of condemnation and death teaches the individual sinner not to seek justification by the law and its work but by personally coming to Christ by faith so that he may make his own radical transition from the law and its wrath to grace.

In other words, to blur the historical transition from wrath to grace is inevitably to blur what goes on in the personal salvation of each individual believer.

Jack believed that "passages in the New Testament draw a sharp distinction between the Mosaic covenant and the new covenant." To his mind, an inordinate focus on covenant continuity "minimizes the Pauline teaching with its emphasis on the apostle's dichotomy between law and gospel, wrath and grace, servitude and sonship."

IN MAY OF 1977, after much discussion, the faculty of WTS formally voted concerning Shepherd's teaching, and a narrow majority affirmed that Shepherd was not out of the bounds of the confessional standards. Reports from a significant minority, however, disagreed. Jack himself had firmly concluded that Shepherd was "substantially out of conformity with Scripture." Following this vote by the faculty, Jack wrote to the seminary's board of trustees and said, "My brother [Shepherd] gives the appearance to me of having a theology which instinctively pushes Romans 3–4 and Galatians 2–3 into the background—and pushes them so far into the background that in his theological thought processes, 'justification' seems to be something other than what is set forth in these classical passages treating justification without the works of the law."

Since the seminary had not taken action against Shepherd, Jack and Kuschke returned the matter to presbytery by filing charges against him, based on his 1976 study paper, at a meeting on May 27. However, they ran into several difficulties. Jack was not present at that meeting, and the presbytery disallowed the moderator to read the charges without him. Then, soon after the meeting, Edmund Clowney—a friend of Shepherd's who tried to remain a neutral party throughout the discussions—protested the fact that Shepherd's confidential study paper, which Kuschke had placed in the hands of the moderator without Shepherd's permission, was being used in the filing of the charges against him. Probably as a result of this procedural objection from Clowney, Jack dropped his name from the charges—though he continued to oppose Shepherd in less public settings.

Kuschke continued to press charges without Jack. In September of 1977, despite objections from Shepherd and Gaffin, who was a primary supporter of Shepherd at the time, the presbytery approved the formation of a three-person committee to conduct a preliminary investigation. Though the presbytery disallowed Shepherd's study paper to be used as evidence without his permission, it did allow faculty members to be witnesses against him and to testify regarding faculty discussions—which would cover most, if not all, of the same material that was in the study paper. As the faculty and board of WTS themselves had, the Special Committee to Conduct a Preliminary Investigation found itself divided, which resulted in its submitting a majority report and two minority reports. It ultimately recommended that the presbytery institute charges against Shepherd—though the presbytery decided not to act on the recommendation.

Disagreements within the faculty and board of WTS continued

to intensify. As matters surrounding Shepherd's teaching remained unresolved, Clowney came under increasing pressure from participants on every side of the controversy. To Jack's disappointment, the long conflict began to negatively affect conversations that had been in the works about a possible denominational merger between the OPC, the Reformed Presbyterian Church, Evangelical Synod (RPCES), and the PCA.

In January of 1978, Shepherd presented a new study paper to the faculty and board of WTS. After two years of intense discussion with members of the board and faculty, which included many conversations with Jack, Gaffin, and Kuschke, he had rewritten and revised many of the statements that were originally presented in his 1976 study paper. And, while Jack had been impressed by the apparent progress that he and his colleagues had been making in their attempts to bring Shepherd's teaching in line with the confessions and with Scripture, the follow-up paper disappointed him. Although Shepherd had, in Jack's eyes, clarified his meaning, Jack thought that he was continuing to err. He wrote, "The fine statements that [Shepherd] made so often in our [prior] discussions did not seem to me to come forward in the manner that would put the spotlight on the unique office of faith in our justification in a manner to silence the objections."

After taking some time to think and pray, Jack wrote a letter to Shepherd that he copied to Gaffin, Clowney, and Strimple. The controversy had become a strain to those who were involved, and Jack noted that "most of us have listened and talked until our mental circuits were overloaded." While he acknowledged that Shepherd had improved his formulations in his new paper, he maintained that he still did not see—in Scripture, Luther, Calvin, or the Westminster Standards—any support for Shepherd's position that "obedient faith justifies" nor any use of phrases such as "obedient faith" or "working faith" when those sources speak of justification.

Jack respected Shepherd and the WTS faculty and considered

his own theological training to be inferior to theirs. Nonetheless, the scholarly background that he had in interdisciplinary studies along with his experience in the area of practical ministry gave him a multifaceted perspective that few others at WTS shared. After praying and poring over Scripture to make certain that he was confident about the positions he was taking, he wrote a letter in May of 1978 to the WTS board of trustees that explained why he remained unsatisfied with the narrow majority vote that the faculty had cast in favor of Shepherd's latest paper.

As he explained why he had signed the dissenting minority report, he sought to distinguish his own view from that of others who opposed Shepherd and to show appreciation for Shepherd's concern about compromised discipleship. His letter detailed his maturing Reformed position on redemptive history, which was in contrast to that of some on the WTS faculty who, as Jack saw it, were in danger of reducing the confession's two-covenant structure to a one-covenant structure by overemphasizing covenant continuity.

I am gripped afresh with new understanding of the striking way the Apostle Paul draws a sharp line between the Mosaic law and the gospel. It has struck me that he is saying with all the volume of a gospel trumpet that the Old Covenant was a way of condemnation and death (2 Cor. 3) and that the law was added for the specific purpose of increasing guilt so that men might be driven to see their desperate need of the gospel.

In other words, not just in man's regeneration-conversion is there a passage from death to life and from wrath to grace, but in redemptive history itself God has brought about a radical change from law to faith, from wrath to grace, and from death to life. And what is crucial now in my view is that the pattern of redemptive history is the teaching model for each man's personal coming to Christ. In redemptive history and in my own personal renewal, "the very commandment which promised life proved to be death to me" (Rom. 7:10), and therefore I am driven by the ministry of death to claim by faith alone "the righteousness of God" which "has been manifested apart from the law" (Rom. 3:21).

Clair Davis, who was then the chair of the WTS faculty, indicated that the faculty had basically divided into three groups regarding the issue: those who opposed Shepherd, those who supported him, and those who were uncertain what to think but were unwilling to declare his views as being out of accord with Scripture and the Standards. And, while Jack himself opposed Shepherd, he, in the words of Robert Godfrey, "did his own thing"—finding himself in the peculiar place of opposing him in a way that differed, at least in Jack's estimation, from other opponents of Shepherd, who were focused primarily on the doctrine of justification by faith alone and on Shepherd's multiple justifications. Jack acknowledged to the board, in the letter that he wrote, that he "found this position exceedingly difficult."

BY THE FALL OF 1978, the whole subject of the role of works in justification had stumped the most highly trained Reformed scholars in the world and nearly torn the faculty and board of WTS apart. For three years they had tried to address the controversy within the context of the seminary; but, when both the board and the faculty finally acknowledged that they were at an impasse, parties on both sides ironically took steps to return the matter to presbytery. The board overrode Shepherd and lifted the restriction on his controversial 1976 study paper so that it could be used as evidence for charges within the Philadelphia presbytery. Four days later, Shepherd responded by presenting a letter to the presbytery in which he asked for their help with reaching a solution. He offered the presbytery a set of improved formulations, which he presented in the form of "thirty-four theses in relation to faith, repentance, and good works," in order to avoid their having to rely on an older, more controversial paper.

The presbytery subsequently met as a whole for six hours on

December 16 to conduct a preliminary hearing on the theses. John Mitchell, a highly respected member of the presbytery, was elected to the unenviable role of moderating that hearing as well as subsequent meetings.

At this crucial moment in the controversy, the Millers were away on a family vacation to visit Jack's mother. Jack wrote to Shepherd from Pistol River, Oregon, to inform his colleague that he would be unable to attend the presbytery meeting and also to commend Shepherd for the "more balanced" approach he had taken in his thirty-four theses—though Jack added that he continued to see some problems. While on the vacation, he prayed, studied, and wrote—returning to his familiar pattern of researching an issue and writing a personal study paper to get his thoughts in order about it. Influenced by Herman Dooyeweerd and Cornelius Van Til, he sought to engage with Shepherd while also assessing his own presuppositions about the Bible's teaching on justification. The unpublished essay that he wrote as a result, "Justification by Faith in the Twentieth Century," is worth examining at some length, because it represents a rare positive contribution to the topic of justification that arose from the controversy.

Jack began the essay by noting that conflict regarding justification by faith alone, along with the role of works, was not new. The Heidelberg Catechism, which was written in the sixteenth century, states in answer 56 "that God, for the sake of Christ's satisfaction, will no more remember my sins, neither my sinful nature, against which I have to struggle all my life long; but will graciously grant unto me the righteousness of Christ, that I may never come into condemnation." Many people in the time the catechism was written, Jack said, saw this teaching as "a threat to Christian moral life and even an invitation to sin. . . . Offer [the Christian masses] the certainty that the Last Judgment had already been borne for them by Christ, and it wouldn't take much imagination to see how they would live." Jack saw a different sort of problem in modern times: a tendency in the church for people to be indifferent to "the whole

(1) God is personal-Supreme   (2) His law enables us to see our sin against Him.

subject of justification by faith and its central message: the free forgiveness of sins through the righteousness of Christ imputed to us and received by faith alone." This left modern men and women, both within and outside of the church, trying to deal with a "troubled and restless conscience" on their own terms.

Shepherd taught that believers needed works in order to continue in justification. Jack affirmed the opposite: that the Bible teaches justification by faith alone. This, he argued, presented a great opportunity for the church to recover the gospel in the twentieth century. As he responded both to Shepherd and to the apathy about justification that Shepherd had identified, Jack sought to "affirm certain of [his] own convictions about justification by faith and its place in the modern world."

The first three affirmations that he made in the essay laid the groundwork for why justification by faith alone was necessary. In the first, Jack wrote that "justification by faith has, as a founda- (1) tional presupposition, a *consciousness* of the majesty of God and the absolute demands of his justice." God is not abstract but is personal—"the Lord God of the Bible"—and his law is likewise personal; it expresses his "exact and unchanging justice." As long as modern man's idea of God on his throne is just "an idea on paper, an empty metaphor," it is a "barrier to any effective communication of a teaching like justification." In order for the Bible's teaching on justification to be embraced, God must be recognized as the "Supreme Lord of all existence," whose judgments are just.

Jack's second affirmation was that we will view justification by (2) faith alone as a "most precious gift" only if we experience "a personal encounter with God's law and the conviction of sin which arises from that encounter." In contrast to the "isolated and only loosely related commandments" of nonbiblical religions, God's law is a "single mirror" in which we see both our own sin and the "awesome Face" of God himself. The law, like God, is "holy, just, and good" and "promises life to those who obey it"—and condemnation to those who break it. After all, if God "does not act justly in keeping with

107

3) All are under His wrath b/c of sin
4) Law requires absolute obedience. Jesus perfect obed. is life

Cheer Up! Justification Is by Faith Alone, Even in the Twentieth Century

His own holy nature, then He is less than a merely human judge who is fair and equitable in condemning or acquitting men according to their guilt or innocence." Jack concluded that since "the law calls for endless judgment to fall upon those who persist in refusing to give the All-glorious God thanks and praise and service from a joyous heart," we can see that "our sin is infinitely worse than anything we had imagined."

Jack next raised a concern in his third affirmation about "the tendency in modern Reformed circles virtually to exclude either the elect or children of the covenant from the divine wrath against sin. . . . The idea is that the elect being in Christ were justified in the counsel of God from all eternity"—which made it "hard to take seriously the Scriptural teaching that the elect are in a real sense under God's condemnation before their regeneration and conversion." He noted that the apostle Paul was referring to the elect—the chosen of God—when he told Christians in Thessalonica that Jesus is the one "who delivers us from the wrath to come" (1 Thess. 1:10). If the church teaches that "men are born Christians and not reborn as Christians," then it "practically [loses] the necessity of conversion." Jack emphasized the necessity of justification by faith alone through his affirmation that "the Scriptures clearly teach that before the new birth and saving faith *all* men are in a state of condemnation."

After making these three affirmations regarding God's holy justice and the dire condition in which man was left in light of the law, Jack turned to an important distinction between the law and the gospel. The law promises life on the condition of obedience, whereas the gospel makes an *unconditional* promise—one that is based on Jesus's perfect legal obedience. This, Jack said in a fourth affirmation, is a "fundamental distinction"—and "to blur the distinction between the gospel promise and the legal promise . . . will inevitably move one in the direction of justification by works."

These first four affirmations led climactically to a fifth: that the gospel promise, which is unconditional, "is received by faith alone."

It is through the gospel promise, not the conditional legal promise, that we are saved. Drawing from Romans 3:28, Jack wrote that "justification is grounded in a substitute righteousness provided by God through faith without any admixture of human law-keeping." He continued, "Justification is through Christ and His righteousness *alone*. Justification is through Christ's merits freely imputed to us. There is no plus, no 'and' possible after the name of Jesus. Nothing can be added by way of human work or effort to what He has done on behalf of His own. Only Jesus, our propitiation, can placate by His blood God's just indignation over our ungodly ways (Rom. 3:24–25)."

Jack responded indirectly to Shepherd by addressing the idea that "non-meritorious works" (works that are done by grace) play a role in justification. Faith, he wrote, "is the sole doorway . . . into the house of salvation." To say that faith and non-meritorious works together "function as the means or instrument of justification . . . would take away from the unique office that faith performs. . . . That function is to receive Christ, something works can never do, no matter how you describe them." Only after a person lays hold of Christ through faith and is justified will he or she experience the other benefits of Christ's salvation, such as sonship and progressive sanctification (the process by which the Christian grows in holiness).

"So far," Jack wrote, "I have been focusing on [faith's] unique role in God's act of justifying the ungodly. In such a discussion, I refuse to give any place to talk of love, works, or obedience. It does not belong there." However, his previous five affirmations now necessitated a sixth: that "faith which embraces Christ is neither dead nor empty" but has "unlimited resources for working by love (Gal. 5:6)." He continued, "By faith [the believer] possesses Him whose power is unlimited. . . . [This] kind of power . . . accomplishes the impossible through weakness" and "leads me joyfully to embrace the First Commandment as the supreme goal of life and thereafter to do all good things possible to my neighbor out of love for the Father and the Lord Jesus Christ. . . . I am able to put myself in another's place in my human relationships just because that is what the Lord did for me in His death."

Jack had seen a systemic issue in Shepherd's teaching that went beyond that of justification by faith alone: namely, a strong emphasis on covenant continuity. He was most concerned by "the idea that the governing principle of this 'covenant continuity' is covenant obedience. . . . Of course, God does require covenant obedience. . . . But it is just this kind of covenant obedience which we can never supply." Thus, in a seventh affirmation, Jack argued that there is in the New Testament "a sharp distinction between the Mosaic covenant and the new covenant." The dominant note that Paul found in the Sinaitic covenant was one of obedience—not promise—whereas the new covenant emphasized the gospel promise as its dominant theme.

Jack brought systematic theology, biblical theology, and practical theology together as he wrote, "If there is little stress on the Pauline teaching on the radical change in redemptive history brought in by the gospel replacing the Mosaic ministry of condemnation and death, then there is likely to be little stress on the personal transition from death to life of the individual sinner."

Jack next affirmed that declarative justification leaves believers with no cause whatsoever for boasting of themselves. Paraphrasing Exodus 34:6–7, he said that "the Lord is full of compassion and delights in showing mercy" and yet that "He may by no means clear the guilty"—which leaves sinful humanity with a problem that only God can solve. Thus God, in an act of his grace, enacts declarative justification and makes righteous the utterly ungodly through Christ. "In this generous outpouring of grace there is not a single thing that a man can do to boast in as his accomplishment. All the glory is God's because all the undoing is by man and all the successful doing is by Christ."

For Jack, this eighth affirmation led to an immediate application. If all the "doing" of justification is by Christ, then we can have "a firm and healthy assurance in the Christian life. Having given up all our boasting which is rooted in self-righteous human effort, we have a new identity as forgiven, thankful sons of God." Jack continued,

> So long as believers try to work out the gospel from the foot of Mt. Sinai, they are denying the validity and power of the cross. We do not find ourselves boasting in Christ but doing bitter penance over our sins. Pastoral counseling may temporarily relieve us. But we can have no lasting peace of mind because we are forgetting about our overarching peace with God. We feel no courage to witness to the world because we are talking about a message that we have at least half-forgotten ourselves. However, we are yet the sons of God if we have trusted in Jesus. We have a radiance in Christ and a power to be different through the Spirit of grace. Be what you are! Glory in your sure salvation! Daringly boast in full and free forgiveness! When under Satanic attack, take your troubled conscience to God.

The ninth and final affirmation that Jack made in his essay was that "declarative justification properly understood does not cancel out discipleship," as Shepherd had concluded, "but makes it a reality." Justification is not "dead and inert" in its application to the believer who is in union with Christ. Jack wrote that "under a new dominion, the disciple is able to reckon himself dead to sin. His union with Christ also includes a new mind-set (Rom. 6:11). . . . Doing good is inherent in his new nature." Justification, he argued, is inseparable from sanctification. He quoted Geerhardus Vos, who wrote that "justification and sanctification are not the same, and an endless amount of harm has been done by the short-sighted attempt to identify them. But neither are these two independent one of the other; the one sets the goal and fixes the direction, the other follows."[4] So, while good works are not necessary for us to be justified, the Reformed tradition does teach that they are a necessary "part of our comprehensive salvation." Good works "are the evidence *demonstrating* that our faith is the real goods" and that "we have come through faith to a death to sin and a new life in Christ."

Having laid down these nine affirmations, Jack was then ready to address the issues Shepherd had raised regarding justification and works at the last judgment. He admitted that a startling contradiction seemed to arise upon a surface reading of passages that were pertinent to the controversy: Paul argues that "the doers of the law . . . will be justified" (Rom. 2:13) while James says three times that people are justified by works (see James 2:21, 24–25).

Yet Jack explained that a closer examination of these passages indicates that Paul and James both have the day of judgment in view. "This fact in itself supplies us with clear indication that Romans 2 and James 2 are describing something other than the definitive justification [without works] of Romans 3 and 4 and Galatians 2 and 3." An indication that James intended this interpretation comes in verse 21 of chapter 2, where he shows that Abraham's faith was justified as living faith when he offered up Isaac. Jack writes, "It would seem rather obvious that 'justify' here does not mean to declare righteous as in definitive justification but to demonstrate that Abraham's faith is alive. . . . Thus, the verb 'to justify' as used here means 'shown to be righteous,' not 'declared to be righteous.'"

Still, he admitted that James 2:23, which quotes from Genesis 15:6, "does not [speak] of declarative justification." He explained that "apparently James is saying that works will have a certain forensic character at the Last Judgment. Or if you reject the idea that the chapter is oriented toward the Last Judgment, then it would seem to follow that works relate to a present judgment." Jack's conclusion was that works "will have a key role in the Last Judgment seen as a final vindication of the faith of God's people. It appears to me that such a development warrants the language of 'reckoning' found in verse 23 [or being 'counted,' in the ESV]. Works are necessary as a fulfillment-vindication of our faith (James 2:22)."

He wrote that, in the end,

> Just as [Christ's] righteousness was my hope and boast on the first
> day I trusted in Him, so it will be my hope and boast on that Day
> of days (Gal. 5:5). In a word, this means that the One who will
> judge me has already stood trial for me and provided me with a
> sure verdict of acquittal. Therefore, at the last judgment seat it will
> be his righteousness which will be brought forward as the basis
> for a final acquittal. This is a forensic or legal hope since it rests
> entirely on what Christ did for me and apart from me at the cross
> and the tomb.
>
> At the same time, the believer's works must harmonize with
> this verdict and vindicate the work of faith in his life. After all, it
> is a judgment according to works, though it is never a judgment
> based upon works as its grounds. These works demonstrate to all
> that the believer's life has been righteous and, as such, pleasing to
> God (2 Thess. 1:5). . . . Cleansed by the blood of the second Adam,
> these evidences of grace will be heralded as deeds worthy of the
> kingdom. . . . They become our crown of life received in the way of
> faithful obedience to Christ. . . . Yet it is a crown-gift which we will
> quickly cast before the throne of the Lamb lest we intercept any of
> the glory which is His due alone [see Rev. 3:18–4:11]. *yes,*

God's gospel produces in every disciple a saving faith that continues to work by "unfeigned deeds of love" throughout the believer's life. Therefore, in the day of judgment, God is vindicated as both
just and justifier (see Rom. 3:26), and he vindicates the works that
men do through faith in Christ (see 1 Cor. 3:13–15).

Having thought through the matter of justification in the twentieth century, Jack was now prepared to engage constructively with
Shepherd's thirty-four theses.

HE RETURNED FROM his Oregon vacation and reentered the ongoing meetings that were being held in the presbytery about the

controversy over works in justification. In meetings that took place in January and February of 1979, he expressed significant reservations about theses 3 through 6 of Shepherd's paper, although presbytery minutes from December of 1978 suggest that in that earlier meeting, the first six theses had passed the scrutiny of the presbytery without objection.

In the February meeting, Shepherd went on the offensive. During previous conversations among the faculty, he had accused Jack and others of being Lutherans and pietists, of overemphasizing justification by faith alone, and thus of not being truly Reformed. He had also questioned Jack's qualifications for engaging in such a scholarly theological debate, since Jack's doctorate was in literature, not theology. Now, using Jack's *A New Life* booklet and his book *Repentance*, he directly challenged Jack before the committee, questioning why his colleague saw the two of them as differing when, in Shepherd's estimation, they were saying the same thing.

Jack gave Shepherd the benefit of the doubt and accepted his challenge in good faith, taking it as an opportunity to explain their differences. On April 11, 1979, he presented the presbytery with two essays. In a cover letter, he explained that he planned to publish the first essay, "Continuance in Justification," as a chapter in a book or as one of a series of pamphlets. The title of the essay played on the language of Shepherd's multiple justifications—language that Jack saw as leading to "shakiness and doubts" regarding justification that are not found in Scripture. The second essay, which Jack did not intend to publish, focused on Shepherd's thirty-four theses.

The first essay gave a brief exposition of Philippians 3 as a way of providing biblical rationale for Jack's position that works cannot be a part of the believer's continuance in justification. Before Paul became a Christian, Jack wrote, the apostle trusted in his keeping of the law. As a Christian, "Paul did not see his struggle with Judaism and the way of law-keeping as a mere phase of the past." Instead, Paul's struggle against trusting in works of the law was an ongoing problem for him, and he saw the works-righteousness of his Judaism as "a symptom of the threat to grace inherent in man's sinful self-importance." Thus, the battle against trusting in one's works is every Christian's present-tense reality. Speaking of the past, Paul writes, "But whatever gain I had, I counted as loss for the sake of Christ" (Phil. 3:7). Then, speaking immediately in the present, he continues, "Indeed, I count [i.e., keep counting] everything as loss because of the surpassing worth of knowing Christ Jesus my Lord" (v. 8). So when it comes to justification, "we must see works and faith as in opposition," Jack wrote. "I am persuaded this is the Reformed way."

The essay also included support from a number of Reformed theologians—though Jack believed that Calvin had said it best. In Calvin's day, some had taught that "the regenerate man . . . being once reconciled to God by means of Christ . . . is afterwards deemed righteous by his good works, and is accepted in consideration of them."[5] This Calvin utterly rejected—as Jack said, "The law of God always demands absolute righteousness of the believer as well as the unbeliever, 'the only righteousness acknowledged in heaven being the perfect righteousness of the law.'[6] For this reason even the best works of the believer have no place as cause or condition of justification." Jack reaffirmed that "the sole condition for continuing in justification from sins is faith alone. For the Reformed, Calvin says the matter is non-negotiable." This reliance on Calvin and on Reformed scholars and theologians helped to distance Jack from Shepherd's accusations that he had Lutheran leanings.

Jack noted that the doctrine of justification can fall prey to a dangerous caricature—a sense that this justification that takes place through the imputation of Christ's righteousness is "a cold, dead legal issue, settled forever in some remote heavenly courtroom."

This caricature of justification by faith alone ends up either turning confession of sins into a meaningless routine or causing confession to God through Christ to cease altogether. After all, the man thinks: Am I not already forgiven? Are not my sins already under the blood?

But such careless presumption is not the way of faith. Faith knows that further pardon is no charade. It is actual. When we confess our sins in Jesus' name by faith alone, we must know that they are truly forgiven for His dear sake alone. . . . What we are now enjoying as believers is the application of that justification to our present struggle against our sins. In this intense warfare it is of the greatest encouragement to know that the blood of a righteous high priest is forever mine and that in the midst of many sins I can daily claim it as my sure hope before the heavenly Father.

Jack knew that this teaching would cause as much trouble in the twentieth century as it had in the sixteenth—especially for those who were concerned about the modern irreverence for God and his law. Placing faith alone in justification without discipleship sounds too easy—which is why skeptics save "faith alone" for initial justification and then emphasize that covenant obedience is needed in order for a person to continue in justification.

Jack shared the motivation of his Reformed critics who opposed easy-believism. "We do not want to forget that we must exercise repentance and new obedience. But this above all must be remembered: when it comes to the remission of sins, God requires only one thing—faith alone in embracing Christ alone."

The second essay, "Application to Norman Shepherd's Thirty-Four Theses on Justification," directly addressed areas in which he and Shepherd differed. While Shepherd had reworked a few theses that had previously created some difficulty for Jack, the basic problem that Jack continued to see stemmed from systemic errors in theses 3 and 4—errors that, he argued, undermined others of Shepherd's theses.

Shepherd's thesis 3 defined *justification* as "an act of God by which He forgives sinners acquitting them of their guilt, accounts and accepts them as righteous, and bestows upon them the title to eternal life." This broad definition of justification remained inadequate to Jack, since it did not reference "imputation and faith." He wrote, "There is no such thing as justification that does not include in the center of the act of acquittal the free imputation of Christ's righteousness."

While thesis 3 assented to a Reformed understanding of justification, Shepherd immediately redefined the term in thesis 4: "The term 'justification' may be used with reference to the acquittal and acceptance of a believer at his effectual calling into union with Christ, or with reference to the state of forgiveness and acceptance with God into which the believer is ushered by his effectual calling, or with God's open acquittal and acceptance of the believer at the final judgment (Matt. 12:36–37; Rom. 3:22, 24; 5:1; 8:1; Gal. 5:5)." Jack argued that this extended definition of justification that thesis 4 presented introduced immediate ambiguities that undermined the value of Shepherd's "capsule definition" of the term in thesis 3. These ambiguities created problems for the next two theses, 5 and 6, whose wording left it unclear whether Shepherd believed that justification was an *unrepeatable* act of God.

He critiqued the definition of justification in Shepherd's third thesis by offering a definition of his own: "Justification is a final and unrepeated act of God by which He forgives sinners acquitting them of their guilt, accounts and accepts them as righteous, and bestows upon them the title to eternal life, on the sole ground of the righteousness of God supplied through Christ's obedience and received by faith alone." Such a definition would render thesis 4 and its multiple justifications, as well as most of the following theses, largely unnecessary. He wrote, "Since I am of the view that there is only one justification in the absolute sense, then it becomes a serious problem when someone speaks of obedience as 'necessary' to continuing in a state of justification. . . . When we speak of justification as forgiveness of sins and acceptance we have in view, if we follow biblical language, the priestly work and sacrifice of Christ. In such a context faith alone is what continues us in justification, not works or obedience."

He concluded, "Mr. Shepherd insists that he does not want

works brought in as a meritorious ground of justification. Granting the sincerity of Mr. Shepherd without any question here, we still need to see whether or not he has avoided a formulation which, because it is not sufficiently guarded, will mislead both students and the people of God."

In July of 1979, the presbytery as a whole was locked in a stalemate over Shepherd's thesis 22: "The righteousness of Jesus Christ ever remains the exclusive ground of the believer's justification, but the personal godliness of the believer is also necessary for his justification in the judgment of the last day (Matt. 7:21–23; 25:31–46; Heb. 12:14)." Referencing Colossians 4:3–4, Jack held that in order to be considered in accord with the Westminster Standards, any theological formulation regarding the gospel needed to be clear. In his estimation, Shepherd's continued lack of clarity undermined the gospel message. This was seen in two specific ways in thesis 22. First, it was unclear which of Shepherd's three justifications the thesis intended by its first use of the term *justification*. Second, it was unclear what was meant by the phrase "necessary for his justification." The language of necessity in that phrase suggested that works were, as Jack feared, again overshadowing the language of faith.

When the presbytery could not decide on a position regarding thesis 22, the frustrated moderator, John Mitchell, broke its tie vote by voting that Shepherd's thesis was in accord with Scripture and the Westminster Confession. In an open letter to the presbytery, he expressed his frustration and regret over the whole situation: "If I had refrained from voting . . . it would have been in order then to bring a formal complaint against Presbytery for (1) its failure to resolve the question of doctrine, and (2) its failure to declare that Thesis 22 is in harmony with the teaching of Scripture and the Westminster Standards. That . . . would have confronted the presbytery with what I can only suppose would have been an impossible dilemma."

In October of 1979, Jack challenged in writing some ambiguities that he saw in theses 23 and 24. Shepherd used *justification* four times in thesis 23 without clarifying which sense of the term he was speaking about. Thesis 24 introduced a whole different set of ambiguities, with respect to "good works" and "works of the flesh," such that Jack could not comprehend how the presbytery could let the confusion that these ambiguities introduced pass theological examination. He wrote, "In Thesis 24 we are told that the works which are excluded are of a certain class, i.e., 'works of the law' which are the equivalent to the works of the flesh. The works which 'are excluded from justification and salvation are not "good works" in the Biblical sense of works for which the believer is created in Christ Jesus. . . .' I find this an amazing statement! For the whole strength of the Reformation teaching and life rested in the exclusion of any works whatsoever from justification." He said that, in contrast, "there is to be found in [Shepherd's thirty-four theses] such an urgency for *doing* and *obeying* as a covenantal response that there seems to be insufficient concern with the foundations of assurance which are grounded in one definitive act of free imputation received through faith alone."

Jack said that, in the end, Shepherd's primary problem was not with those who opposed his teaching but instead with Scripture and the historic creeds of the Reformed church. Jack argued that if WTS and the presbytery of Philadelphia allowed Shepherd's teaching to continue unchecked, they would share in the guilt of supporting teaching that was out of accord with Scripture and the Westminster standards.

Engagement in the controversy within both the presbytery and the seminary thinned toward the end of 1979 as increasing numbers of exhausted and skeptical participants dropped out of the discussions. In a December presbytery meeting, a vote regarding whether Shepherd was in accord with Scripture and the Westminster Standards ended in a tie, which meant that the deeply divided group still could not reach a decision—and Mitchell announced his intention to file a complaint with the OPC's general assembly. "Failure to resolve this question of doctrine is harmful to the peace and unity of the church, to the ministry and well-being of Mr. Shepherd, and brings the name of Christ into disrepute among us," he wrote. The helpless presbytery members determined to have a season of prayer, and they elected a five-man committee to make a final recommendation for how the controversy should be resolved by the time of their September 1980 meeting. When that meeting came, the presbytery agreed to take no further action.

As the controversy had unfolded, Jack had continued to pastor NLC and to speak at PEF conferences. He had also begun ministries in Ireland and Uganda and, as a result, was frequently out of the country and unable to vote when presbytery meetings were held. Nonetheless, he remained deeply concerned about what was happening within WTS and the OPC. In a letter to Gaffin that he wrote in the summer of 1980, Jack said,

> I want to drop you a note asking if you see any value in our getting together to talk about ways of furthering reconciliation in the matter of the "justification problem.". . . . I have been increasingly out of touch with matters but fear that it has ended up with at least some of the participants alienated from one another.
>
> . . . As you know I am very much interested in a most intense way in the gospel and justification, but I'm left totally downcast at our inability to work through these matters in a gospel manner.
>
> Is there anything to be done to preserve Christ's honor in our midst? I think it is a great shame that the Spirit of Christ cannot give us the oneness of mind and love which is held before us in Phil. 2:1ff.

He continued by saying, "We seem to need to be more humble in our relationships with one another if we are ever to get the objective questions ironed out" and proposed that the two of them gather some participants in the controversy to pray together. "I don't think prayer is a form of near-sightedness but a way of getting to know God better and His will in a situation which is far beyond any human power to correct, and also to seek His blessing in our desperate straits."

Later, while sitting with Gaffin over lunch at Howard Johnson's, Jack told him about "the way that justification by faith has become a liberating power in [his and Rose Marie's] lives together and in the ministry [they] share[d]." Gaffin told Jack that he wished Shepherd could hear some of the things that Jack had shared with him.

IN JUNE OF 1981, Shepherd presented a series of five lectures at Sandy Cove, a retreat center in Maryland, that was titled "Life in Covenant with God." He gave recordings of the lectures to Clowney a few weeks later. Clowney had been in support of Shepherd, but when he listened to the tapes, he called their contents "unwholesome" and reversed his stance. He then listened to Shepherd's course on the Holy Spirit, which raised additional questions in his mind. As a result of his withdrawing of his support, the seminary moved in October to suspend Shepherd from teaching for the first half of 1982. In November, after further discussions, the WTS board of trustees voted 13–8 to remove Shepherd from being professor of systematic theology at the seminary.

When Jack heard the news while he was ministering in Kenya, he sent a personal letter to Shepherd in which he emphasized the love that he had for his colleague, despite strongly disagreeing with him for seven long years.

> I want to take this breather to write you and let you know that I keenly regret your dismissal from WTS. My hope has always been that a reconciliation among us would keep that from happening. I know how much teaching at WTS has been a part of your life, and such a development means a pulling up of some deep roots for you—and also for Connie. You have both been very much in our [his and Rose Marie's] prayers. Our love for both of you has deepened and strengthened as we have prayed for you and understood the burdens you have been bearing.

Jack did, however, tell Shepherd that he agreed with the board's decision to dismiss him from the faculty.

Motivated by love for you and the gospel, I am of the opinion that . . . matters have come to a stage that functioning [in your position at the seminary] is practically impossible. I could not wish upon you the ongoing tension and conflict and suspicion that you now bear. It is not good for your person and ministry and certainly not for your family. . . . God has called us to peace—not to this!

I am also concerned about the functioning of the Seminary as well. The issues have gone on for several years and are no closer to resolution so far as I can see. There is a responsibility to protect your rights, and I have attempted to be faithful to you in this matter. On some points I am closer to you than brothers like Arthur [Kuschke] and Palmer [Robertson]. On the basic issue I think I am further away from you than they. . . .

At the same time, I do believe that the heritage of the gospel at Westminster is bigger than any one of us, including myself. My concerns are not just prudential but to preserve the life and integrity of an institution dedicated to preparing men for the gospel. The conflict simply cannot go on in this form simply because it undermines the clarity of the gospel and confuses the faith of all of us.

Even though Jack saw no reason to try to save Shepherd's faculty position at WTS, he continued to aim the gospel at his colleague's heart. Shepherd had questioned Jack's integrity and reinterpreted his words as a means of claiming that the two men agreed when they did not. Now Jack wrote,

Such sharp-edged style neither serves the interests of truth nor is evidence of that "faith which expresses itself by love." I mention these things not because I have any grudge. I have fully forgiven you. My purpose is only that you might understand that your style at times was not one of reconciliation and mutual love.

Again, reconciliation on a personal level and learning to think together is hindered when you tell us who disagree with you either that our ideas or our theology is not Reformed. What that does is make it difficult for you to learn from us, who are your fellow elders in the church of God, and it leaves us feeling that such labeling reduces the value of the discussion. It puts us in an adversary position with you, one that I certainly do not want. I am your friend. I do not know about others, but I hold you in my heart with all good will and wish to be held in your heart with all good will.

The Lord had humbled Jack in 1970, and, from that low place, his Spirit had worked mightily in Jack's weakness—and Jack wanted the same for Shepherd as well.

He encouraged Shepherd to seek reconciliation with Clowney despite the seminary president's sudden turn against him. He wrote,

I personally know that [Clowney] has sought through some pretty hard times to maintain a firm friendship for you. I am sure that his defense of you over the past several years has damaged his public reputation. He has given a good deal for you and your cause, and as hard as it is for you to see him take a position against a key element in your thinking, you need to follow the new covenant in forgiving him and doing everything in your power to maintain the unity of the Spirit.

We are all getting older. Life is slipping by quickly, and soon we shall all stand before Him who will ask us to give an account according to our works done in the body. When that happens, it will be important for us all to say in our final vindication that we led a life of ongoing mutual kindness and forgiveness at Westminster. Even though you may feel wronged by others, it is still crucial for our standing under the Father's blessing that we work hard to have no personal alienation and continue to work for that oneness in spirit and doctrine which is so pleasing to the Spirit of unity. At a time of what must be unbearable burden bearing for you, I would yet encourage you to seek out Ed and be at peace with him. Shall we not "make every effort to keep the unity of the Spirit through the bond of peace"? Together we must hear the voice of the Spirit saying, "Be kind to one another, tenderhearted, forgiving each other, just as in Christ God forgave you."

Through prayer my affection for you and Connie has grown greatly, and I want to see our lives together full of Christ's reconciling Spirit. That means I am most ready to hear you point out sins and faults in me. I have found such correction given in the right spirit (and even in the wrong spirit) can bring into lives the power of the Kingdom like nothing else. If such reconciliation comes more to the forefront, who knows what mighty works of God may follow? I think you will agree that sometimes we must all be humbled to the dust in order to be lifted up in praise and service.

Jack gave his last word on the matter in December of 1981, when he sent another letter to the WTS board of trustees in which he summarized his understanding of what had happened regarding the controversy from its beginning to its end. In the letter, he questioned the way that the board had dismissed Shepherd without giving specified reasons for doing so, thereby avoiding concluding that Shepherd was out of accord with Scripture and the Westminster Standards; and, because of the weightiness of the matter, he challenged the trustees to reconsider the "prudential reasons" on which they were grounding Shepherd's removal.

In no way do I deny the Board's right to dismiss someone for inadequacies of various kinds. But I believe Mr. Shepherd's situation calls for something more. What I am asking the committee to do is recommend that Mr. Shepherd be dismissed for holding views that are contradictory to Scripture and the Westminster standards. I believe that such an approach is fairer to Mr. Shepherd and to the Seminary community.

I understand, of course, that the Board has already acted, but I hope that it would not be too late for consideration to be given to the question: Has he or has he not been faithful to his views as a Westminster faculty member to uphold the Westminster Confession?

Jack had opposed Shepherd's teaching since the outset of the controversy, and he still opposed it in late 1981. Throughout the unfolding of the controversy, he had kept his conversations with both Shepherd and others private and had avoided criticizing Shepherd publicly except when he was pressed into open conflict. Additionally, he had limited his interactions with other participants in the controversy to as small a group as possible. Nonetheless, he expressed regret.

> I believe that if I had been a more mature person with greater wisdom and courage perhaps this could have been prevented. I am not positive on that point, but I can see that greater grace in my life might have made a difference. What strikes me, however, is the common failing we have all shared in. What is the gospel all about? It is the reconciliation of sinners to God through the blood of Christ and the reconciliation of men to one another as the fruit of that reconciliation to God. I believe that is the priority which is on the heart of the Lord—and one that we sadly neglected in our relationships to one another. It must be greatly offensive to the Lord to see us defending the gospel in a manner that puts us at a distance from one another. . . .
>
> I fear that we have acted hypocritically as brothers together in debating issues that we know little about as part of our own obedience. Who among us has been practicing covenant faithfulness? I do not mean that we have always been at each other's throats, but it seems clear to me that the kind of love which is produced by a living faith has been in mighty short supply. If it had not been, I believe these issues would have been resolved long ago. The whole matter makes me sick at heart. I see little honor for Christ in what has happened, and no victors, only mutual shamefacedness.

The seven-year-long controversy over justification was a painful and humbling experience for almost all who were involved. For Jack himself, however, it had not been purely negative. By raising important questions about justification, Shepherd had helped Jack to sharpen his own theological understanding. And although the conflict was confusing and destructive for many, Jack used it as an opportunity to constructively articulate a vision for Christians of his day: "Cheer up! Justification is by faith alone, even in the twentieth century." Soon, this justification by faith alone would empower a whole movement of discipleship and missions—both across the United States and around the world.

5

CHEER UP! GOD'S KINGDOM IS MORE
WONDERFUL THAN YOU EVER IMAGINED

The Missionary Church and the Missionary Family

In April of 1973, in a party at the home of Hans Rookmaaker—a professor at the Free University in Amsterdam—Edmund Clowney, the president of WTS, met a man named Kefa Sempangi. Sempangi was serving as the professor of art history at Makerere University in Kampala, Uganda, and was the founding pastor of Redeemed Church—a Pentecostal church that had grown out of the charismatic East Africa Revival Movement. Concerned about the shortage of educated Christian leaders in Uganda, Sempagni discussed with Clowney the possibility of sending some leaders from his church to WTS. Unfortunately, he himself was the only such leader who met the seminary's admission requirements, and he had no plans of his own to leave Uganda in order to study in the United States.

For two years, he and his family had avoided the attention of Idi Amin, "Uganda's Hitler," who had staged a military coup in 1971 and was "killing anyone whom he suspected of opposing him."[1] But in the fall of 1973, Sempangi along with his family were forced to flee for their lives when he became marked for execution. He, his wife, Penina, and his daughter, Damali, escaped through Kenya and traveled to Amsterdam, where they were granted temporary asylum. A refugee without a home, Sempangi wrote to Clowney to officially request admission to the seminary for the spring semester of 1974.

Once WTS accepted Sempangi's application, Clowney immediately contacted several churches, including NLC, and informed them of the family's pending arrival. Both WTS and New Life Church (NLC) welcomed the Sempangis with love and open arms. Jack sent William Stump, an elder-in-training at the church, to WTS student housing to greet them when they arrived and to find out what they would need in order to settle comfortably. Kindhearted people who were connected with WTS, and especially those who were from NLC, provided them with supplies and tried to help the family to forget the horror they had endured. For the first time in two years, the Sempangis could make plans that reached beyond the present day. Soon Sempangi, Penina, and Damali had made New Life their church home, and Sempangi, along with Stump, went on to become founding elders of NLC once the plant became a particular church.

"Any time Sempangi showed up in your life, things happen[ed]; none that you would have ever imagined, some that you might regret, some that are very exciting, some that you look back on with fondness, and some you look back on with consternation," Stump said in an interview. And, according to Stump, Jack himself had a similar effect. Few people other than Jack and Sempangi (and perhaps also Stump) could have imagined the expansive mission opportunities that would emerge when the two worked together—first in the United States and then in Kenya and Uganda.

Jack himself was eager to get to know the new student. Sempangi, in turn, was particularly drawn to Jack since he was a Calvinist who, in his estimation, was also a charismatic preacher. Jack assisted Sempangi with the seminary's language requirements and helped him to understand the Reformed theology that he was learning in class. When he explained the different approaches to Reformed theology that different scholars took, Sempangi was able to overcome the negative reaction he had to Calvinism as it was taught by some who were at WTS. Sempangi, for his part, talked to Jack about how Christians in Uganda, many of whom were Pentecostals, approached the Bible. Seeing the interest that Jack had in missions, education, and practical theology, Sempangi also explained the best way for him to teach Reformed theology in East Africa.

In an interview, Sempangi remembered telling Jack that "every time you [go] to preach in Uganda, you go to preach your last sermon"—that, in other words, a preacher in Uganda did not expect to survive. Jack wanted the American church to hear how an underground Ugandan church had both survived and grown in the midst of persecution, and he found ways for Sempangi to share the story of his escape from Amin's reign of terror.

But Sempangi was a seminary student in the United States now. "In the security of a new life and with the reality of death fading from mind," he wrote later in his book *A Distant Grief*, "I found myself reading Scripture [at WTS] to analyze texts and speculate about meaning."[2] As he engaged in theological discussions with fellow WTS students that he found to be intellectually refreshing and enjoyable, his former students and congregants in Uganda became increasingly distant to him.

Sempangi noticed that this shift to more abstract theological thinking was being accompanied by a negative change in his prayer life. He recalled that "with the new sense of security, new environment, everything secure, I was finding myself praying in abstract, and . . . God was challenging me, 'You used to pray so and so, for this child and another child. Now your prayer is very generalized.' . . . Comforts made me begin to think in terms of general things, and [my prayer] didn't have much substance." In response to this realization and the conviction that it brought, Sempangi started an all-night prayer meeting, and Jack joined him.

Even after this conviction took place, when he would receive letters from Ugandan refugees in Kenya, it would have been all too easy for Sempangi to ignore them. Though his family was far safer than they had been in Uganda, they still barely had enough to live on themselves; and the needs of the other Ugandan refugees seemed staggering. But as he regularly met with Jack to pray with and be mentored by him, Jack challenged him to help his friends in Kenya.

In cooperation with NLC, the two men began to raise missionary and financial support for Ugandan refugees. The Orthodox Presbyterian Church contributed $15,000 after Cornelius Van Til approached its foreign missions committee with the refugees' overwhelming need, and NLC raised money to send to Nairobi from other Christians and churches around the United States that wanted to help. After Stump graduated from WTS in 1975, he worked full time to help Sempangi with setting up a ministry, the Africa Foundation, that could continue broadening support. And, after he himself graduated from WTS in 1977, Sempangi continued to draw attention to the suffering of Christians in Uganda by writing his first book, *A Distant Grief*, with encouragement from Jack and others.

NLC sent Dan and Betty Herron, the former houseparents of Hillside House, to Kenya as missionaries to Ugandan refugees in early 1977. By May of 1978, Christian leaders in Kenya had helped the Herrons to start four discipleship groups in refugee camps that were in and around Nairobi. NLC then sent Bill Viss, an elder at the church, and his wife Charlotte to replace the Herrons in August of 1978. By the time they arrived, the Herrons had started two additional Bible study groups and planted a Presbyterian church in Kenya amongst the Ugandan refugees.

AROUND THE SAME time that the Herrons were first heading to Nairobi, NLC also sent Jack and twenty-two other short-term missionaries to Ireland to work with Grace Baptist Church in Dublin, whose pastor, Chris Robinson, Jack had met while caravanning around Ireland on his sabbatical a year earlier. That short-term missions trip that the team took to Ireland would be the first of many.

In the late 1970s, sending short-term missionaries was a pioneering venture for most churches, since they more typically supported full-time missionaries instead. Moreover, to send such a large team that was almost entirely from one church was groundbreaking, at least among Reformed Presbyterians, and the team members raised their own support, which was uncommon at the time. In order to prepare the team, Jack along with NLC elder Bill Viss created and taught an evangelism and discipleship course.

Dan Macha, another elder at NLC and the leader of the Ireland team, said that "the three weeks we spent in Dublin back in '77 felt like a walk through the book of Acts." The team held worship services on St. Stephens Green near Grafton Street. They prayed, sang, and gave testimonies, and Jack and other members of the team preached. One man, who had been tormented until then by the memory of killing his wife during a drunken rage, surrendered his life to Christ as a result of the team's street preaching.

The team from NLC worked with members of Grace Baptist to incorporate creative methods of engaging Dubliners with the gospel. For instance, as a way of confronting viewers with the life, death, and resurrection of Jesus Christ, they performed a skit in which four men dressed in tuxedos, with their faces painted white, carried a coffin up Grafton Street. As the provocative skit confronted people with the gospel in a fresh way, it nearly caused a riot. Police officers intervened to control the crowd and allow the men enough time to share the gospel. The team also took a puppet show to low-income-housing flats and to the Dublin Children's Hospital, where a little boy named William came to Christ.

In an especially effective form of local hospitality evangelism, the Irish-American team invited people to eat with the American missionaries at the Dublin church. As these local people ate together, heard testimonies, and listened to Jack preach, they received the warmth and welcome of Christ from sinners who were saved by grace. One night, a nineteen-year-old named Peter came to deliver a tape recorder to a friend and stayed for dinner. That very evening, he prayed to receive Christ.

BACK IN THE United States, NLC, which was now seven years old, had a lot going on. Not only had it been involved in the ministry in Ireland and Uganda; it had also, under the leadership of the Kaufmanns, been active in pursuing children's and youth ministries at home. As a result, the number of children who now attended NLC had grown so much—with preschoolers alone numbering eighty—that the church was looking for an even larger space than the gym it currently occupied.

In a 1981 church newsletter, Clair Davis wrote, "The big news for the year . . . is really a lot of little stories: marriages healed, tragedies faced up to and met by God's grace, a lot of people cutting back so our new budget with its 45% increase was met, and all of those times we shared each other's burdens, rejoiced with those who rejoiced, mourned with those who mourned, seeing again the Lord's marvelous work in our midst." The young church, under Jack's pioneering leadership, looked forward to another year of experiencing growth at home as well as making an extraordinary impact in the United States and around the world through its church planting and missions work.

NLC recognized the need that it had for leadership training if it was going to take advantage of the exciting growth opportunities that God was placing before it. This meant that it needed to mobilize significant financial resources and administrative support even as it was launching new ministries. Yet for Jack, the budget committee that was handling such considerations was more than a finance team trying to allocate limited resources among a seemingly unlimited number of gospel opportunities. He wanted the committee to be able to help the leaders and congregation to gain a vision for "the grace of giving in an orderly manner." In a letter to the budget committee, he wrote, "It seems to me that one of the weaknesses in our giving has been a failure to emphasize giving as an act of total devotion to the Lord in worship. The offering time traditionally in our worship services has been one of the most casual and unfocused parts of our time together. . . . Personally, I want to catch the excitement of bringing my gift to Jesus without any thought of anyone else as recipient. I want to be Christ-oriented in my giving before I am cause-oriented—even when the cause is most urgent." Such giving required faith: "You simply cannot come and pour all the anointing oil on Jesus's head if you think that the poor of the world will starve because of your waste in worship."

In his letter, Jack proposed a "faith partnership with God." After all, he continued,

> His very nature is that of abundant provider for those in fellowship (literally "in Partnership") with Him. If He is the Senior and Sovereign Partner who owns and supplies all my property, then I can give confidently in worship. Furthermore, I have a right to ask Him to increase my income and bless my frugality so that I may have more to give to Him and His kingdom work. It is out of this partnership with Him that I understand that the weight of world hunger is on His shoulders and that He is willing to increase my resources so that I may give generously to the support of the poor and the teaching ministry of the church. Our people need this faith-freedom in giving so that they are not oppressed by the size of the church general budget or the ache of world hunger and lose their joy.

Jack recommended that the church pay its own administrative expenses last and prioritize its outward-facing expenses, such as mercy ministry, church planting, and foreign missions. Yes, he acknowledged, this might mean that its pastors, which included himself, would not get paid sometimes—but that would help to make them more cautious about putting new items on the budget and might encourage them to pray. "This would be all to the good."

He and NLC cast a vision for, and would eventually organize, a network of like-minded missional churches (before such a network of Reformed Presbyterian and Baptist churches actually existed) that could partner together to support ministries that were connected to NLC—especially the Uganda mission.

SEMPANGI TRANSITIONED FROM pastoral ministry to politics by traveling to join a new Ugandan government that formed in exile in Tanzania in March of 1979. A month later, the Tanzanian military invaded Uganda and deposed Idi Amin. As the fragile new government set up its cabinet, Sempangi was appointed to the position in that cabinet of deputy minister of rehabilitation.

That August, he officially requested that NLC send Jack to plant a New Life church in Kampala, the capital of Uganda—one that would draw back members of the Redeemed Church that he had originally founded before it had been dispersed and driven underground by Idi Amin. After discussing the idea with the elders of NLC and with others who were close to them, Jack and Rose Marie decided to go if the violence in the area died down. Rose Marie wrote that "Kefa kept saying, 'You must come, but it still is not safe.' Finally in November of 1979 he said, 'It is safe. COME.'"[3]

When the time came for Jack to go to Uganda, he found himself conflicted about doing so, for reasons of personal health and safety. He had a history of health problems—including the recurring sinus infections that had brought his initial studies at WTS to an end—and was afraid of getting sick in Uganda. He later told Rose Marie, as she relates in her book *Nothing Is Impossible with God*, "I cried for two weeks because I really didn't want to go." Rose Marie too was hesitant: "I thought I might die there."[4]

The Lord had restored Jack's confidence by the time he and Rose Marie boarded their plane on November 28, 1979—though Rose Marie remained anxious. They remained in Uganda until mid-February of 1980—a few weeks later than they had originally planned—as they looked for ways that NLC could minister to the war-torn country. Four other men from NLC—David Powlison, Phil Gross, Walt Kendall, and Bob Heppe—arrived in Kampala on December 24, 1979. When that first NLC team left Uganda, Gross stayed behind to become more familiar with the city. In the course of that first exploratory visit, the team identified four near-term ministry opportunities that they then reported back to NLC: helping orphans, evangelizing in public, training church leaders, and performing outreach to special groups—such as lawyers, doctors, government officials, and university students.

"I loved the people of Uganda and the ministry I found there,"[5] Jack wrote later. A number of Ugandan church leaders had stayed in the country during Amin's rule in order to lead the underground church, and these young men had been tested by fire. "Pastors Peterson Sozi, Edward Kasaija, Joseph Musuitwa, and Patrick Kamya led us to a spot in Kampala between Owino Market and Kisenyi slum. Here we preached our hearts out. . . . Rose Marie went with us, worked with the women in the Africa Foundation Orphanage, and at night we witnessed to the Asians and government leaders confined with us in the big International Hotel."[6] Through Sempangi's government connections, the NLC team developed contacts and relationships with many important government officials, including President Godfrey Binaisa and his family.

Jack and Rose Marie found living in Uganda very difficult. Though they had experienced poverty early in their marriage, they were unprepared for what they experienced in the war-devastated country: "Ugandans were victims of a city where law and order simply disappeared at dusk," Jack wrote later in the book *Come Back, Barbara*. "The demons of disorder and revenge rode the streets at night. In the morning city officials would often pick up between twenty and thirty bodies of those slain the night before. Old grudges, bitterness, tribal strife, and murderous greed were the terrible heritage of the Amin years."[7]

After spending a little over a month in Uganda, Jack and Rose Marie took a much-needed two-week break to Mombasa, Kenya, where they boarded comfortably at an Episcopal guesthouse. When Jack was invited by local missionaries to evangelize in a nearby marketplace, he startled and infuriated Rose Marie—who had been peacefully watching ships in the harbor nearby—by suddenly announcing that she would speak next. Despite her frustration, she was so used to doing what Jack wanted that she spoke to the group anyway.

When she later asked Jack why he had wanted her to speak, he responded, "They were not listening to me and I thought maybe they would listen to [you]." Forty-five years later, Rose Marie reflected on this experience that had so angered her and concluded that "[Jack] cared, and I didn't. I mean, that's my take on it. He cared, and I didn't."

While they were on a layover in Geneva, Switzerland, on their way home, Rose Marie started to cry while walking along the clean Swiss streets with Jack. As she thought about the three months they had spent in Uganda, the dam burst, and she sobbed uncontrollably. "Why couldn't I love people more? What's wrong with me?"[8]

"Sometimes you act like an orphan—as though there was no Holy Spirit to help you," Jack replied, as Rose Marie quotes in *Come Back, Barbara.* "Don't you know that you are in partnership with the Father and that he loves you and wants to help you?"[9]

In Uganda, Rose Marie had encountered countless orphaned street children, and in the orphanage she had cared for sixty orphans herself. Now Jack was telling her that she herself was displaying an orphan-like mentality of her own—one that showed her unawareness of the Spirit's presence with her. She had been acting as if her heavenly Father had abandoned her—as if he had not given her the Spirit of Christ.

The Spirit used Jack's words to cut Rose Marie to the heart, and she halted in the middle of the road. "That is what I was missing all along, a connection with the Spirit."

Four months later, she and Jack were again part of another team that NLC sent to Uganda for a second mission trip. By this time,

Godfrey Binaisa's government had been overthrown by a military coup. Jack wrote that "the country was in severe disorder. A soldier had been shot and seriously wounded a few days before near where we were preaching at the entrance to Owino market in Kampala." The team moved their worship service to the market in an effort to prevent further killing. Yet, even with all of that being the case, the Lord had now filled Rose Marie with so much love for the Ugandan people that, this time, she could not wait to return. "I especially marveled at Rose Marie's JOY and nonchalant courage in facing . . . automatic rifles," Jack wrote. ". . . She stood there without flinching because she loved the Ugandan people more than her own life."

Even as he marveled at Rose Marie, however, Jack felt a lack of courage himself—one that he feared would soon be exposed. In a letter to his daughter Roseann, he wrote,

"No weapon that is formed against thee shall prosper, every tongue that shall rise against thee, thou shalt condemn" [Isa. 54:17]. This verse Rose Marie claimed, and so did Edward Kasaija, as we walked down from the Rohanna Sports Club to Owino Market where it joins Kisenyi slum. It was downright scary. I don't mean scary with evil lurking beneath the surface. I mean scary with evil right up front and highly visible and armed. Inside the office at Rohanna we had just had prayer for Lydia, whose brother was killed the day before yesterday. It was a brutal murder by hoodlums who blew off the top of his head before his small children. Lydia was crushed in total agony of soul. . . .

The Christians with her were enraged. Really angry in a way that I've never seen them before. What to say? Only to pray, "Father, forgive them, for they know not what they do." My prayer beginning in feebleness turned into a cry of triumph as together we forgave and blessed these murderers.

After prayer, a number of us headed down the steps to Owino. As we came to the street in front of Rohanna Club, we saw a small group of uniformed men coming toward Namirembe Rd.

They almost walked into us as they walked by. Only one has a[n] AK47. Enmity and murder [are] written all over their faces. I think they are drunk with kerogi and hate. They go on like zombies. . . . I stand by the curb, holding my Bible high to identify us. They are gone.

I think my reputation for courage is about to be blown. Man, I can feel fear. Well, they are gone. "Edward," I call, "let's stay together as a group. And let's sing and keep singing." We praise Jesus as we go. It's thin and feeble, but it identifies us as we pass through the Kisenyi slums. We are now going past whorehouses, bars, houses, stepping over open sewers still singing as we go. As we draw near to Owino Market at the edge of Kisenyi slum, I can hear Rose Marie and Mamma Kawooya behind me laughing uproariously at some joke. I think they have courage.

Fear is beginning to fade as we assemble to proclaim the Word of God at the point where the stalls of Owino meet the shops of Kisenyi. The Spirit is coming on us with power as we converge on our preaching spot.

Roseann described her father's letter as "Vintage Dad—involving everyone in a somewhat crazy scheme. Full of faith, bold preaching of the gospel, then the results that were always at once inevitable and surprising: people coming to Christ. And then putting it all into a dramatic story."

According to Sempangi, Jack also demonstrated an excellent awareness of cultural issues—one that Sempangi often found to be lacking in others. To make his point, he mentioned how Jack handled questions from skeptical Pentecostal leaders concerning baptism. When the church plant in Kampala officially became the Presbyterian Church in Kampala, its elders asked Jack to baptize over twenty recent converts. Most of the church leaders, including Sempangi himself, had come from a Pentecostal background that taught that full water baptism by immersion was a necessary part of "true baptism."

Initially, Jack expressed uncertainty about how to proceed with baptizing these converts, but the Westminster Confession of Faith, to which he subscribed, gave him freedom with respect to which mode of baptism could be used. The elders gathered the Ugandan church together to worship outdoors near a local well. Jack arrived to preach holding a bucket. After explaining the significance of baptism, he lined up the new converts. Then he filled the bucket with water and used a ladle to pour it over each person, saying, "I have immersed you, so this is full water baptism [in the name of the Father, the Son, and the Holy Spirit, Amen]." According to Sempangi, Jack's approach was acceptable to the former Pentecostal leaders and helped the church in its early stages, when its skeptical leaders had questions and concerns about Reformed theology. (Jack was also open enough to different modes of baptism to go on to perform full-immersion baptisms in Lake Victoria.)

Sempangi also recounted an incident that took place when he, as a former professor at Makerere University, opened doors that gave Jack the opportunity to speak there as a guest lecturer. The first time Jack did so, a university student asked him a question about the practice of polygamy and drew attention to differences regarding the views of American and Ugandan culture concerning this topic. The student wanted to know how Jack would address this problem. Sempangi recalled Jack's response:

> "Well, I will tell you something. I've been a professor for a long time. I've been a Bible scholar for many years." [Jack then told a] long story about a man with more than one wife, and out of that [story about a] bad marriage, Jack preached a sermon [to the class]. Jack Miller now [said], "When it comes to marriage, we should be very, very careful not to prejudge. But we know . . . the Bible says that for somebody to be a deacon or elder he had to be a man of one wife. So maybe [some in] the Corinthian church may have had two or three wives, [but] we know that the Bible does not teach that."

According to Sempangi, this response showed respect for the student and handled the cultural differences effectively while also providing biblical clarity in a way that impressed Sempangi himself, the students in the class, and the faculty. The faculty requested that Jack teach again and also asked him to recommend professors that they could appoint to teach at the university.

EARLY IN JUNE OF 1980, after the second team arrived, a group of New Lifers and Ugandan Christians preached in Nakasero Market. But they found that no one was listening to them—the market was too full of stinking, rat-infested garbage for anyone to pay attention or stick around. The debris had piled up so high that dead bodies were found underneath it.

Phil Gross managed to commandeer the only two garbage trucks in the city, and he invited local Anglican bishops to join the NLC team as they cleared away the trash, which they did—still in their white collars. The team stuck a sign that read "Jesus is the answer" on one of the garbage trucks and took turns climbing atop it to share testimonies and preach while other team members shoveled garbage in order to clean up the market. "When Jack came back, he stunk to high heaven," Rose Marie remembered.

Ugandans watched in amazement as these white men shoveled garbage all day long. They had seen only a few white men in their country at all throughout the previous decade of Amin's dictatorial and anti-American rule—and they had never seen a white man shoveling garbage. One reporter, while interviewing Jack, accused the missionary team of having an undisclosed political agenda behind their work.

Gross had gotten away with commandeering the two garbage trucks that first time, but in order to continue using them, the team would need official permission. So, a week later, Jack and Gross went to the new city engineer, an Oxford graduate, who greeted the two Americans warmly. He explained that in 1970, Kampala had had over fifty garbage trucks that were being used to serve a much smaller population. By 1980, the city's population had increased to over a million people, and now it had only one working garbage truck along with a second one that was undependable. The city engineer speculated that the other garbage trucks had irreparably broken down or been used by workers for their own purposes. Gross had stumbled onto a real problem.

Jack explained what the team had done with the garbage trucks the previous week. He asked for permission to use the trucks to continue cleaning up the markets and suggested that city employees be allowed to cooperate with them. As the missionaries sought to help the people of Uganda without taking advantage of them, the people began to see the city systems starting to work again. To Jack's delight, the city employees brought garbage containers to the market so that people could throw away their trash rather than continuing to dump it on the ground. They had been empowered to keep their markets clean, and the city workers were encouraged to see the progress that was being made.

Jack also asked the city engineer for advice on how to communicate effectively with the people of Uganda. He explained, "It was not easy to get people to understand why we [were] out there. A reporter . . . thought we must be supporters of [former president] Lulu. Others thought we were trying to clean up the market because Europeans don't like all the flies from the garbage fouling the markets where we shopped." He wanted to understand "how to help people understand our motives." The city engineer replied, "Here in Uganda we can only understand two motivations: force and money. Amin taught us this for eight years. We learned to do things out of fear of punishment or for money. It's a deeply-seated way of life now, and we find it hard to understand that anyone would volunteer to do something for another reason. We didn't [used] to think that way."

As members of the team shoveled garbage in the Nakasero Market and the nearby Owino Market, Jack and some other members climbed onto the garbage truck. Together these Ugandan and American team leaders, covered in dung like Joshua in Zechariah 3, preached the gospel of God's omnipotent grace to the people of Kampala.

MOST MISSIONARY AGENCIES refused to send people into Uganda until they were confident that they could provide for their missionaries and secure their safety. Jack, by contrast, thought like a pioneer. Steve DeMoss, who came to Uganda as part of that second team of missionaries, said that "Jack brought us there and basically dropped us off. . . . When he left, he gave me the instructions, 'Steve, fit in any way that the leaders of the church want to use you, for diaconal purposes or whatever, just make the gospel practical.'" DeMoss was around twenty years old at the time.

> I always saw Jack as someone that was really affected by his faith. [As a result], he was open to doing things differently. Along those lines he would make some mistakes by stepping out. Common sense to him was, "Let's go to this country that was beat up and war-torn." When I was there, no other mission organization would ever go to a place like that at that stage. The U.S. embassy [officials] came and found me and said, "Look, we are not going to be able to protect you. We need you to leave the country. There are only seven Americans registered here, and we need to let you all know you need to get out of here." And Jack looked at me and said, "Steve, I want you to stay here. If you leave there is not going to be any [Americans]." At that time, I was the only American who had not left.

During the nearly three-year term that DeMoss went on to spend in Uganda, three changes of government would take place. The situation was chaotic, and he ended up losing fifty pounds. "We were eating food, and on the side of the container it would say, 'Not for human consumption.' The stuff we feed our pigs is the stuff the US would send for aid. It was like this cornbread, but it was very hard, very coarse. We would dip it in some kind of juice, some kind of soup, or curry. Basically, it was watery soup and you would dip it and basically just try to get something in your stomach." DeMoss saw people who were normal one day lose their minds from malnourishment the next.

Originally, DeMoss lived in a house with the other NLC team members—including Bob and Keren Heppe. But he and Heppe went on to start a successful painting company in the country that occasionally provided DeMoss with a check for $200, which was enough for him to rent his own place—something he decided to do without consulting Jack or NLC. He was trying to adjust to life in Uganda and felt that he needed to be talking directly with the Ugandans and asking them questions rather than listening to other Americans talk *about* the Ugandans. Although Jack disagreed with DeMoss's decision, he respected the bravery that the young man showed by living on his own in the country.

ALL THESE MINISTRY activities in Uganda were happening at the same time as some key events that were taking place in the lives of Jack and Rose Marie's two youngest daughters, Barbara and Keren. Years beforehand, in 1972, Barbara had informed her parents that she intended to pursue her own personal freedom without being bound by the restraints of Christianity. Jack reflected, "I [got] the stuffing kicked out of me in the conflict with my daughter. I did not like to live year after year with the tension of the battle and the constant feeling that things were completely out of my hands. But . . . Barbara's change was not a fluke. . . . It came about because God was weaving a web of love around us all, and an important part of that web was his working through my being humbled."[10]

When Barbara rejected the Christian faith, Rose Marie stubbornly argued with her, and Barbara just as stubbornly refused to listen. Two months later, she left home to begin her freshman year at Dickinson College in Carlisle, Pennsylvania. Instead of coming home the following summer, Barbara moved in with her college boyfriend, and in early 1974 she married this young man whom she had met a couple of semesters earlier. Jack's doubts about the marriage's survival were vindicated the next year when, in a search for "glamour and excitement,"[11] Barbara divorced her husband and moved in with a drug dealer named John.

Jack and Rose Marie had been in Europe while this was happening. When they returned and heard about Barbara's latest decisions, Jack met with her immediately. Rather than lecturing his wayward daughter, he asked her to forgive him for the failures and sins he had committed as a father. He also told her that he forgave her for sinning against him. The conversation "broke down a barrier between them," Rose Marie wrote in her book *From Fear to Freedom*—and although "Jack came home exhausted" he was "remarkably relaxed and at peace."[12]

After Jack asked for his daughter's forgiveness, Barbara came home more frequently. In April of 1977, she finally left John and returned to her parents. She did not exhibit true personal change quickly or easily, however—she continued to hide behind Christian language as a way of deceiving her parents as she slipped back into her old behaviors. God, however, gave Jack and Rose Marie the strength to not allow her to take advantage of them. They laid down an ultimatum: she could stay, but only if she submitted to the standards of their home. Barbara argued, insisting that she had a right to personal freedom as a grown woman—but Jack and Rose Marie held their position.

Unwilling to live by the rules of the Miller home, Barbara moved into her own apartment two miles away and got a job as a waitress. The family pitched in and helped her to decorate the new apartment. With these new boundaries in place, their friendship continued to grow.

Soon afterward, Barbara came back to her parents' for a visit—this time accompanied by a new "friend," Angelo Juliani. In many ways, Angelo was like the other men Barbara had dated. A bartender at the restaurant where she was waitressing, he was a self-confident young man who had a weak moral center. He thought nothing of taking a little money from the register or dealing a few drugs. Barbara, however, truly loved him, and they were good for each other. Angelo helped Barbara to leave the glamorous and dangerous lifestyle that John had represented. She had enrolled at Temple University and was making excellent grades. She, for her part, made Angelo stop selling drugs, and he enrolled at Temple as well and studied to become a public-school teacher. By early 1978, the couple were talking seriously about getting married.

Barbara no longer viewed her parents as enemies, and she was gaining an increased moral sensitivity. With the aid of a local self-help course, she began to confront her habitual deceitfulness and visited the local IRS office to pay back taxes that she owed. This wasn't yet coinciding with an increased *spiritual* sensitivity, however—she and Angelo visited church one Sunday but were bored by the sermon. They had also met lots of other relatively moral people who were outwardly successful and seemed happy without needing all the religious baggage of Christianity.

When Jack began revising his evangelism-training booklet *A New Life* in 1978, he decided to ask non-Christians, including Barbara and Angelo, to help him with making its language more relevant. Angelo especially took an interest in helping him. Barbara, however—suspicious of her father's agenda—warned Angelo that Jack was trying to convert him to Christianity. For the first time in his life, Angelo was looking closely at Scripture and understanding something about the gospel and what the Bible said about sin and grace.

In 1979, Barbara was accepted into the graduate program at Stanford. As she prepared to move there for the fall, she asked Jack if he thought she should marry Angelo. She was surprised when he encouraged her to do so—and even more surprised by his advice regarding Angelo's career path. After she described Angelo's gifts and aptitudes, as Jack tells the story in *Come Back, Barbara*, "an interesting picture began to emerge. [Angelo] was a good counselor, a good teacher, an able public speaker, and a genuine people person." Jack's answer was the last thing that Barbara expected him to say: "Sounds like he'd make a good pastor."[13] Together, they laughed at the irony.

Jack writes,

> The key to winning a lost child, or any lost person for that matter, is to reach the conscience. The primary way to do that is by building a friendship based upon truth and love.
>
> But to do this God's way, Christian parents must constantly work to rid themselves of negative feelings and attitudes toward the erring child. You cannot deny the past, of course, for you have been hurt—and hurt many times. You must learn to accept the past and not cram all these negative thoughts into the basement of your life, close the door, and deny them.
>
> Crippled parents—those who have never had the basements of their lives thoroughly cleaned—will inevitably interfere with Christ's work in the child's life. Christ wants to reach the young person, to find that lost child, for he loves that wandering spirit. But the Spirit's convicting work will be severely hindered by a parent's unconscious rejection.[14]

The Spirit was cleaning out the basement of Jack and Rose Marie's lives in a way that gave them access to the inner sanctum of Barbara's and Angelo's consciences as well.

Dick and Elizabeth Kaufmann had taken a special interest of their own in Barbara—when she and Angelo ended up needing five hundred dollars for their move to California, the Kaufmanns organized a collection for them. When Jack presented the money to them at a going-away celebration, Angelo had to step outside the house so that no one could see him cry. He had never experienced unconditional love from Christians, and both he and Barbara were astonished by the generosity and love of the very people they had rejected.

As Barbara and Angelo prepared to move, Jack was anticipating his first trip to Uganda. He knew that, before he and Barbara could go their separate ways, "there was something painful Christ wanted [him] to do."[15] Despite the changes that had taken place in her life, Barbara was not yet saved. Jack girded himself for a last battle with his daughter—one in which he was committed to tell her "simply and forthrightly how it made [him] feel that she would not be with [him] in heaven."[16]

When the time came, he told Barbara how pleased he and Rose Marie were with her—that they were excited to see her go to Stanford and prepare to marry Angelo. "But," he said, "there's a burden on my heart I feel I must share with you. It's simply that when it's all said and done, this life is soon over. I have been thinking that of my own life. And I want you to know that it seems so sad to me that when I go to heaven, I will only take you along as a beautiful memory."[17]

At his words, Barbara became so furious that she would not allow him to say more. Rose Marie happened to walk into the room just as Barbara began to shout at Jack, and she turned and left the room again in tears. Barbara vehemently denounced her father for several minutes. As she raged against Jack and said that he was always fighting with her, Jack prayed for the strength to listen to her and to remain quiet as well as for "God to touch her conscience with his Spirit, to convict her of sin, and to give her an awareness that it is insane to organize your life as though this present world was eternal."[18]

When she stopped, Jack prayed for courage before calmly saying, "Why should it seem wrong for me to tell you what I really feel? And I do feel that way. I do not want to go to heaven and only take you there as a beautiful memory."[19]

Barbara blew up again, lashing out at her father with equal intensity. When she eventually stopped once more, Jack replied, "You and I haven't been fighting all our lives. That's just false. I can only remember two or three fights when you were growing up— and you won them all. Really, we should have had more conflicts and settled some things. It seems to me that there's nothing wrong in what I just said. What's wrong with my telling you that I want you to go to heaven with me?"[20]

The tension broke, and Barbara's whole demeanor changed. She fell down, suddenly in tears, at Jack's feet. "With tears streaming down her face, she looked up and said, 'Dad, we are going to have to do this more often.'"[21]

As he held his daughter, Jack agreed. "Barb, I want to ask you to do only one thing. Will you ask Jesus to reveal himself to you? Just that. Will you ask him to show himself to you? . . . That's all I ask. That's enough. He'll hear your prayer, I know he will. I love you. God be with you."[22]

After that, Jack, knowing that the battle was over, entrusted Barbara to the Lord.

ON FEBRUARY 13, 1980, Angelo Juliani and Barbara Miller were married in Palo Alto, California. Soon afterward, Rose Marie called Barbara to tell her daughter about the experiences she had had in war-torn Uganda. In a conversation that is quoted in *Come Back, Barbara*, she described the terrible living conditions and how the culture shock had been too much for her. "I didn't have the resources to handle it," she told Barbara. "I became angry and withdrew." Then she told the story of the breakdown she had experienced in Switzerland—how she had cried to Jack, "What's wrong with me?" only to receive his answer: "You act like an orphan. . . . Don't you know that . . . the Father . . . loves you and wants to help you?"[23]

Rose Marie heard her daughter choking up on the other end of the phone as she replied, "Mother, that's the way I am too." Without really knowing what she had been doing, Rose Marie had offered an example of repentance, and the Spirit used her "confession of weakness [to win] Barbara's heart."[24]

A few weeks later, Barbara became a Christian—and a few weeks after that, Angelo did as well. The couple returned from California in June while Jack and Rose Marie were on their second trip to Uganda. Keren welcomed her sister and brother-in-law home—though with skepticism. Having decided to follow in her older sister's footsteps, she had thrown off what she perceived to be the restraints of Christianity and become pregnant while her parents were away, and now she wondered whether Barbara and Angelo's professions of faith were genuine. The two of them soon recognized the path that Keren was taking. "As Barbara pursued her," Jack wrote in *Come Back, Barbara*, "Keren began to rethink her values, and to her dismay she learned that the love of many non-Christians was only superficial, while the love of Christians like Barbara was remarkably enduring."[25]

When Keren was later in the hospital following the delivery of her baby, Bob Heppe, who had known her for years, visited her—and also showed romantic interest in her for the first time. The next week, he went to Uganda; and while he was there, he and Keren started writing to each other regularly. When Jack learned about this, he talked to Bob about marrying his youngest daughter. Keren explained, "We had a semi-arranged marriage. We didn't date at all. The phone lines [from Uganda] were really bad. So, we wrote letters back and forth. Then we decided to get married, and he proposed in April [1981] and I said yes." On April 25, Jack praised the Lord as he recorded in his personal journal that Keren had called to tell him that she had surrendered her life to Christ and to announce her engagement.

When Bob returned to the United States for about a month that September, he and Keren were married. He had already committed to serve in Kampala long-term, Rose Marie thought that it was important for Keren and the baby to bond with Bob, and Keren wanted to be with her husband. So, in December, the newly married couple traveled to Uganda with their baby girl.

UGANDA ITSELF OFFERED Jack a ministry opportunity that was unparalleled by even the other promising ministries in which he was involved. Even as the Shepherd Controversy raged at WTS and in the presbytery of Philadelphia, he continued to travel there during his winter and summer breaks. Seeing the increased demands that Jack was facing around the United States and overseas, NLC's session recommended in 1981 that he discontinue teaching at WTS the following year. Although he loved the school as well as his students, he agreed in principle that he needed to balance his work and ministry better, and he resigned from WTS despite being on the verge of tenure. He did, however, continue to teach in an unofficial capacity by moving his practical theology training to the church and, later on, by frequently coming to the campus to speak.

NLC's session was "more convinced than ever that Dr. Miller should be using his gifts to minister to other parts of the body of Christ." They divided his time among key areas: 20 percent of it to foreign ministry, 20 percent of it to his writing ministry and to rest, 40 percent of it to ministry at the church itself, and 20 percent of it to ministry to other churches in the United States. This division of his time enabled Jack himself to act as a pioneer and a catalyst and to leave others in the field—whatever field that might be—to organize and execute his suggestions.

The session of NLC grappled with the immensity of the opportunity that Uganda presented. The need within the country was monumental, even with four full-time missionaries there—Alan Smith, Steve DeMoss, Bob Heppe, and Phil Gross—and with short-term teams, including Jack and Rose Marie, traveling back and forth. Fortunately, the teaching that Jack was doing at national and regional pastors' conferences that were hosted by Presbyterian Evangelistic Fellowship (PEF) was revitalizing and having a major impact on pastors and church planters in the Presbyterian Church in America (PCA)—which enabled NLC to recruit other Reformed leaders from outside the OPC who could help in Uganda. Jack invited Henry Krabbendam, a professor at Covenant College and a long-time friend and OPC colleague, to come to Uganda and bring some of his students. Harvie Conn, professor of missions at WTS, also came and brought with him a team of eight WTS students to serve the Ugandan-American team. To handle the growing interest in Uganda from Christian leaders around the United States, Jack and others put together a curriculum for short-term American missionaries and Ugandan leaders that included teaching on discipleship, spiritual warfare, and sonship.

The NLC session soon experienced tension over, as a church newsletter said, "how much time to give to the Africa Foundation [the ministry that Sempangi had started, which placed an emphasis on orphans] and how much time to give" to the Presbyterian Church in Kampala (PCK), which was becoming hard to differentiate from the Africa Foundation's orphanage—according to David Powlison, an elder at NLC, "the [Kampala] church had become the 'orphanage chapel.'" The church was seeking to establish an identity of its own and to place an emphasis on church planting, and work needed to be done to make it a separate entity that would be distinct from the orphanage and have its own administration and location. As leaders from NLC and the Presbyterian Church in Uganda (PCU) debated how much time should be dedicated to church planting versus dedicated to the care of orphans, Alan Smith began to focus on the latter alongside the Africa Foundation while Phil Gross worked directly with the Presbyterian church.

The Ugandan government gave Sempangi a building to be used for housing orphans, but the sheer number of orphans in the country immediately exceeded its capacity. A Ugandan church leader approached DeMoss about the prospect of DeMoss's taking the children into his house. Since Jack had encouraged DeMoss to do what the Ugandan leaders asked, DeMoss agreed, with Sempangi's blessing. As the nephew of Arthur DeMoss—the founder of National Liberty Insurance—he had access to a large network of wealthy people and quickly raised the additional funds that he needed to house the children.

NLC AND THE PCU hosted two conferences in Kampala for pastors: one in June of 1981 and the other in February of 1982. Jack reported to NLC that his trip to Uganda during the time of the first conference, had been "the best trip yet." The church had found a new location so that it would no longer be identified so closely with the Africa Foundation orphanage, and Jack along with other team leaders whom he had recommended had been given opportunities to hold lectures and speak in classes at Makerere University.

The Lord was breaking down barriers that had existed between Pentecostals, Anglicans, and Presbyterians in Uganda. At the 1982 pastors' conference, Jack taught on Galatians, and Reformed leaders prayed for "a great outbreak of conversion power," in his words. Christian leaders from around the country continued discussing, late into the evening, what they had learned at the conference. And soon after the event, as the pastors who attended it went on to share the gospel with renewed faith, several hundred people in Uganda were converted to Christ—including a number of politicians and bankers, plus a well-known lawyer. A Ugandan pastor who had planted sixty-six churches identified with the PCU and asked them to send him as a missionary to unreached tribal areas. Ugandan pastors and foreign missionaries from different denominational backgrounds who had been disillusioned about evangelism or had refused to permit it in their parishes began to have a whole new outlook on it as they saw the gospel turning people—including some who were already ordained pastors—to Christ. Isaac Ijolk, Uganda's minister of education, encouraged Jack to expand his seminar from the pastors' conference to other parts of the country, and the PCU took steps to translate Jack's book *Repentance* (which had previously been published as *Repentance and Twentieth Century Man*), along with other Christian literature, into the tribal Lugandan language.

After returning from Uganda, Jack taught his Bible study on Galatians to an American audience. In the study, which focused on the nature of spiritual power, Jack explained,

> If you open to [Galatians 3] and begin to read, you see that Paul's whole argument is about the power and the vitality—and the protecting of that power and vitality—of the ministry of the Spirit. . . .

Now the logic . . . goes something like this: that you find the power of the Spirit not through some mystical or strange experience but simply by taking and keeping justification by faith as your foundation. . . . Now if you keep justification behind you as something kind of on the shelf—Oh! Yes, once I really trusted in Christ and in his blood shed for me, but that's way behind me—once you do that, you've lost spiritual power. So, by the Holy Spirit's power we are always maintaining the foundation of justification by faith.

In other words, the book [of Galatians] is not primarily about justification by faith. It is about [spiritual] power—that the way you get the power is always staying on that foundation. Don't think of [the Christian life] simply as "There is justification by faith back there—and here is adoption, and here is sanctification, and here is glorification" so that you kind of leave justification behind. Rather, justification is the permanent foundation, and you build on it, and as you grow up [in maturity], you are always in an utterly humble state with respect to justification. You can never do anything you can trust in for your own justification. And your [spiritual] power then lies in your continuing to forsake any righteousness of your own, and always trusting in Christ's righteousness. And that gives you the power of sanctification.

As Jack and his son, Paul, were leaving the Galatians Bible study one evening, Paul asked Jack what the teaching material should be called. Jack stopped and thought for a moment, then said, "Let's call it Sonship." Because of the Bible study's connection to the teaching Jack had originally done at the pastors' conference, Bob Heppe explained that "Sonship [originally] started in Uganda."

IN 2010, during a celebration of the thirtieth anniversary of the PCU, Steve DeMoss stood next to Sempangi and fellow church leader Edward Kasaija on a mountain overlooking eleven Ugandan villages that lay in the valley where Sempangi had grown up as a child. In 1980, none of those eleven villages had ever heard the gospel. By 2010, six had been claimed for the glory of Christ. DeMoss said to the Ugandan leaders as he looked over the valley, "In my mind [this] all began with Jack Miller and his stepping out . . . in faith when everyone else said no." In a later interview, he elaborated, "People were against it and said, 'You are crazy.' But he went forward with it, and as a result [60] churches have been planted [in the Kampala area]. And he instilled the evangelistic spirit in [the 220 PCU churches planted in] Uganda as a whole [a spirit] that still exists to this day."

Jack was a pioneer in Uganda. He helped to found PCK—leading to the formation of the PCU—led teams to the most dangerous areas of Kampala, went east to plant a PCU church in Mbale as well as a second church in a nearby Muslim village, and traveled west on exploratory mission trips to Fort Portal and Bundibugyo. What impressed Ugandan leaders the most was when he was willing to take a pioneering team to the tsetse-infested Buvuma Island in Lake Victoria. DeMoss described that life-threatening trip to Buvuma as one more example of how Jack would say, "Why not?" when others said no. For Jack, "the joy of bringing the gospel to 'forgotten people'" was worth the risk of becoming infected with sleeping sickness.

Jack took Kasaija, missionary Bob Heppe, and two other Ugandan leaders to Buvuma. And, while the visit itself was a success, their return trip to the mainland became a nightmare. The ferry, which was already packed with too many passengers, was caught in a terrible three-day storm that nearly capsized it. Jack described those ominous days that they spent on Lake Victoria in a sermon that he titled "Election: The Power Source for Life."

[Initially], I rather thought we were going to get through this. . . .

But as we went deeper into the darkness and the storm, those poor people [crammed onto the small boat] were trying to hide in the bottom. They were vomiting, and we were getting everything from every possible direction. And the rain, there must have been about thirty gallons of water in the boat. It was not a very big boat

154

either. . . . Finally, the pilot even turned off the motor in the darkness. That had been my own last hope [that we still had the engine running]. You know, we Americans, we always have a Plan B if Plan A doesn't work. I do. And then if plan B doesn't work, I've got Plan C, and if Plan C doesn't work, I've got plan D, and I work my way right down to Z. Now there was nothing left to do except say, "God, you are sovereign."

I remember Edward [Kasaija]'s prayer. He may not remember, but I couldn't forget it. I was the one who encouraged Edward to start singing and said, "Make it loud!" I wanted to keep the people who [were] not Christians from panicking, and they were already to one side of this small boat, almost tipping it over. That was what I was especially afraid of. Edward kept singing and praying, but pretty soon, it was too wet to sing. So, he kept praying: "God, this is a revelation of your power. God, this is a revelation of your glory and your majesty." And I was praying to myself, "Yeah, and why don't You quit. I have seen enough."

. . . The wonder of God is that He's not to be measured by human instruments. And the thing that just hit us [in that storm on Lake Victoria] is that God is God. Not just here on this lake, but God is God everywhere. And we little puny human beings are being compelled to admit it here on that lake and to pray out of the knowledge that if He simply touches this boat with His finger it goes to the bottom. And yet if He touches those waves with His finger we go right on into Tommy Bay, and all is well.

The frightened yet grateful team made landfall, albeit three days later than they expected to. They had met themselves in their weakness, Jack said—but they had also seen how absolute God is.

Since the beginning of their work together, NLC and the PCU had been blessed by a spirit of unity—one that went on to last through early 1982. The relationship between them deepened as the American missionaries and Ugandan Christians evangelized together, planted churches together, and endured great dangers together—such as the storm on Lake Victoria and attacks from rebel forces. Tragically, however, the partnership between them would eventually be severed by problems that stemmed from money coming from the United States.

Since 1975, Jack and NLC had encouraged William Stump, in partnership with minister and civil-rights activist John M. Perkins and his ministry Voice of Calvary, to help Sempangi and the Africa Foundation to establish a fund for Uganda that could raise financial resources independently from NLC. Sempangi, for his part, had already been pursuing resources like this by fundraising himself throughout the United States. The church in Uganda had significant challenges to address, which Paul Miller described well:

> Diaconal ministries [tend] to overrun gospel ministries especially when diaconal needs in a country like Uganda are unlimited. Diaconal projects multiply and grow until the national church is unable to manage them. . . . Our model of operation is like the US Army in Vietnam, requiring many support people and large infusions of cash to operate, instead of stream-lined guerrilla operation where every man is a soldier. Yet the needs of the people are very real and pressing. It is hard to disciple someone if they are unemployed and hungry. Unemployment in the PCU congregation in Kampala is as high as 80%.

In the summer of 1982, Paul McKaughan of Mission to the World (the PCA's missionary-sending agency) and Nelson Malkus of World Presbyterian Mission (a mission organization that was associated with the Presbyterian Church in the USA) met with Jack and Harvie Conn back in the United States. Their own agencies were not willing to commit resources to Uganda because of the continued instability and danger in the country, but they encouraged Jack and NLC to take the lead in forming a mission that would partner with other Reformed churches for the purpose of providing resources despite this. Thus, NLC joined with other churches in the PCA and with Reformed leaders from PEF to form World Harvest Mission (WHM) on January 10, 1983. The formation of WHM gave other churches in the OPC, the PCA, and PEF an opportunity to broaden their partnership with Jack and NLC in Uganda and Ireland.

The first WHM board meeting was held on that date at McLean Presbyterian Church (PCA) in McLean, Virginia, and Jack was named the mission's executive director. The board of the new mission drew up a constitution that established twelve distinctive features of the mission, beginning with a focus on "church planting, evangelism, and discipleship." WHM also envisioned having a diaconal program that would be "secondary [to] and supportive" of this main focus. The new board made a point of stating that the mission was "NOT a diaconal-relief organization with an emphasis on evangelism and discipleship added" and "NOT basically a channel or clearing house for expediting and coordinating requests from Uganda or other countries."

As Jack prepared to go back to Uganda in the late spring, Rose Marie told him, "You have two mistresses—one black [PCU] and one white [NLC]—and you give all your time and your attention to them, and there's nothing left for me." She challenged him, "You often say you want to be a man controlled and compelled by the promises of Scripture, a man of prayer and patience, and a perpetual learner. God is making you all of this, but I rarely hear you desire to be taught how to nourish and cherish your wife as Christ does the church. . . . I have often thought that I lost a husband when you took your first pastorate, and I'm not sure I have ever gotten him back." While she had "followed [Jack] all over the world," she did not want to return to Uganda. Perhaps ironically, Jack went on to participate in a conference on pastors' wives before heading to Uganda without her.

When he arrived in the country, he found that the PCU leaders in Kampala were frustrated over the way WHM had been formed without their involvement. In response, Jack and Bob Heppe—who was an executive committee member—offered to appoint additional PCU leaders to join the one Ugandan, Peterson Sozi, who was on the WHM board. Jack also suggested that the leaders create a list of practical ideas for how the growing church could create small businesses that would be able to provide jobs for its members. He had in mind low-cost business ideas such as Heppe and DeMoss's painting business, which had started up using a small investment of $5,000 that was paid out over about four years and that achieved a gross revenue of $60,000 in 1983. However, throughout two weeks of difficult meetings that were held on the subject, the ideas that the leaders presented were bigger and costlier than what Jack had in mind and would have required significant funding from the United States. Uncharacteristically, a frustrated Jack shook his head and laughed at the proposals. Although the ideas may have been impractical, his offhanded dismissal of them did not help matters.

A low point of the meetings, and a source of great strain for Jack, came about when a PCU leader accused Jack of stealing money. He may have thought that WHM was using Uganda as a pretext to raise funds for other ministry activities that were directed outside the country and to enhance the personal reputations of the board members. DeMoss, however, suspected that the angered Ugandan leader had actually seized on a misunderstanding that had taken place between DeMoss and Jack.

Before he had left for Uganda, Jack had unexpectedly been handed $2,500 that had been collected in the United States as part of DeMoss's personal fundraising for the orphans who were living in his home. Without accounting for the tension that existed between NLC and the PCU over American funding, DeMoss, in an act that he now regrets, asked Jack for the money in front of the Ugandan leaders. Jack gave him only $900 of the $2,500 that he had raised. When DeMoss questioned him, Jack told him that he would discuss the remainder of the funds with him later. And he did so—meeting privately with him to discuss his concern regarding

DeMoss's decision to board orphans in his home and the implications that this would have for his other responsibilities as part of the NLC Uganda team. During this meeting, he gave DeMoss the remainder of the money.

But the damage had already been done. The church leaders' frustration over US funding in general was exacerbated by what they interpreted as Jack's withholding of money that had been designated for supporting Ugandan orphans. PCK-PCU and NLC-WHM decided to sever their binding partnership in favor of an agreement to work together when opportunities arose. This new arrangement allowed PCK-PCU to pursue American funding in its own ways and allowed WHM itself to maintain a healthier, more balanced relationship between evangelism and church planting as well as diaconal ministry as it continued to work in Uganda.

THE CONTENTIOUS MEETINGS with the PCU leaders quite literally broke Jack's heart. On Thursday, June 30, a day before his scheduled departure from Entebbe Airport for the United States, he began having severe chest pains. The waves of pain were so unbearable that he had to be carried into the doctor's office he was taken to.

Initially he was diagnosed with angina and prescribed nitroglycerin. Bob Heppe still hoped to get him onto the plane back to the United States so that he could receive better medical care. But when his excruciating pain continued, Jack was admitted to Saint Francis Nsambya Hospital. No indication of a problem showed up on his EKG, however; and he was at the hospital for more than seven hours before Heppe managed to get a doctor to give him something for the pain.

Unfortunately, by the time Rose Marie received word of his emergency, it was Friday morning—too late for her to get a visa to enter Uganda. Still, now that Jack's pain was finally under control, she encouraged Heppe to return on his own scheduled flight so that he could be with his family in Philadelphia while she and NLC leaders made plans for her to get to Uganda as soon as possible.

The hospital's dated medical equipment finally showed that Jack's pain was the result of a heart attack—a severe anterior infarction, as the doctor was able to determine. Jack later told Rose Marie, "The pain was so intense that I couldn't remember any verses from the Bible and I couldn't pray. *I was a weak man.*"[26] In a sermon that he later delivered on the last judgment, however, he said, "God gave me strength in spite of the agony to begin witnessing to my nurses. I became so concerned that nobody had to go through this kind of agony, and the thought of [anyone] going through it forever and ever was just overwhelming."

Jack was too weak to hold his large NIV Bible, so he asked his English-speaking Ugandan nurses to read the book of Romans to him. When they read that "God presented [Christ] as a sacrifice of atonement, through faith in his blood. He did this to demonstrate his justice" (Rom. 3:25), Jack asked them, "Do you know what this means?"[27] Though he was too tired to discuss it with them at the time, he told them to take his Bible home and read all of Romans 3 so that they could talk about it together. The following day, Rose Kaijuka was the first of his nurses to surrender her life to Christ. Afterward, several of the other nurses made professions of faith as well—although one of them, after further discussing with Jack the conversion she believed she had experienced, realized that she had made her own profession simply because she was caught up in the emotions of the mini-revival.

The sound of singing and praying that came from Jack's hospital room after these conversions drew a group of medical personnel, who asked, "What's this good news that everybody is talking about?" The Lord greatly encouraged Jack during his weakest moment as he watched the power of the gospel start a "little church . . . in that [hospital] room."[28] Rose Marie wrote,

Jack's church planting was extended to [Nsambya] Hospital!
The same grace that changed these young women also gave Jack strength. Soon he was sitting in a wheelchair outside in the

hospital grounds, sharing his faith with an ill and very distraught Hindu.

Jack said, "I will pray for you that God will heal you, but I will pray in the name of Jesus Christ, the Son of God, who is not one of your gods." He kept repeating this as he talked to the man. After many similar conversations, the man put his faith in Christ and was healed. Jack repeated, "Now who are you going to say healed you?" The Indian replied, "Jesus Christ healed me, the Son of the Living God."[29]

God's omnipotent grace had replaced the pain and suffering Jack had been experiencing with the joy of the gospel. In a letter that he wrote to his daughter Ruth and her husband Jim Trott, Jack said, "I certainly would not want to go through the experience of a heart attack again, but by grace I have even been able to look squarely at the prospect of death itself and God appears to have taken away the fear of that . . . at this time."

Rose Marie arrived in Uganda at 11:00 a.m. on July 4, accompanied by Bill Viss, who had left an NLC missionary team that he was leading in Ireland in order to meet her in Brussels and fly with her to Kampala. As they came to the hospital, Rose Marie wondered if Jack had died. She was overjoyed to find him weak and pale but alive. Jack himself told Ruth and Jim that Rose Marie looked to him "as radiant as the sun."

Rose Marie and Viss did, however, notice a drag in Jack's mental abilities. Over the next several days, his awareness fortunately improved—though he continued to remain sluggish. When Rose Marie told him that he was repeating himself, it frightened him. Every pain or weakness that he experienced made him fear that he was having another heart attack.

The nurses were horrified when they gave him his first bath and discovered that he had red bedbug bites all over his back. Rose Marie added to the letter that Jack was writing to Ruth and Jim by saying, "There is so much in this country I hate. Yet God has filled me with peace and contentment. It is right to be here. I'm not sure I could have prevented this if I had been here. . . . It is back to spit baths, cockroaches, smelly toilets, no indoor water, ants, and lizards. Last night there was a shooting quite close, but fears were gone." She wanted to get her husband out of Uganda and back home as soon as possible, but Jack needed to build up his strength before doctors would allow him to travel.

Dr. Arnold Gash—a cardiologist at Temple University, a member of NLC, and a friend of the Millers—asked the elders of New Life to allow him to travel to Uganda so that he could care for Jack and bring him back home. His willingness to accompany Jack to Philadelphia relieved the patient himself, Rose Marie, and the staff of the hospital. Gash contacted Jack's doctors in Uganda to consult with them. When he arrived in Uganda, he immediately got Jack out of his bed and had him walking up and down the stairs—though Jack found the movement alarming as every twinge of pain made him think he was having another heart attack.

The return trip to Philadelphia was taken in stages. The party traveled from Entebbe to Nairobi and then to Brussels; then, after an overnight stay there in Belgium, they made their final flight to the United States. Gash had brought a portable defibrillator with him from Philadelphia in case Jack suffered another heart attack. And, while Jack himself was fine, Gash ended up using the equipment on another passenger who suffered a heart attack during that final flight.

WHEN JACK FIRST returned home, he was too weak to climb the stairs to the house's master bedroom, so he slept on the lower level. Gash continued to care for him, and he slowly recovered. He resumed his teaching and preaching responsibilities on a limited basis, as he was able, and attended important NLC-WHM leadership meetings in September. By late October, the results from his heart stress tests had improved by 50 percent—though he still required two hours of sleep in the afternoon in order to make it through each day. Gash indicated that Jack's heart would remain unstable for another six to twelve months. The earliest that he would be able to travel would be May of 1984.

The PCK-PCU leaders grieved when Rose Marie told them that Jack didn't think he would be able to return to their country. Jack's deep love for PCK-PCU made the fact that he had to remain separated from them during an unsettled conflict all the more difficult for him. From Rose Marie's perspective, however, God had taken away one of the "two mistresses" that were in Jack's life through his heart attack. He had sidelined Jack from being able to travel and instead focused his attention on his family, on writing, and on ministry that he could take part in from the confines of the Philadelphia area.

Larger-scope ministries did, however, feel the effects of Jack's reduced level of involvement. John Julien, a WTS graduate and former houseguest of the Millers, had agreed to plant New Life Church Northeast in urban Philadelphia—with the understanding that Jack would help to launch the new church plant and preach at it regularly after he returned from Uganda. Julien had not felt ready to plant a church by himself; but, as a result of Jack's heart attack, he found himself doing just that.

While short-term teams continued to travel to Ireland from NLC, WHM, and PEF after Jack's heart attack, his health problems did delay the launch of a permanent team that was coming together. After the team successfully launched, WHM turned its attention to Amsterdam and London. Eventually, in August of 1986, WHM recruited a short-term team, which included Bill Viss and Paul Miller, to travel to Amsterdam and explore the possibility of beginning a permanent mission there.

Meanwhile, a church-planting team that was bound for the eastern part of Uganda collapsed. An outbreak of hepatitis in 1984 as well as civil war in 1985 forced the missionaries who were in western Uganda into survival mode. Jack could not travel to be with them, but he could pray for them—and he could gather others to pray as well. Once the dangers subsided, a newly reorganized team in western Uganda was able to plant a church in Fort Portal by 1986. And, from 1987 to 1989, the team also began taking the gospel to hidden mountain tribes who lived farther to the west of Uganda and in Zaire.

Jack took advantage of his new limitations and weaknesses by calling people to pray with him. He invited both the leaders of NLC and WHM, as well as others who wanted to attend, to join him in this spiritual work every Thursday morning at his house from 7:00 until noon. These meetings became "a school of prayer to train believers to pray for a larger vision of the whole church," Jack wrote in an article called "Let us Pray." "We especially used the format of praying for the inward life of the church, its upward worship, and its missionary outreach." As the group prayed, NLC's ministries became revitalized—"the youth ministry stabilized, the daughter church was well launched, and [they] were making progress on calling a new pastor." Jack noted that "our congregation is a praying one. But we have much to learn and must constantly fight the tendency to let prayer decline into intercession for emergencies and felt needs. Our burden is to become more God-centered in our praying and to see his name glorified through great revival and missionary expansion in our time in response to the prayers of his people."[30]

Although NLC itself had moved to a large gym a few years beforehand, it still had to add a third service to its Sunday schedule in order to accommodate an increase in its attendance. In April of 1985, the church called John Yenchko to be an associate pastor who could help to serve its growing congregation. Yenchko had been attending the Thursday-morning prayer meetings since Jack started holding them at his house and, with encouragement from Jack, had taken the lead in the meetings and started running them.

AS A GENERAL PRINCIPLE, the weaker Jack became, the more he prayed; and the more he prayed, the more he rejoiced as he witnessed the glory of God's kingdom. God used Jack's own weakness to draw him to others who were weak—and were even considered by evangelical Christians to be unclean.

One example of this was his response to the AIDS crisis. During the mid-1980s, many evangelical Christians angrily condemned homosexuality, indicted gay people for the AIDS epidemic, and blamed them for creating fear about the contagious disease. Jack, however, had already seen the devastating effects of AIDS in Uganda. Now, he visited patients who were dying from AIDS in order to share the gospel with them and took others from NLC along with him. He joined Dorrit Sterner, a medical doctor at Temple and a member of NLC, to speak publicly on the topic of "Understanding the AIDS Crisis," when few conservative evangelical leaders were offering a constructive response to that crisis. "We must become the society of the forgiven and the forgiving," he wrote—"not the community of the frightened."

He also had the courage to graciously confront evangelical leaders when he thought it was necessary or to address controversial subjects that others refused to touch. In a July 1988 letter to the *Philadelphia Inquirer*, Jack wrote, "As an evangelical pastor I deplore the rise in violence against homosexual persons . . . attributed to the growing feeling that homosexuality and AIDS go together." He offered a possible solution: "Let's begin by each of us taking a hard look at our attitudes and prejudices, apologizing to each other, and forgiving one another." He then led the way in repentance: "As an evangelical Christian let me be the first. I apologize to the members of America's homosexual community for the harshness and tone of superiority that has all too often issued from the evangelical community." But he also asked, "Can anyone escape the conclusion that at least some homosexuals have spread the AIDS virus with a self-centeredness that seems totally indifferent to the lives of others? Therefore can a case be made for repentance in the homosexual community too?" If homosexuals would join with Christians in repenting, and if both groups would humbly seek forgiveness, he concluded that "our example together might create a climate that would make it difficult for 'anti-gay violence' to thrive."[31]

John Freeman, the founder of Harvest USA, writes, "Jack's steady hope and expectation of 'seeing what God's going to do now' . . . is something I've carried with me for the past twenty-five years . . . that God is always at work—and is pleased to use redeemed sinners like us to accomplish his work, as we step out of our comfort zones, by faith."

JACK'S SCHEDULE FOR April 3, 1984, provides a sense of the daily rhythm of his activity and rest nine months after his heart attack. From 5:30 in the morning until 6:15, he had personal devotions; from 6:30 to 7:45, he participated in a men's prayer time; from 7:45 until noon, he took part in a men's breakfast, counseling, and one-on-one prayer. By 10 in the morning, he was "getting a bit groggy and had to rest." After also needing to rest over lunch, he then participated in a three-hour staff meeting in the afternoon before resting again for two hours. Finally, after dinner, he taught on Romans 7 for a leadership training class as a substitute for Bob Heppe.

During this period of recuperation, Jack also committed himself to completing a book that he had been working on for several years: *Outgrowing the Ingrown Church*. He had promised Sue Lutz—his editor and the wife of Ron Lutz—that he would complete a preliminary draft of the book by February 1, 1984. While he had taught English to high school and college students and earned his doctorate in literature, the solitary work of writing a book was a significant challenge for him. He found the dialogical work of talking with people and communicating the gospel to them in teaching and preaching contexts to be far more energizing.

He rose to the challenge, however—along with completing *Outgrowing the Ingrown Church* in 1986, he also used his time from 1983 to 1987 to write many of the letters to missionaries, church planters, and Reformed leaders that are found in *Heart of a Servant*

Leader (which went on to be published in 2004) and to further write *Come Back, Barbara* in 1988.

JACK'S PHILOSOPHY OF ministry had always involved a strong emphasis on teams, and his teaching on this subject became a module in NLC's early leadership training. As a pioneering leader, Jack was committed to taking other leaders who were more gifted than he was and training them to be able to take over specific ministries and help them to grow after he left the field. As he recovered from his heart attack, he focused his time and attention on the area of leadership development so that he could multiply the number of missionary leaders who were at NLC and WHM and help to equip them.

For nearly a decade, NLC had been teaching every-member ministry, under Jack's guidance and using his *A New Life* booklet that had first been published in 1973, in small groups. Church small-group leaders and emerging missionary teams needed leadership training of their own, however, which necessitated a separate course. While that separate course had officially begun in February of 1983—six months before Jack's heart attack—with a class of twenty-five people, Jack and NLC had laid the groundwork for it in 1977, through a course that the church's Ireland leadership team had prepared for the purpose of training the first missions team from NLC that went to Dublin. That initial 1977 course contained seminars that focused on prayer, evangelism, and discipleship, and much of its subject matter in these areas of evangelism and prayer had come from Jack.

As the Uganda mission had expanded, Jack's son Paul had organized and developed leadership training material for NLC and WHM. He now integrated his father's teaching on Galatians and spiritual power into the material and expanded the 1977 course's focus on the three areas of prayer, evangelism, and discipleship into four different modules: "Sonship," "Discipleship," "Evangelism," and "Teams." Paul explained, "In Sonship you learn about God's love for you. In Discipleship you learn to communicate that with another Christian. In Evangelism you learn to communicate the gospel to non-Christians, and in Teams you learn to do that with a group of Christians."

"In Jack's mind," Rose Marie said, "you never give the gospel without discipling somebody with it, and without sending them out. In his mind, there was no disconnect." Accordingly, the syllabus for this 1983 training course explained that "each student is expected to learn how to do evangelism so as to form those who have been evangelized into disciples who in turn will be able to disciple others. Since the heart of disciplemaking is the effective communication of the gospel message, the course begins with training in personal evangelism and involves each trainee in evangelistic calling. At the same time, effective evangelism involves the whole life of the witnessing Christian. For this reason, strong emphasis is placed upon witness and meditation in the Scripture as the basis for behavioral change for the person being trained."

Paul continued revising the Sonship module between 1983 and 1989. Jack himself did most of the teaching for the course until 1987, along with help from Paul and Rose Marie, and other leaders helped with mentoring the participants and following up with them. WHM took over the teaching of the course and administered it to its missionaries as well as to PCA and PEF leaders, and NLC required its leaders to participate in the training as well.

Enrollment in the program continued to rise, and demand for the Sonship module began coming more and more from outside Philadelphia, as leaders in the Reformed church began to hunger for material that married missions with spiritual renewal. Paul along with Dave McCarty, a graduate of the course, distributed copies of the tape recordings as well as homework by mail to individual people who applied for the leadership training program. When a student would complete and return one lesson, WHM would mail out the next one—and so on until the sixteen-lesson course had been completed.

TOWARD THE END OF 1984, Jack became able to travel again—albeit on a limited basis and, at first, only within the United States. Then eventually, from December 30, 1985 to January 17, 1986, he went to Kenya to talk to leaders at a WHM missionary retreat about perfectionism and effective team ministry. On his return trip, he also stopped over in Ireland. Josiah Bancroft, the current senior director of mission at Serge (the new name of WHM), recalled one of many stories he had heard about that visit:

> When I got to Dublin [in 1991], one of my friends said, "Yeah, Jack's coming back. You know he's kind of crazy on the evangelism stuff. . . . Last time he was here, we went to a pub together, and there was a drunk that Jack started talking to. The drunk kind of got loud and belligerent. Jack turned to him and said, 'Well, the New Testament said we should love our enemies, so I need to get to know you better, so I can love you better.'" [The friend said that] the guy stumbled out of the pub and went across to lay down on a green. Jack went [over] and laid down beside him and witnessed to him while he was trying to sort through his drunken stupor. And when [the NLC team tried to locate him, they] looked outside and saw Jack lying next to this guy talking to him about Jesus.

Ireland missionary Hunter Dockery recalled another instance from that trip, in which Jack took him to see a group of Travellers—Ireland's itinerant people—who had been funneled into a compound to keep them from squatting on private land. The Travellers had pulled the wood out of the houses that had been built for them and were using it for their campfires—to Dockery's eyes, it looked as though the place had been bombed.

> We went in and [Jack] banged on the door [of one of their caravans]. [When] they opened the door, his opening line was, "Does anyone know anything about Jesus?" And I'm like, "Oh my gosh. I've taught evangelism. That was not the opening line anyone

ought to be using." But they invited us in, and we had an amazing time talking. Jack told them straight up, "God saved me from a heart attack, so I came here to talk to you." And these folks were superstitious . . . so they loved that. And the craziest thing, after bringing them to this beautiful place, he says, "Hunter, I want you to pray for us as we finish."

Now you have to understand, we took my car into this place, and all I could think about was the fact that my car was going to be stolen. That was all I could think about, and I was worried. I was not prepared to pray by faith. So, I did some sort of "God is great, God is good" prayer and was out of there.

When we got into the car, [Jack] looked at me and was angry, and said, "What happened; you weren't worried about your car, were you? Where is your faith?" . . . There were so many times like that he would teach us.

Due to how much demand for Sonship was increasing, Jack's PEF speaking engagements eventually gave way to Sonship conferences that were organized by WHM. In October of 1986, when he came to Missouri to teach a Sonship conference in St. Louis, Paul Kööistra, the president of Covenant Theological Seminary (the PCA's denominational seminary), invited him to speak on campus. In a later interview, Kööistra described a challenge that Jack issued to him, over a lunch conversation, to "build [Covenant Seminary] on grace"—something that Kööistra was determined to do.

As president, Kööistra had been working to confront "Reformed fundamentalism" at Covenant. He defined this fundamentalism as "a tendency to make a screen by which we sift people finer and finer and pretty soon it is me and me alone." Under his leadership, as he did so, many faculty members left Covenant, and Kööistra came under intense criticism for his restructuring of the seminary. Jack encouraged him not to let the "Christian intimidators intimidate you." In Jack's own experience, while persecution in most parts of the world came from outside the church, in the United States—where

Christians had the freedom to worship—it more often came from inside the church.

In a letter that he wrote to Jack a few years later, Köoistra explained the influence that Jack had had on his life.

> I think it is very important for you to know that I consider you in many ways a spiritual father and mentor to me. I have gone on the attack in a very big way concerning the matter of grace here at Covenant Theological Seminary. I have been battling what I consider to be legalism couched in a defense against liberalism. It has stifled the growth of this institution, and I think has also been stifling the growth of the PCA for some time. . . .
>
> . . . You were the first one who opened the door to let me peek in just a bit and to see that there are only two alternatives—self or God, works or grace. I have also come to realize that antinomianism and legalism are not opposites but are in fact on the same end of the continuum, and the only cure of both is a healthy understanding of God's grace. I am sure you have known, as well as I have, of those who have been legalists and no longer could live under such bondage that swung over to antinomianism and vice versa. I praise God for your ministry in my life.

By June of 1987, it appeared that Jack had fully recovered from his heart attack, and he returned to a full schedule of his normal activities that month. In an unpublished essay called "Learning about Limits: God Rebuilds a Man and His Ministry," Jack described his schedule on one particular week.

> On Tuesday afternoon, I . . . review[ed] the doings for the rest of the week. I found: four seriously ill people to call on, my own doctor's appointment, several requests for counseling, a sermon outline to be completed by tomorrow morning for the church bulletin, a letter to be written to the congregation by Thursday on behalf of the fund-raising program for our new building. In addition: five

meetings were scheduled between Tuesday evening and Friday noon! But there was more. Friday night and Saturday, I was speaking three times to our leadership training class and preaching twice on Sunday morning.

Two months into this schedule, while speaking at Western Carolina University, Jack began running a temperature but put it down to allergies. Around August, he was surprised by rapid swelling that he was experiencing in his abdomen and went to his doctor in early September. The doctor found two hernias in Jack's lower abdomen, which he thought explained the swelling and pain that Jack had been experiencing. Jack underwent hernia surgery a couple of weeks later. The next day, he was back at work and speaking at a leadership training retreat that was being held for a new NLC church plant in nearby Fort Washington—however, by the end of September, his swelling and pain had intensified and he could hardly eat.

On Saturday, October 3, while he was teaching lesson 6 of Sonship to forty or more students who were gathered at NLC, he asked them to pray for a doctor's appointment that he was scheduled to have on Monday. At the appointment, the doctor put off a second hernia surgery and instead ran tests in order to locate the source of Jack's swelling and abdominal pain, since he still could not eat and was losing weight rapidly even though his stomach was distended. The doctor assured him that "he was 98% sure" Jack did not have cancer.

Three days later, however, doctors informed Jack that he had lymphoma. In fact, cancer was growing in his abdomen so rapidly that it soon caused his kidneys to shut down, and his cardiologist feared that Jack's heart, damaged as it already was from his earlier infarction, would also fail. His chances of surviving the cancer looked bleak. The spring semester of Sonship leadership training was cancelled. Ella Mae and Frances, Jack's older sisters, traveled from Oregon in the hopes of seeing their baby brother before he died, and other family members and friends also gathered to say their goodbyes. In the unpublished essay "Love Defined: Love Is Intelligent Self-Sacrifice," Jack described the thoughts and feelings that he had at the time:

> You think the American way: every problem has a solution. If you go bankrupt, start again and work harder. If your marriage fails, adjust to singleness or find another wife or husband. If you are sick, get another doctor or change your medicine. Make the right choice and you'll be O.K. But when you face the prospect of your own death and suspect that you have only a few hours or days to live, your power of choice disappears. What troubles you about death is that for the most part the matter is entirely out of your hands and you face it alone. You have a desperate urge to do something, but there is nothing to do but wait all by yourself. As you wait, the words "death" and "irrevocable" seem to be exact synonyms. . . . There is in each of us a sleeping fear of "the great unknown": death. I could now feel this fear waking up in me. But perhaps harder for me was the thought I would never again see my family and friends. Never again share intimate family life with my wife and children and grandchildren, never again talk and laugh together on holidays in our home . . . the loss seemed so very great.

Emergency surgery followed Jack's lymphoma diagnosis. The next evening, Paul stayed by Jack's bedside and the father and son spoke together. "We are very close friends," Jack wrote in his essay, "and what [Paul] . . . did was natural. He began crying. Not despairing or weeping, but tears of caring and love. His love touched me deeply. We both knew this moment might be the final goodbye in this life. I wept with him, many tears, father and son embracing. These tears did much to ease the pain of an anticipated final leave-taking."

The surgery had relieved some of the pressure that the large tumor had been causing, and, in the absence of that pressure, Jack's kidneys began to function again. He remained in intensive care for four days, during which he was hooked up to medical equipment and intravenous lines.

He next had to decide whether he would accept or reject chemotherapy. A letter from a Christian friend urged him to reject chemotherapy and fly to Mexico for alternate treatment. He did not know what to do. His family and friends encouraged him to take the recommended chemo, however—his daughter Ruth, a trained nurse, told him, "Maybe your purpose is to give hope to people who are taking these drugs. Many cancer patients have lost hope; they're really scared and hurting, feeling alone, and wondering if chemo really helps. They need what you have to tell them. Give these sufferers some hope."

Eleven days after his surgery, Jack decided to undergo an intensive regimen of chemo that would last for five days in a row and take place every nineteen to twenty-one days. The first round of this treatment substantially reduced his tumor—though it was difficult for him to sleep during those days of chemotherapy, as well as during the hospitalizations he received for future rounds, and he woke up hallucinating on at least two occasions.

His journals show that he had no idea how to find the strength and hope to endure his next four grueling months of heavy chemotherapy. He had always been the one who had cared for others; now he had to humble himself and allow others to love and care for him while he was in the midst of his own helplessness and unable to offer them anything in return. He noted in his journal that one friend—a man who was in the medical profession—had written to him, "You are fighting for us in the battle of life. Don't be afraid; be our champion. We are all for you, and we have a part in the struggle."

The more Jack turned his thoughts from his own health problems and toward the love God had shown through the gift of his Son, however, the more his tears of helplessness were replaced by joy. John Yenchko described visiting him during this time while he was receiving chemotherapy: "We would laugh and laugh together about how God was going to have to use weak people if he was going to use us. . . . A lot of people may not have experienced the privilege that I had to just enjoy . . . the mirth of heaven, the mirth of the Lord [with Jack]. And Jack was a man [who had] a lot of mirth in his life." Jack liked to reference Martin Luther's adage that "you have as much laughter as you have faith"—and God not only gifted Jack with laughter of his own but also used him to bring the mirth of heaven into the lives of those who were in the cancer ward alongside him, among the healthcare professionals who were caring for them, and to his visitors as well as those of other patients in the hospital.

Jack was discharged from the hospital on October 31, 1987—only to return ten days later when a slight fever he was experiencing became more severe. Doctors feared that he'd contracted an infection and hospitalized him for ten more days. He became increasingly lonely as a result of having to remain isolated during this latest recovery. And, despite being isolated, he still felt a need to share the gospel; so as soon as he had the opportunity, he dictated a pamphlet to his daughter Barbara entitled "How to Deal with a Personal Crisis."

Being in the hospital gave him plenty of time to think. "I simply could not turn [my mind] off. When I first went into [the] ICU my busy mind was asking: If I went to be with the Lord, how would this affect my family—and especially my wife Rose Marie? What will happen to our church stewardship campaign—and to our other pastors? More questions followed. What did I do to deserve this? Does God really love me? Then came feelings of sadness because I seemed far from the divine graciousness." As he grappled with his finitude, he began to recognize his limits and adjust his priorities. Up to then, he had essentially been working multiple full-time jobs; now, however, out of necessity, he began to wonder where he should focus his efforts.

Rose Marie recalled an instance when, after a round of the chemo was over, she and Jack went away for a couple of days to a retreat center in Lancaster. While they were there, Jack began experiencing a lot of pain and became alarmed. Was the cancer returning? Was he having a heart attack? Rose Marie called his doctor, who said that he didn't think the cancer had come back but suggested that Jack spend the night at the retreat center and then go home.

"That night was crucial for Jack," Rose Marie said. "I knew he was really upset, and I said, 'Jack, why do you want to live? What are you holding on to?' . . . And he just got down on his knees and he gave his family, gave the ministry, gave the mission, gave the church, gave all the people—he just gave it all to God, and God gave him a good night's rest."

6

CHEER UP! COME ON, LET'S DIE TOGETHER! IT'S A GREAT WAY TO COME TO LIFE

The Sonship Movement and Dying in Faith

IN THE EARLY 1970S, a revival movement had begun that was centered around Jack's life as well as his ministry at Mechanicsville Chapel, New Life Church (NLC), and Westminster Theological Seminary (WTS). This revival led in turn to church plants that were inspired by New Life, and impacted by Jack's teaching, throughout the Orthodox Presbyterian Church (OPC) and Presbyterian Church in America (PCA), as well as in other churches and denominations across the country, in the late 1970s and early 1980s. This New Life movement directly contributed to the formation of World Harvest Mission (WHM) in 1983, which further expanded Jack's influence by saturating the missionary and educational institutions of the PCA with a movement of grace that became known in the 1990s as the Sonship movement. Jack had become the pioneering leader of a growing and increasingly extensive network of gospel-centered, Reformed leaders who were teaching in seminaries, planting new churches, revitalizing existing churches, and recruiting and training missionaries who would go on to be sent around the world.

Sonship emphasized the historically neglected Reformed doctrines of justification, adoption, and the fatherhood of God, as well as how partnership with the Holy Spirit enables Christians to maintain access to the spiritual power and freedom that is theirs in Christ. Paul Miller explained that "Sonship wasn't a movement even in 1990. It was pretty small even at that point. It wasn't until [1993] that Dad would start talking about *Sonship theology*"— picking up on a term that critics had used to describe Jack's teaching. Paul wondered if that terminology implied that Scripture was being "interpret[ted] . . . through one lens," and Jack agreed with him—though he did believe that Sonship captured his Reformed understanding that evangelism was the foundation of discipleship.

In his 1980 book *Evangelism and Your Church*, Jack had written, "I fear that Reformed Christians today have fallen into the error of preaching the doctrines of grace theoretically instead of preaching them practically and using the truths of Scripture to draw men to Christ. . . . Biblical doctrine has become our grounds to exclude those—even other believers—who disagree with us. Instead of using the Scripture as the sword of the Spirit to conquer men for Christ, we spend our energies defending it, as if it were fragile and easily broken."[1] Although he believed that the church must protect its flock against false teaching, he also warned the church against allowing a spirit of protectiveness to cause it to neglect "God's first priority for His church"—which is "to proclaim the gospel to the lost, bringing them to salvation."[2] After all, as he pointed out, "We have seen throughout history that God's power and blessing have been most evident not on those who have assumed a defensive posture toward the lost of the world, but on those whose first concern is to see God save [the lost]."[3] Only when such a concern for the lost was prioritized could the church pursue "a cultivation of the life and unity which that gospel produces among [God's] people" and "[defend] herself against error."[4]

JACK HAD BEEN converted in the Orthodox Presbyterian Church and had great personal attachment to the denomination. By the late 1980s, however, he was struggling with what he called the "OPC outlook." In a letter, he described the attitude that he meant: "It is not the accepted style to confess to one another sin and weaknesses. In three instances where I saw repentance take place publicly in the OPC, the repentance came under strong attack as doctrinally suspect." The OPC had done well in terms of avoiding liberalism; but in the process, in Jack's view, "its priorities [had become] defensive and negative. It came to exist less and less to proclaim the gospel and more and more to defend itself by pointing out sins and weaknesses in others." The denomination in general did not place the priority on evangelism, missions, and repentance that Jack did. He was willing to continue to call OPC leaders and church members to repentance, but what mattered most to him was "the basic calling . . . to serve the Lord of the church and to obey His command to go and preach the gospel."

Jack believed that both NLC and WHM would function better if they were aligned with the PCA instead, since as a denomination it was "more in step with [NLC's] general direction and priorities" than the OPC was. The PCA had already evidenced a commitment to evangelism, both within the United States and beyond. Its Mission to North America, which focused on reaching cities with the gospel, had tasked former PCA pastor Timothy Keller, who had attended NLC for five years and served there as an elder, to find a candidate who could plant a church in Manhattan. When he couldn't find anyone, Clair Davis and Harvie Conn challenged Keller to accept the call to plant Redeemer Presbyterian Church himself—which he did. Mission to the World, the PCA's missionary-sending agency, had also partnered with WHM by putting all their full-time missionaries through Sonship leadership training.

For a time, it had seemed possible that the PCA and OPC might merge, themselves. Discussion of such a denominational union had begun in 1973, when Jack and Francis Schaeffer, among others, had encouraged a merger between the OPC, the Reformed Presbyterian Church Evangelical Synod (RPCES), and the PCA.

At that time, however, the PCA had opted against joining the other two Presbyterian churches.

The OPC then had another opportunity to join the PCA and the RPCES in 1982. That time, however, though the presbyteries of the PCA voted to receive the RPCES, they voted against receiving the OPC—due, in large part, to the unsettled controversy surrounding Norman Shepherd's teaching on works in justification. This frustrated those in the OPC who were working diligently to resolve, in good faith, the matters that surrounded the controversy.

Jack was disappointed and embarrassed by this failed denominational union. Among other things, he felt that it set a negative example for the recently formed Presbyterian Church in Uganda. The PCA's decision forced him to explain to Ugandan church leaders how the OPC and PCA were able to work together in the far more difficult environment of Uganda while not being able to settle their differences in the United States.

As the tensions around the Norman Shepherd justification controversy seemed to diminish, the PCA reissued an invitation to the OPC in 1984 to join them. At the OPC's 1986 general assembly, its voting members rejected the PCA's latest overture. Some churches and pastors in the OPC, along with some professors at WTS, reacted to this decision by exiting the OPC in order to join the PCA. Their exodus further amplified what Jack had hitherto considered to be small differences between the two Reformed Presbyterian church bodies, which derailed any prospects for a denominational merger in the future. "Those of us who believe that the union of these two virtually identical churches is a biblical imperative made clear in our Lord's will for Christian unity . . . have been very disappointed," Jack wrote. He and NLC found themselves in a hard position: "We now have a decision forced upon us in the absence of such union."

The NLC in Glenside, where Jack attended, began discussing the possibility of realigning with the PCA instead of the OPC six months before Jack received his cancer diagnosis in 1987. Several other New Life churches moved forward with transitioning into the PCA while NLC Glenside was deciding: New Life Northeast transferred into the denomination in November of 1987, and New Life Fort Washington and New Life Presbyterian Church Escondido joined it months later. Meanwhile, as Jack recovered from his cancer, the leaders of NLC Glenside spent nearly two years "exchanging and reading many letters, articles, memos and papers" before making a recommendation to the congregation. One reason for their delay was the fact that, even after sending hundreds of its members to plant several large daughter churches, NLC Glenside was the largest congregation in the OPC, and Jack and the elders of the church "did not want to take action that would be 'precipitous'"—they were aware that if NLC left the denomination, a number of other churches might follow its lead. Nonetheless, on December 12, 1989, "after much prayer, repentance and searching of hearts," the elders of NLC recommended that the congregation leave the OPC and join the PCA.

Leading up to the decision, Jack had found himself "wanting to do almost anything to avoid leaving the OPC." There was already bitterness in the denomination over the churches that were leaving for the PCA. In addition, Jack knew that many people in the OPC blamed him as well as WHM for the decline that the denomination's missions program had been experiencing—once NLC and WHM had started drawing, training, and sending their own missionary teams, enthusiasm for their work had drained people and financial resources away from traditional OPC missions operations. "To go to the PCA," Jack realized, "would be to leave in the lurch those brethren [in the OPC] who are seeking to fulfill the Great Commission." Could New Life, he wondered, better serve the OPC and these members he was describing by offering the denomination correction from within rather than from without?

After much prayer, however, Jack finally concluded that God's will for him was "not to become the prosecuting attorney in the OPC but to fulfill [his] calling in obedience to the Great Commission."

He wrote, "I am not able to reform people who are not ready or willing to listen to me or anyone else call them to repentance" and acknowledged that "no church or institution can ever become an end in itself. . . . God can take care of Himself. He never permits us to make Him a prisoner of our institutional priorities." In a letter that he wrote to the congregation of NLC, he explained,

> It has been inexpressibly humbling for me to confess that denominations, unless revived by repentance, usually fade after fifty to seventy years. To admit that this is what happens in history and that I cannot change this history is crushing to my pride. Somehow, I feel in my heart there ought to be one more thing to do, one more attempt to call men to repentance, one more way of rationalizing this chaotic aspect of life, or some way to minimize, wish away, the dreadful effects of sin in Christian movements.
>
> But it is also freeing for me to recognize my limits. . . . I am not the Holy Spirit. I can trust the OPC to His working. I can and must endure the pain of seeing my beloved society of fellow Christians become more and more ingrown and to avoid repentance as a thing of shame. To leave may mean that we shall be misunderstood and judged by them. Oh, I love to preach about being forgiven like the publican, but I hate to be treated like one by the church where I found Christ!

Thus, on March 10, 1990, the PCA's presbytery of Philadelphia received New Life Church into the denomination. The OPC, in turn, dismissed NLC to the PCA on May 5, 1990.

MEANWHILE, in the fewer than ten years since its founding, WHM had recruited, trained, and sent thirteen full-time missionaries to Ireland, twelve full-time missionaries to Uganda, twelve missionaries to Amsterdam, and two missionaries in London. By 1992, it was also sending one to two hundred short-term missionaries each year to support the work of existing teams by participating in evangelism or service projects. Rose Marie Miller described the lasting impact that her husband had had on the organization: "Jack left an amazing legacy in [WHM]. . . . Someone was asked why they chose Serge as their mission and the reply was, 'They care for their missionaries.' When the mission was growing, Jack and I visited the fields encouraging the workers, spending time with them, and I did the same with the women." This personal interest that Jack had taken in the missionaries, along with his vision for missions and for renewal in the area of leadership training, continued to define WHM even long after he was gone.

Throughout these first ten years of WHM's expanding missions work, enthusiasm for Sonship had also been spreading—almost entirely by word of mouth from missionaries and Reformed leaders who had been personally impacted by WHM's renewal ministry—and while WHM's church planting results in the United States and overseas were encouraging, the positive response to Sonship in North America surprised everyone, including Jack. The Sonship Course, which had once been one of four modules in the leadership training series, had begun to take on a life of its own. As WHM trained more leaders through the course, the leaders in turn used it to train their own church leaders and missionary teams. Paul began to adapt Sonship to be able to be used effectively in different formats, including small groups.

In 1989, WHM had hired Jeff Salasin, a former student of the Sonship course, to train other leaders using the course's materials. Salasin helped Paul Miller and course graduate Dave McCarty to manage the increasing number of people who were taking Sonship through the mail. This naturally led WHM to begin offering Sonship by phone as well, which quickly filled Salasin's schedule by allowing him to mentor Reformed leaders and their wives from across the United States.

In order to handle the increasing demand for Sonship training, WHM formed an International Renewal Team (IRT). Drew Angus, another graduate of Sonship leadership training and a

WHM missionary who was working in Ireland, returned to Philadelphia in order to lead this new team. He then hired six American missionaries to be mentors who could disciple the influx of Reformed leaders who were asking to take Sonship training.

Many of these applicants were surprised to find that Sonship training was no small commitment. Many of them remarked, "For a course on grace, I have never had so much work." The training required a minimum of four hours of work for each session. The ideal schedule for a small-group format involved fifteen minutes of worship, forty-five minutes for a lecture, twenty-five minutes for discussion, five minutes for the following week's homework to be introduced, and sixty minutes for small-group interaction. During this hour that was set aside for the small-group interaction, the group members initialed one another's homework as a means of mutual accountability, shared something specific that they had repented of during the week prior, prayed together, and preached the gospel to one another. The ideal schedule for taking Sonship by phone required sixty minutes for listening to the lecture, sixty minutes for completing homework, five minutes for mailing or faxing (or emailing) the homework, and fifty minutes for further discipling with a Sonship mentor. Sonship also included Scripture memorization, prayer partners for each member to recruit and pray with weekly, and supplemental readings.

As time went on, Paul and Bob Heppe began noticing some unintended consequences of the Sonship movement that were arising among some of the course's disciples. As early as 1991, a sort of "Sonship cult" (in Paul's words) began to emerge in some American church contexts—and especially among PCA leaders. Jack responded with dismay:

> It grieves the heart to think of anyone taking the message of grace and using it to scorn fellow Christians with a most ungracious spirit.
> There may be things we can do to work against such strange perversions of grace, at least things I know I need to do daily. One

is just to avoid any tone or stance of superiority as I present the teachings of grace and the wonders of our Father's forgiving and adopting love. Such humility requires much grace, because the sin of elitism is so subtle, and I am so slow to see it in my own heart and life.

Another is to guard against ingroup exclusiveness, and the practice of having little to do with other Christian groups. Such going it alone feeds the feeling that we are not just special because of grace, but special because we alone understand grace. That's a tough distinction to maintain. But it helps when we just have more contact with other Christians and other Christian groups and show ourselves eager to learn from them—without compromising the gospel.

By the time IRT was formed and Angus was hired, thirty churches had already started Sonship courses—and, as word of mouth about the courses spread, additional requests for Sonship training came in every week from congregations around the country. Jack's speaking engagements with Presbyterian Evangelistic Fellowship (PEF), his books and pamphlets, and WHM's book and tape ministry added to the impact that he and Sonship were having on believers in the United States and around the world.

By the end of 1992, over a thousand people from twenty states and nine countries had gone through Sonship leadership training. From three to four thousand people were currently taking the training, either by mail or from other graduates of the Sonship course who were teaching the material in their local churches. The transformational impact that Sonship was having on these pacesetting leaders became an advertisement for WHM and Sonship renewal in local churches around the United States—the best advertisement they could have been given.

WTS professor of apologetics William Edgar noted that "[Jack's] influence is all over the place"—not so much through his own name or publications as through the people he influenced and the movements, such as Sonship itself, that went on to come from them. One example is author Jerry Bridges, who is famous for his book *The Pursuit of Holiness*, and who said, "The Sonship teaching has been a tremendous encouragement to me personally. . . . This material is one of the best-kept secrets in North America." Another is Timothy Keller, who, upon accepting the call to plant Redeemer Presbyterian Church, became a well-known pastor and *New York Times* best-selling author. Keller said, "[Jack Miller] taught me how to preach grace no matter what the text." When he planted Redeemer in New York City, he gave Jack's book *Outgrowing the Ingrown Church* to his core leaders. "In a very real sense," he noted, "Redeemer Presbyterian Church, and the ministry we've had up here is one of the fruits of New Life's labors and one of the fruits of [NLC's] ministry."

In a report on Sonship that he helped to write for WHM's tenth anniversary, Paul Miller wrote, "[Our Sonship work] is a unique ministry almost without parallel in the evangelical world." He urged WHM to consider the potential that Sonship had to impact lives. "It could well be that our discipling ministry wins more non-Christians to the kingdom than our church-planting ministry." His reasoning was that many people around the world who claim to be Christians are not truly born again. "Their resistance to the gospel is great, but they have much fewer of the cultural barriers to believing than a typical unreached people group has. The churches are full of people who need to be won to Christ," he said—pointing out both a scary reality for the church and also an unprecedented opportunity for WHM to evangelize Christians and non-Christians within the church.

His prediction about the impact that Sonship renewal could have on the larger church in comparison to church-planting ministries became a reality—but not without cost. WHM's exponential growth was creating pressures that, in Paul's view, caused "Jack's two great passions"—renewal and mission as well as discipleship and evangelism—to be "at war with one another," as the North

American renewal team and foreign missions teams vied for the same resources. The challenge for WHM would be to carry within its DNA both of these two great passions that Jack embodied throughout his life and ministry.

THE EXPENSE OF funding WHM's rapid growth in the areas of both missions and renewal caught up with the finances of the young missionary-sending agency in the early 1990s. In that tenth-anniversary report, Paul Miller explained that "the systems we had when we were smaller simply did not work as we grew in size. The more we grew the poorer we got." WHM could no longer function as a mom-and-pop ministry; it needed a new structure. In order to address its growing financial and administrative crisis, the rapidly growing mission better organized its personnel and created a new infrastructure. Since the founding of the ministry, Jack, as its director, had delegated its day-to-day leadership responsibilities to Paul Miller. Then, in late 1990, Jack resigned as the senior pastor of NLC so that he could better function in his role as WHM's director. Although his time was no longer divided between NLC and WHM, he continued to delegate day-to-day operations to Paul so that he could focus on development, training, and pioneering new fields for ministry.

As a seminary professor, pastor, church planter, missionary, writer, and conference speaker, Jack had always maintained a busy work schedule. He had worked multiple jobs since he was fifteen years old as well as putting himself through high school, college, a doctoral program, and seminary. His resignation from NLC in favor of working full-time for WHM had been encouraged by WHM, NLC, Rose Marie, and Paul, in an attempt, on the advice of his doctors, to allow him to better manage his weakened health—though he continued to have trouble saying no to all the opportunities that kept coming his way.

His transition to full-time work at WHM, however, was more difficult than Jack expected. His first order of business was to raise his own personal support, support for his secretary, and funds for his ministry expenses—and, in a journal entry from October of 1990, Jack noted that "my personal finances are in the red; can't afford to paint even part of my house!!!" He continued, "[I'm] expected to raise money on a major scale, but don't always feel I have tools." He found it easier to help others to raise money than to raise money for himself, and often the money that he did raise for his own needs he then gave away to other people and causes.

In his eagerness to teach and share his faith, he also soon over-extended himself with speaking engagements in the United States and travel overseas. He had an emotional breakdown at a 1991 executive committee retreat in Keswick, New Jersey—one in which, according to Paul, he "push[ed] back hard against gentle inquiries from the board." Paul noted that, as pastor of NLC, "he'd been accountable in his work to the New Life elders and they'd let him do what he wanted . . . not necessarily a bad thing . . . he just wasn't used to a mission organization"—in particular, Jack was not used to the level of oversight that the board represented. Residual effects from his chemotherapy as well as the upheaval of his transition to WHM likely also played a part in this breakdown.

Fortunately, by the middle of 1992, his seesawing health had improved sufficiently for doctors—who were the most effective at getting Jack to slow down out of anyone—to allow him to add to his daily ministry activities once again. The leaders in the Phila-delphia home office of WHM preferred for him to spend most of his time overseas. He focused on helping the expanding London team, writing letters to missionaries, completing his writing proj-ects, and contacting donors. Both WHM and the Heppes, who led the London team, concurred when Jack and Rose Marie suggested that they make London their primary headquarters. An additional home that they had in Málaga in southern Spain became his and Rose Marie's getaway for recovering from sickness and escaping the inclement weather of London.

Unfortunately, the damp climate of the city caused Rose Marie to suffer from recurring thyroid problems, sinus infections, and severe exhaustion. She convalesced with Jack in Málaga during early 1993, which gave her husband time to work on a new book about cancer and to revise his book on evangelism. And, while Jack had attempted to reduce his schedule, doctors warned him that, despite temporary improvements of his health that had resulted, he would likely die within a year as a result of the damage that his heart had sustained if he did not reduce his schedule even further. They did, however, tell him that he could expect to live for another ten years if he slowed down and paid more attention to his health.

In the spring of 1993, Jack and Rose Marie spoke on Sonship to Christian leaders and students in Poland, Russia, and the Ukraine—communist countries that had opened after the Soviet Union had collapsed. During this trip, they also spoke to the psychiatric faculty of Moscow State University, three hundred yards from the Kremlin, about the power that the gospel had to change the lives of the most troubled people. According to Jack, "The response was amazing. The co-editor of the psychiatric journal of Moscow State University asked permission to publish extracts from some of my pamphlets in the journal." WHM had sent a group along with the Millers to support them on their trip; and, after the group returned, WHM began planning to introduce an official Eastern Europe team and to recruit people to serve on it.

During the first six months of 1993, Jack went on from Moscow to make visits to missionary leaders in Uganda, Kenya, Amsterdam (twice), Ireland, and London. In July, he spoke at the 150th Anniversary of the North American Baptist Church as well as at the Church Planters Retreat for the Mission to North America.

Rose Marie, the Heppes, and leaders at WHM continued to work diligently to help Jack to moderate his busy schedule. His health, however, continued to decline—even when he took more drastic measures to limit his schedule to teaching, preaching, and encouraging other missionaries. On May 4, 1993, while he was in Málaga, he wrote,

This was a frightening day. I woke up feeling lifeless, the music of the gospel did not sing for me; it was almost as though I was walking in a desert of death. A feeling of aimlessness had settled on my mind during the night, and the only word to summarize my attitude was apathy. I tried to pray and found I had no desire whatsoever to pray. As I drank my morning coffee, it occurred to me that the devil was attacking me; so I knew I was in for a fight. But I also sensed that God too was speaking to me by his silence.

. . . The devil attacks our minds through stirring up fleshly dependence. That afternoon I knew what I had to do. I must firmly resist the devil who was stirring up unspiritual self-dependence in me. Having spotted the enemy, I resolved to lean on God and pray for grace to fight against the deep rebellion of the human heart.

. . . I still felt completely alone, but now I could see a purpose in God's silence. In the desert of self, God was calling me to die to my self-competence (real or imagined). He wanted me to see its ugliness. So I confessed to God that apart from his grace I was a desert and left to myself I would make a total mess of my own life and ministry. That was a confession unto death. Die, Jack, die!

As the day went on, the sense of spiritual danger that he was feeling faded—and he had learned from the experience in a most personal and practical way. "[The Lord] wanted to wrestle with my soul, like his wrestling with Jacob at Jabbok until something died and something new came to life." Jack realized that faith "brings death as a prelude to new surgings of the Spirit's life and joy"—the Christian dies to self-righteousness, self-effort, and self-competence. "This is a hard death because in itself competence is a commendable quality—if it is competence based upon grace. But we only arrive at such grace-competence through seeing with faith our incapacity to do God's work God's way." Jack saw that dying by faith was a great way to come to life.

When he and Rose Marie returned to London in April, they expected their housing arrangements to be in order. However, their housing arrangements had fallen apart at the last minute—leaving them homeless and scrambling to find acceptable accommodations. They were forced to move five times in just ten days before their housing situation was finally settled. In the city, Jack met Raju Abraham, an Indian-born Christian medical doctor, who asked him to come to India in order to explore the possibility of a new WHM India team. Jack made plans to travel to north India in early 1995.

On March 11, 1994, he spoke together with Joni Eareckson Tada and John Templeton at a WTS conference, where he addressed hard questions about death and dying. After attending a missionary retreat in southern Germany and a church-planting seminar in Kiev, he returned to the United States in order to speak at the Annual Prayer Breakfast of the 4th Federal Judicial District Court of Appeals in Washington, D.C. Rose Marie's book *From Fear to Freedom* was published around the same time.

In late 1994, Jack had a series of ministrokes. When he went on to suffer a major stroke on March 6, 1995, his trip to India was cancelled so that he could go to the hospital, where he spent nine days. The stroke also prevented him from attending a WHM missionary retreat that was scheduled to be held in Bavaria in May or from participating in a Sonship conference that was to be held in Colorado Springs that June. Recurring ministrokes that he suffered throughout the next year further reduced his ministry activities.

Jack wrote in a letter, which can be found in *The Heart of a Servant Leader*, "At times there were struggles . . . tough ones. But the gospel of grace really caught me up with the power of the Holy Spirit so that my sense of humor and love were triumphing over my weakness and fears." After his hospital stay in March, for example, he had noted that "one nurse seems to be near conversion, and another [nurse] promised to visit New Life Church in Glenside."[5]

JACK'S PHYSICAL POWERLESSNESS did not mean that he was spiritually powerless. The weaker he became, the more he gave himself over to "effective praying based upon a stronger knowledge of Scripture."

When he and Rose Marie would leave NLC on their travels, Jack would buy a notepad and ask the congregation to write down any prayer requests that they had on it. Then he and Rose Marie would take the notepad with them and pray their way through it. "One time we came back," Rose Marie said, "and this man came up to Jack and embraced him, and said, 'Oh, thank you. That prayer you prayed just solved everything.' So, Jack got to thinking about this (he's very methodical) and he knew he hadn't come to that man's prayer yet. We didn't do all the prayers, but the very fact that the man put his request in [the notepad] and was honest, God saw that and answered [his prayer]." Just as he had been since 1970, Jack was "convinced that field work, leadership, and personal growth depend entirely on our learning to prevail in prayer." Being married to Jack, Rose Marie said, was like "being married to a twenty-four-hour prayer meeting."

This combination of his spiritual power and physical weakness could be seen in his preaching as well. Doctors had warned him that the passionate preaching he did increased his risk of another stroke, and thus every time Jack stood up to preach, he was fully aware that he might be preaching his last sermon. On one occasion, he confronted some pastors in London who were debating whether personal illustrations should be used in sermons. Jack did not have the time or energy to argue with them—instead, he preached to them. Missionary Hunter Dockery described what happened:

> The Spirit came on [Jack] that day and I remember him . . . with this passion; that anger at the people's hard hearts. And I remember him yelling at the top of his lungs when he said, "I am a dying man preaching to dying men!" They had no idea that he was literally dying. . . . And I remember sitting there and I realized that my face was streaming with tears. He had this intensity, and the coolest thing was that he loved these men who were so hard. They were just nit-picking . . . trying to poke holes in something. And as he preached, he just humbled himself enough to become passionate.

It was like the breaking in of the Spirit, and these men were overcome with their [sin].

In 1993, the staff of Die Arche (The Ark)—a large Pentecostal church in Hamburg, Germany—gave their pastor, Wolfgang Wegert, a series of books that had been written by the Reformed Baptist preacher Charles Haddon Spurgeon. Wegert was amazed by what he learned through Spurgeon's sermons about God's providence and the cross of Christ. As he plowed through Spurgeon's works and then additional works by Martyn Lloyd-Jones and John Calvin, he "began to understand the Bible in a brighter light" and came to "love the Reformed doctrine of sovereign grace."

Later, in 1995, Die Arche invited Joni Eareckson Tada to speak at a conference. After she spoke about "confidence in God's gracious providence" and her "joy in election," Wegert asked her to recommend someone who could talk to him with sensitivity about these gospel truths. Tada answered, "Jack Miller." Wegert immediately contacted WHM to make arrangements for Jack to come to Hamburg and organized a conference at Die Arche at which Jack could speak. Its theme was "Grace Runs Downhill: Powerful Grace Working through Powerless People."

Jack was so weak by this time that he could hardly stand. Nonetheless, he desperately wanted to preach the gospel in the land of Luther—so WHM assembled a team to help him and Rose Marie to teach at the conference, mentor groups as part of the training that accompanied it, and explore a possible new field opportunity in Germany. Jack spoke at Die Arche from February 15 to February 23, 1996. On Sunday the 18, in what would be his final sermon, he preached on the theme that had stood as a banner for his entire life and ministry since 1970: the glory of God and the grace of the gospel.

People have asked me a question: "You plant churches, you have a mission, and you go all around the world, and you build everything on this idea that God loves his sons and daughters. But have you noticed how much suffering you do?" A friend of mine, who has known me for many years, said, "I am deeply moved when you talk about God as Father, but then this question comes into my mind. I wonder if God is so loving why does he send such hard things to you? . . . It doesn't sound very safe to have God as your Father. The question comes to me, 'If I have God as my Father, what is He going to do to me next?'"

Jack laughed. "Well," he said, "the Lord has given me the Spirit, and I don't see it that way any longer. It is entirely a gift of grace." He continued,

Why is it so difficult to hear . . . about God's perfect plan? It's very hard to see it as a perfect plan if you don't know how much God loves you, because hard things are going to happen to every one of us. But if you trust the Father's plan, it makes such a difference. And the only way you can trust the Father's plan is by growing in the grace of knowing the gospel. The gospel is not only that Jesus died for sinners. That is wonderful. But there is more. The gospel comes to us as a promise. And promises are designed to kill anxiety.

Thinking back to that final conference that he preached at in Germany, Rose Marie said, "Simply put: the entire event was divinely appointed."

ON FEBRUARY 28, 1996, Jack and Rose Marie returned through London to their home away from home in Spain. The cold climates of first Hamburg and then London caused Jack to become sick. While they were on the plane from London to Spain, Rose Marie began to cry. She looked over, exhausted, at her sick husband and confessed to him and to God that "I'm just tired of traveling." When they arrived in Málaga, Jack was so weak that he could hardly walk.

He had finally given up trying to write a book about cancer and costly love. Paul encouraged him to write instead on the subject that he most loved. With the help of his family, Jack wrote *A Faith Worth Sharing* during the final three months of his life.

Jack's health deteriorated rapidly, and he experienced repeated angina attacks. He attended a leadership retreat in Spain that WHM had scheduled for the end of March of 1996—and when WHM leaders arrived at the retreat, they were shocked to see for themselves how severely weakened and fragile their founder had become. Jack was too sick to join them for more than a few meetings—and, when he did, WHM leaders had to carry him up and down the stairs that led to the meetings he felt good enough to attend. Nonetheless, as Dan Herron recalled, "he was still very enthusiastic . . . challenging, encouraging, involved in prayer for the different fields, gathering around the different leaders to try to help them work through different issues. . . . Even the sickness and weakness would not hold him back as long as he could move."

After the retreat, in order to locate the cause of his recurring angina, Jack received a heart catheterization—which revealed that he had two blocked arteries and badly needed surgery. His cardiologist in Pennsylvania coordinated with his doctors in Spain to determine whether Jack was strong enough to travel to the United States for the operation. As the days passed, his angina intensified, and his Spanish and American doctors concluded that he required immediate open-heart surgery. They scheduled the surgery for Tuesday, April 2, at Clinica San Antonio in Málaga.

Jack's doctors were generally optimistic about his likelihood of having a successful surgery and recovery. Rose Marie recalled that "I was thinking in my mind [that] he was going to make it through surgery and [that] now I'll be able to stay [with him] longer in Spain." However, everyone had wrongly assumed that Jack's heart was stronger than it actually was. When his surgeons opened his chest, they saw what his catheterization had failed to reveal: that the combination of the massive heart attack he had sustained in

1983 and the chemotherapy that had been used to treat his lymphoma in 1987 had inflicted severe damage.

After completing the surgery, Jack's doctors hoped that allowing him to remain on life support for a few days would enable him to gain enough strength so that he could breathe without the help of a ventilator. Sadly, though, when his oxygen mask was removed, Jack could not breathe on his own. He briefly regained consciousness and gathered enough strength to look at Rose Marie, Barbara, and Keren and say three final words: "I love you."

His kidneys began to fail by that Saturday. On Sunday, Paul arrived in Spain. While driving to the airport to pick him up, Rose Marie made her peace with God. "I was praying the Lord's prayer, and as I prayed 'Thy kingdom come,' it was as if God said to me, 'Are you really willing to believe me and pray, "Thy kingdom come" if it means I take Jack?' 'Yes,' I replied. I still kept praying that [Jack] would live, but I also knew that there was a transaction from heaven. I had moved into a dimension that was bigger than my own will."

Twenty-six years earlier, the sovereign Lord had brought Jack, Rose Marie, and their three youngest children to Spain, where Jack had studied the promises of God and been transformed. "Once again, our heavenly Father had brought us to Spain," Rose Marie wrote, "this time to say goodbye to Jack."

C. John "Jack" Miller died in Málaga, Spain, on the morning of Monday, April 8, 1996 with his son, Paul, his daughters Barbara and Keren, and his wife, Rose Marie, standing beside his hospital bed. He was sixty-seven years old.

CONCLUSION

CHEER UP! THE WAY UP IS THE WAY DOWN

ON APRIL 13, 1996, over seventeen hundred people from across the United States and around the world gathered at Calvary Chapel in northeast Philadelphia to worship the Lord by celebrating the extraordinary life and ministry of C. John "Jack" Miller—a twentieth-century pioneer of grace. William Stump, a founding elder of New Life Church, recalled Jack's memorial service as being "transformative": "There was a presence of Jack there, because so many people had been so touched by him. . . . [When the service was over,] most people just sat there. . . . It was like they were riveted to their seats. I remember Rick and Donna [Buddemeier] standing up in front of me, [as] I was sitting directly behind them, and Rick turned to me and I said, 'I don't want to leave.' It was such a blessed experience."

Tom Hawkes, director of the Arrowhead Leadership Program, vividly recalled his thoughts upon hearing of Jack's death:

> We all knew about [Jack's] surgery and had been praying for him. We didn't think he was going to die; he died somewhat surprisingly. . . . My very first thought [when I heard the news] was, "You made it. Thank the Lord, you made it, Jack. You finished well." . . . Most leaders don't finish well. . . . And I remember thinking, "He finished well. Way to go, Jack." . . . And my very next thought was, "Who will lead us now?"—thinking of the church planters

and pastors in the PCA and beyond; the missionaries. [Jack] was such a forerunner in mission and renewal—both those things. My immediate thought was, "Man, he leaves a vacuum; who will lead us now?"

Jack Miller was the unprecedented leader of several interrelated movements of grace that began among Reformed leaders and extended across the United States and around the world; he was what sociologist James Davison Hunter describes as a primary leader of leaders within a complex of elites, networks, technology, and institutions.[1]

Culturally transformative movements necessarily face difficulties, challenges, and criticisms that must be addressed and, when necessary, corrected in order for those movements to continue to flourish. The Sonship movement was no different. Both the year before and the year after Jack's death were marked by challenging leadership transitions that took place at New Life Church (NLC) and World Harvest Mission (WHM). WHM also experienced a severe financial crisis after it unknowingly invested in a pyramid scheme. Providentially, however, these leadership transitions and complicated financial problems did not swallow up Jack's legacy or lasting contribution.

The Sonship Movement and Mission to the World

In 1994, Paul Köoistra resigned from being president of Covenant Theological Seminary in order to become coordinator of Mission to the World (MTW)—the PCA's missionary-sending agency. By that time, MTW was fully invested in Sonship. It had worked cooperatively with WHM as early as 1982, and in 1989 it had entered into an agreement with WHM to use Sonship Training as the primary spiritual-training program for all its full-time missionaries.

When Köoistra arrived at MTW's headquarters to assume the position of coordinator, financial concerns required his immediate attention—especially once he realized how much money MTW had been spending for WHM to disciple its missionaries. And he recognized that the money MTW was pouring into Sonship was symptomatic of a deeper issue as well. "I thought it was a crazy idea to turn your spiritual life over to another organization. In fact, I made the statement 'It would seem to me that it would be better if we gave [to WHM] the finance department rather than the spiritual life department.'" In Köoistra's estimation, MTW had essentially given both its spiritual and its financial departments over to WHM. He determined that it was time to bring MTW's spiritual training and missionary care in-house, and he delegated the task of executing the transition.

Before MTW could develop its own spiritual training program, Jack had died. After allowing them time to grieve, Köoistra approached WHM about joining MTW—an alternative way for him to bring MTW's spiritual training in-house. Fifteen years earlier, when Jack and NLC had petitioned MTW to partner with them in the training and sending of missionaries to Uganda, MTW had rejected Jack's request for help. Now, a few years after his death, WHM decided to reject this merger with MTW.

Köoistra, following this, found it frustratingly difficult to replace Sonship. In the end, he had to execute a replacement himself by writing a training program for MTW that he called Living in Grace. According to Köoistra, the main difference between Sonship and Living in Grace was that Sonship's requirement of one-on-one mentoring (a distinctive feature of the course) had not been carried over, which allowed Living in Grace to be taught more easily in a larger group context. Aside from that, Living in Grace is more similar to Sonship than it is different—and Köoistra explained that the reason the two courses have so much in common is because of gospel truths about God's omnipotent grace that he and Jack both found in Scripture.

MTW's slow shift away from working with WHM gave WHM, in turn, sufficient time to transition from mentoring MTW missionaries into providing Sonship for leaders who were in a local, North American church context. This complemented WHM's original motto: "Mobilizing the Local Church to Reach the World."

Concern over the Sonship Movement

In a testimony to the expansive influence that Jack had left on conservative Reformed Presbyterianism, Reformed scholar and theologian Jay Adams wrote in 1999, "Everywhere I go, it seems, someone is asking me about 'Sonship.' . . . People have urged me to write about the movement. Sonship teaching has invaded my own denomination. I am concerned about its uncritical adoption in Christian circles."[2] His response to the Sonship movement, *Biblical Sonship: An Evaluation of the Sonship Discipleship Course*, which was published three years after Jack's death, took an unecessarily harsh polemical tone and argued that Jack was not truly Reformed. Timothy Trumper, a former WTS professor of systematic theology as well as a more measured critic of Sonship and Jack Miller, said about the book that "however valuable [Adams's] claims [were] as points of discussion, it is both certain and regrettable that his arguments [were] overshadowed by . . . *ad hominem* psychologizing of Jack Miller."[3]

Adams had served with Jack in the practical theology department of WTS from the mid-1960s to the mid-1970s, and they had considered each other to be friends. The personal tone that he took was thus unexpected and deeply discouraging to the Miller family. Steve Smallman, a long-time board member of WHM and the director who succeeded Jack, wrote in a brief statement, "There are very valid issues arising out of our *Sonship* discipling ministry, and we are willing and eager to reason about them from Scripture and our Reformation creeds, but [*Biblical Sonship*] is not the forum, and we will await another occasion for that discussion."[4]

Although he had never been through Sonship himself, Köoistra in an interview identified three concerns that he had with Sonship, which stemmed from his observations of some Sonship mentors and disciples. While harshly critical assessments, such as Adams's, wanted to bury Jack and Sonship altogether, Köoistra maintained his appreciation of Jack: "I think if Jack and I sat down and talked, we would agree on . . . most everything." His more irenic concerns about Sonship, some of which are shared by Adams as well, are worth considering here.

Köoistra's first concern regarded the problems that occur when people focus too much on the freeing psychological benefits that result from embracing the doctrine of justification by faith alone without also moving in love toward God and others. In Köoistra's words,

> Grace has become a power word. You just say "grace," and something is supposed to happen. You can't separate grace from Christ. Christ is grace. And the grace that we receive is by the Holy Spirit, but the Holy Spirit is Christ's Spirit. That is what I understand the Bible to mean when it says, "Christ in you, the hope of glory." But what I began to see is if you've got a problem, a serious problem— you know, my ministry is not going well in wherever—I begin to depend on grace. Well, what is that? You depend on the Holy Spirit. It is almost a psychologizing of grace, if you can understand that term or that statement. It became magical, kind of like a pill you take. I saw that.

Köoistra's observation was, at least in some cases, accurate. Rick Downs, a leader and board member of WHM, agreed with it— though he saw this psychologizing of grace more positively than Köoistra did. He explained,

> I do think the . . . Sonship stuff was derivative of [Jack's] evangelistic gift. And I think that what Sonship became I don't think Jack really cared that much about it. The way that Sonship became a vehicle for renewal and people kind of getting ahold of free

justification and the kind of psychological benefits that accrued to them I think were of little interest to Jack. His passion was for the lost. His passion was for people to repent, to wake up and grab ahold of Jesus. . . . So that is kind of my view of Jack. He is this kind of relentless evangelist.

Köoistra's second concern was that Sonship "was highly influenced by . . . Luther's introduction to his commentary on Galatians." He went on to say that those in the Reformed church "believe that Luther was a little bit weak when it came to sanctification . . . and at least in Jack's disciples . . . I saw that [weakness on sanctification]—and the disciples I'm [talking about and] dealing with are MTW [cooperative] missionaries." Again, he took care to draw a distinction between Jack's own teaching and application of Sonship and some of the unnamed cooperative missionaries at MTW who were disciples of Sonship.

Third, Köoistra became uncomfortable with the outworking of Sonship's emphasis on repentance. He explained by way of example: "You had these [Sonship] mentors, and these mentors would be working with you, and a large part of that mentoring process is by telephone, and it was to help you through the process of repentance. And I would see some of our people pushing back and saying, 'Look, lust is not my problem. Or a loose tongue is not my problem.' And these mentors would say, 'You are in denial.' And we would actually sometimes get hostility between missionaries in training."

Jack, during his lifetime, welcomed such criticism more intentionally than most people. He wrote, "I have found . . . correction given in the right spirit (and even in the wrong spirit) can bring into lives the power of the Kingdom like nothing else. . . . Sometimes we must all be humbled to the dust in order to be lifted up in praise and service." Responding to Adams's critique of both Jack and Sonship, Smallman wrote, "I can easily imagine Jack reading what was said of him and breaking out in a big smile and saying, 'Cheer up, Jay,

I'm far worse than you could ever imagine!' and then with a laugh and a delight saying, 'And cheer up, because the power of the cross is greater than we will ever know—we will live by faith in the Son of God, who loved us and gave himself for us.'"[5] Jack would have welcomed talking to Köoistra about his concerns as well.

Jack and the New Calvinist Revival

In 2008, Collin Hansen, an author and a journalist for *Christianity Today*, identified men such as John Piper, John MacArthur, and R.C. Sproul as being the father figures of the new Calvinist revival.[6] *Time* magazine also, in 2010, reported on the Calvinist renewal movement, which it listed as the third of its "10 Ideas Changing the World Right Now."[7] And on January 4, 2014, the *New York Times* noted that "evangelicalism is in the midst of a Calvinist revival. . . . Attendance at Calvin-influenced worship conferences and churches is up, particularly among worshipers in their 20s and 30s. . . . In the United States today, one large denomination, the Presbyterian Church in America, is unapologetically Calvinist. But in the last 30 years or so, Calvinists have gained prominence in other branches of Protestantism."[8] Likely because Jack was more of a pioneering leader than a celebrity preacher, however, Hansen, *Time*, and the *New York Times* overlooked the influence he had left as they named the leaders of this revival.

Ironically, it seems that it is the critics of Jack Miller and Sonship who have most accurately understood and recognized the extent of the impact that he had on today's movement of grace. When one considers the scope and breadth of his influence on Reformed leaders—at Westminster Theological Seminary; Covenant Theological Seminary; Covenant College, where Sonship was taught as a DMin course; Leighton Ford's Arrow Leadership Training; the Navigators; WHM; MTW; Mission to North America; and Reformed Theological Seminary—it becomes difficult to overstate the expansive influence that the Sonship movement has had on almost every major Reformed Presbyterian institution and network that is part of or associated with the OPC and the PCA.

When asked how he would assess the impact that Jack has left on the church today, William Edgar paused for a moment before responding, "Let me put it to you this way. Jacques Derrida, who was famous for deconstruction, was once asked later in his life, '. . . Is [deconstruction] still . . . a hot topic?' And [Derrida] said, 'No, but it's all over the place.' [Jack's impact] is more in the people he affected and the movements that came out of that. . . . I think he had a great impact in that way."

Years after Jack's death, authors such as Dane Ortlund and Trevin Wax made note of the proliferation of the term "gospel-centered" today. Wax called it "a new buzzword in evangelical circles."[9] But such grace- and gospel-centered language dates back to Jack Miller—the phrases "grace centered" and "gospel centered" show up in early Sonship materials, dating back to 1988, and in lectures that Jack gave at NLC and WHM.

The Legacy of Jack Miller

The reporting of the *New York Times* and *Time* magazine on the Calvinist revival anticipates an implosion of New Calvinism through infighting—one that would increase the irrelevancy of the church in modern times.[10] Yet Jack Miller's constructive, gospel-centered Calvinism may well hold answers for discordant Calvinists as well as for non-Calvinists. The fullness of his life, teaching, and ministry may also help to bring unity to Presbyterians who are confessionally and missionally divided. Jack stands as an exemplar of a practical and positive Calvinism—as a man who demonstrated missional adeptness and wisdom while holding fast his confessional commitments, which enabled him to work closely and constructively with people who disagreed with him.

The honesty Jack showed in the way he assessed Sonship, himself as a leader, and his Calvinism could be unnerving to those who were unaccustomed to leading a lifestyle of faith and repentance. Over and again, Jack wrestled with the mortification of his self-centered pride, which taught him that "the way up is the way down," that "grace runs downhill to the foot of the cross," and that a leader must lead in repentance as well as in faith. Likewise, the bold spiritual inquiries he made into the lives of others were not laced with theological superiority. Rather, they were joyful invitations for people to share together in God's welcome with him at the foot of the cross. He welcomed other sinners such as himself—which included Calvinist scholars and leaders like himself—the way Christ had welcomed him, for the glory of God's omnipotent grace (see Rom. 15:7).

Jack's primary goal was not to start a movement or become a celebrity preacher with a large following. His primary goal was, according to Rose Marie, "to show the church [and the world] that he knew he was a deeply flawed sinner, but he also knew where he could find grace and how to share it." She went on to say in her epilogue to Jack's final book, "Once, a dying patient told Jack that she wasn't interested in going to heaven because it would be too boring. Jack asked her, 'What was the happiest moment of your life?' She said, 'The best and happiest times of my life came when I was with someone I really loved.' Jack replied, 'That is what makes heaven so very special. Jesus is my very best friend. And the great thing about heaven is being there forever with your best and truest friend.'"[12]

More than anything else, Jack wanted to introduce his best and truest friend to everyone he knew. *Cheer Up! The Life and Ministry of Jack Miller* suggests a headline writ larger than the one that was published by *The New York Times*: "Cheer Up! God's Grace Is Far Greater Than You Ever Dared Hope." In the words of Jack Miller himself,

[We have] *not* been called to create the mandate for evangelism nor must [we] provide the spiritual power to carry it out. The Lord of the church is the one who has furnished both the mandate and the means for her global witness. We might say that we do not create Pentecost; Pentecost creates us. We are part of God's new creation, joining with Christ as He extends the spread of new life around the globe. All that is asked of us is that we lay hold of Christ in such a way that our lives are daily transformed to share the mind, power and heart of the Lord Jesus.[13]

A LAST WORD FROM ROSE MARIE MILLER

HE WAS AN ordinary man.

Jack was born in Gold Beach, on the southern coast of Oregon, where the swift-flowing Rogue River rushes to join the Pacific Ocean. His six siblings had grown up in the wilds of Oregon, going to a one-room schoolhouse and learning from their father, at an early age, to shoot and to survive in the wilderness. Then, before Jack was born, his family moved to the coast.

His grandmother had come to Oregon on a covered wagon when she was three years old. His mother had the same pioneer spirit and had carved a home in the wilds of Oregon for her family. Jack loved and admired his mother. As far as he knew, she was capable of fixing anything. And, while she did not know much about God or the Bible, she did know that one day Jesus would return on a cloud. This she communicated to her young son—so much so that when Jack coveted a set of deer horns in a neighbor's yard, he checked the clouds to see if Jesus might be coming. The sky was clear, so he took the deer horns. (Later they were returned.) This was the kind of religious education he received at home. He also went to the small Presbyterian church in town, although at first he didn't think it had anything to offer him. Eventually, however, he would ask to preach in it.

Jack's father, a skilled hunter, was killed in a hunting accident when Jack was two years old. His mother remarried, and her husband was verbally abusive to him. Jack's older brother, Leo, nurtured and cared for him, becoming the only "father" he knew. He often spent the summers on Forest Service lookouts with Leo, learning to shoot, watch for fires, track animals, and cook a pot of beans on a cast-iron stove. He experienced a deep heartache at about the age of sixteen when Leo was killed in World War II, causing him to lose a brother, a friend, a father. This was pivotal for him. Although he loved Oregon, Jack refused to put up with his stepfather's abuse and took the bus to San Francisco to live with his sister.

The qualities of rootlessness, pride, independence, and self-sufficiency were handed down to Jack, and he embraced them. Added to this was his firm conviction that God did not exist. He was a confirmed atheist. Also, like many of his generation, Jack believed that you never complained, never explained, and never discussed heart issues. All these things went on to shape our marriage more than we realized while it was happening, and he continued to struggle with them for the rest of his life.

One day God met this proud young man and showed him that Jack was not God. On that day, Jack's pride—his whole independent being—was humbled. Rootless no more, he found a Father.

Jack and I met in a small Presbyterian church in San Francisco. Two people could not be more different than we were. My parents were immigrants from Germany. They too never discussed heart issues—least of all to me. Even when my mother tried to take her life when I was about twelve years old, we never talked about it. Only through God's grace were Jack and I able to see how our marriage was impacted by the legacies that both our families had left in our lives.

We did, however, agree from the outset on some very basic things: Jack (a college student at the time) would finish his education, I would not work outside the home, we would live each day on what God provided, and if God gave us children we would love, teach, and nourish them. We both had a very strong conviction that God was our Father and that he would provide. For ten years I believed that God was for us—was with us . . . until Jack became a pastor. That story is told in my book *From Fear to Freedom*, so I won't repeat it here.

Now, in a sense, I can have the last word after being married to a man who always had lots of words. When Michael Graham asked me to write a "special note from Rose Marie," my first thought was "Yes, I can do this," and my second thought was "I can't do this."

Then I began to seriously reflect on our forty-six years of marriage. Now my last words are *Thank you, Jack.*

Thank you for the Easter hat you bought me when we barely had enough money for food.

Thank you for teaching me how to cook—I learned to put together a tasty pot of beans.

Thank you for not criticizing my cooking when the two of us and our three children were eating on ten dollars a week and I had to stretch.

Thank you for teaching me how to shoot on a Forest Service lookout in Oregon during our first summer together. There were always a lot of empty tin cans to use as our targets, since our staples were canned food that the Forest Service brought us.

Thank you for opening up Shakespeare to me. How could I have gone through four years of university and never studied his writings?

Thank you for being a partner with me as we cared for the four children we had in four years: Roseann, Ruth, Paul, and Barbara. You changed diapers, you washed dishes, you scrubbed floors, you worked to provide for us, and you never made excuses—even when you still had to finish university and later complete your PhD.

Thank you for listening to me when I wanted another baby five years after our first four, which led to Keren's four siblings welcoming her.

Then, after we fast-forward through many tears:

Thank you for listening to the Spirit when you went through your own midlife crisis and, out of that, began to listen to me.

Thank you for listening when I said, "I don't believe in God, and I don't even know he exists"—for not correcting or preaching and, instead, just taking my hand as we walked around the lake in Tennessee.

Thank you for lifting up the cup and breaking the bread in a communion service in Switzerland—an act that God used to reach my stubborn, hard heart. I believe it was the first time I saw how serious my sin against God was—while also being covered by the blood of Christ and totally forgiven.

Thank you for not blaming me when two of our children went, as the Prodigal Son did, to the "far country"—a painful time for both of us, when we simply prayed together, since neither of us knew how to rescue them.

Thank you for humbling your heart and seeking out Barbara when I could not.

Thank you for saying, "Rose Marie, you act like an orphan" when I was devastated by what I had seen in our first trip to Uganda. That was life-changing for me.

Thank you for believing that I had a message to share with women and for not scolding me when I quit in the middle of a week of teaching because I was convinced I didn't know what I was doing.

Thank you for accepting me when I said, "This is it. I am never coming back to Uganda. From now on you can go by yourself."

Thank you for insisting that I write *From Fear to Freedom*—a book that I resisted writing, but one that ultimately allowed me to tell my story.

Thank you for bringing me along on the journey of grace—no easy task, as you spent hour after hour listening to my questions.

Thank you for showing me how important prayer is and for praying at all times, in all places, for all people. This I truly miss.

Thank you for opening up the Word of God to me—especially the books of Romans and Galatians. Even three years of Bible school hadn't taught me the wonders of the truths these two amazing books contain. They are a marvel of pure, undeserved grace that is for desperately needy sinners. "Jesus paid it all; all to Him I owe." Most of the time I did not know how needy I was—and still am.

Another big thanks to you for the vision that you had for helping Bob and Keren to start a mission among Indians living in London. Though you did not live to see it, there are now five church plants in the greater London area—which is where I serve today. To God be the glory!

And, to summarize all of these last words: Thank you, Jack, for the passion you had to spread the gospel and the vision you had to share it with the world. Thank you for loving me enough to insist that I join you on this amazing journey.

I miss you.

Rose Marie Miller
From Fear to Freedom
Nothing Is Impossible with God
Parenting by Grace

ACKNOWLEDGMENTS

THROUGHOUT THE WORK I have done on the Jack Miller Project, of which *Cheer Up!* is the firstfruit, I have been utterly amazed at the team of people who came together to help to make this book possible. Many people have contributed to the project over the years, and in many ways, so if I have left you out please forgive me.

I am deeply grateful to everyone who took part in interviews and exchanged emails with me as I was working on the Jack Miller Project: Raju Abraham, Jay E. Adams, Drew Angus, Saroj Balvinder, Josiah Bancroft, Frank Barker, William Barker, Jerry Bridges, Steve Brown, David Clowney, Jean Coley, Ruth Correnti, Robert Custer, D. Clair Davis, Robert DeMoss, Steve DeMoss, Hunter Dockery, Rick Downs, William Edgar, Meredith Elder, Sandy Elder, Paul Elliot, Sinclair Ferguson, John Frame, John Freeman, Ben Gardner, David Garner, Robert Godfrey, Clyde Godwin, Dave Green, Tom Hawkes, Steve Henderson, Barry Henning, Keren Heppe, Robert Heppe, Dan Herron, Ian Alastair Hewitson, William Iverson, Dennis Johnson, Angelo Juliani, Barbara Miller Juliani, John Julien, Elizabeth Kaufmann, Richard Kaufmann, Timothy Keller, Dick Keyes, Patric Knaak, Paul Köoistra, Henry Krabbendam, William Krispin, Allen Lawrence Jr., Jack Lonas, Johnny Wade Long, Ron Lusk, Ron Lutz, Sue Lutz, Dan Macha, Dave McCarty, Mary Ann McGuire, Jeff McMullin, Paul E. Miller, Rose Marie Miller, Charles Morris, Gary North, Joe Novenson, Bob Osborne,

Wy Plummer, Vern S. Poythress, Harry Reeder, Mark Rushdoony, Jeffrey Salasin, Kefa Sempangi, Stephen Smallman, John F. Smed, Scotty Ward Smith, Robert B. Strimple, William Stump, Mike Tannous, Roseann Trott, Tim J. R. Trumper, Paul Tsou, William Viss, Jeff Whitted, and John Yenchko.

Additionally, New Life Church Glenside, the PCA Historical Center, the OPC's Presbytery of Philadelphia, the Philadelphia Presbytery of the PCA, Westminster Theological Seminary, New Growth Press, and other groups and organizations gave me access to media, newsletters, minutes, and other important archival material related to Jack Miller. Thank you for your help.

A large team of outside readers reviewed the chapters of the initial dissertation (and sometimes revisions of those chapters) in order to ensure their accuracy. In particular, I would like to thank the scholars who helped to edit and more clearly articulate some of the sections that contain important historical and theological nuances regarding Jack's life and ministry.

My special thanks to Rose Marie Miller and Bob and Keren Heppe, who opened their home and gave me the opportunity to hold days of recorded interviews with them about Jack's life and ministry. Thank you for your hospitality and your participation in the Jack Miller Project. Rose Marie prayed, and recruited others to pray, that this biography of her husband would bring glory to God—a goal that I adopted as my own, as well. I also want to express my gratitude to Paul Miller for the multiple recorded interviews and follow-up conversations he had with me, which improved the content of this study. I am humbled by and grateful to the entire Miller family for allowing me to have such open access to all things Jack Miller for the purpose of writing a useful biography.

My desire has been to handle with integrity the trust that has been granted to me by those who participated in the research for this book. Although I did not directly quote from all of the invaluable interviews I had with these participants, they together provided the well-rounded picture of Jack that I needed in order to write a biography of his life and ministry.

Hickory Grove Church (PCA) played a vital role in the completion of this biography. Its leaders would likely have asked me more questions at the outset if they had known beforehand how much time and energy would be required to complete the book. Hickory Grove has been the ideal church partner for this labor of love.

Those who know me know that I need an entire team of excellent editors, and the sovereign Lord provided exactly the team I needed. I would like to give special recognition to these editors, who took Jack's biography from being a dissertation to being a published book—beginning with Pamela White, a long-time member of Hickory Grove Church. She made this biography exponentially more readable, which in turn made P&R's decision to publish it much easier. I would also like to express my gratitude to Dr. Stephen Stout for the patient help he provided with SBL's style requirements during the biography's dissertation phase. And when I began working with P&R, the sovereign Lord again provided a stellar team of editors who had just as much patience with my circular and confusing thought processes. I don't know what I would have done without the excellent wisdom and work of Amanda Martin, editorial director at P&R Publishing, along with the detailed and thoughtful help of Aaron Gottier, P&R's senior copyeditor.

I am grateful to my daughter Molly Lukić, who spent the summer of 2016 transcribing interviews and who proofread the final version of the dissertation. She has also managed the Jack Miller Project's Facebook page, and my son James Graham and son-in-law Michael Pollard have helped to build the Jack Miller Project's website.

Dr. Daniel Akin deserves credit for the prophetic vision he had that led him to graciously challenge me to "record the life and ministry of Jack Miller for the church while so many people he impacted were still alive" and for taking over as my doctoral supervisor when I decided to change my dissertation into a biography. Clearly the sovereign Lord appointed Dr. Akin to wisely oversee and patiently guide Jack's biography to its completion. I am equally grateful to John Hughes, the academic project manager at P&R, for taking such an interest in Jack's biography, introducing me to P&R, and guiding me—a new author—through the book-proposal process.

My wife, Vicki, has sacrificed more than anyone else has to enable this biography of Jack Miller to become a reality. When she returned to working full-time so that our children could graduate from college without debt, she did not plan on going on to also underwrite my doctoral studies for the past seven years or the research and writing that this biography required during the last four years. She has encouraged and pushed me when over and over again I wanted to quit. Thank you, Vicki, for partnering with me in the Jack Miller Project and, more importantly, for your steadfast love and encouragement throughout the past thirty years of marriage. And yes—my doctoral research and the writing of Jack's biography are finally over. Sovereign Lord, thank you for knowing the lifelong marriage partner whom I would need—one who is so much like you!

Above all, I want to praise the Lord Jesus Christ for affording me the great privilege of researching and writing this biography of the life and ministry of Jack Miller. It has been among the greatest joys of my life. Along with Jack, I pray that the sovereign Lord would use his story to help many people discover and rediscover "what has happened to all [their] joy."

NOTES

PUBLISHED SOURCES THAT are quoted or referenced throughout the book are cited below. Any quotations in the book that are not cited are taken from unpublished writings, audio recordings, and interviews, many of which are stored in extensive archival collections (see p. 228).

Introduction: Cheer Up! What Has Happened to All Your Joy?

1. Dennis E. Johnson, *Him We Proclaim: Preaching Christ from All the Scriptures* (Phillipsburg, NJ: P&R Publishing, 2007), 54.

2. Timothy Keller, in turn, often repeats these two most familiar of Jack's "cheer up" statements—for example, he has written, "The gospel is this: We are more sinful and flawed in ourselves than we ever dared believe, yet at the very same time we are more loved and accepted in Jesus Christ than we ever dared hope." Timothy Keller with Kathy Keller, *The Meaning of Marriage: Facing the Complexities of Commitment with the Wisdom of God* (New York: Dutton, 2011), 48.

3. C. John Miller, *Outgrowing the Ingrown Church* (Grand Rapids: Zondervan, 1986), 74.

4. Steve Brown, "Who's on the Pedestal?" *The Plain Truth*, May/June 2001, http://www.ptm.org/01PT/MayJun/sbremind.htm.

Chapter 1: Cheer Up! God's Grace Is Far Greater Than You Ever Dared Hope

1. C. John Miller, *A Faith Worth Sharing: A Lifetime of Conversations about Christ* (Phillipsburg, NJ: P&R Publishing, 1999), 48.

2. Miller, 51.

3. Miller, 50.

4. Miller, 50.

5. Miller, 51.

6. Miller, 77.

7. C. John Miller, *Powerful Evangelism for the Powerless* (Phillipsburg, NJ: P&R Publishing, 1997), 53.

8. Gary Kamiya, *Cool Gray City of Love: 49 Views of San Francisco* (2013; repr., New York: Bloomsbury, 2014), 14.

9. Miller, *A Faith Worth Sharing*, 24–25.

10. Miller, 29.

11. Miller, 28.

12. Miller, 27.

13. Miller, 31.

14. Miller, 34.

15. Miller, 34.

16. Miller, 41.

Chapter 2: Cheer Up! You Are Far Worse Than You Think

1. Rose Marie Miller, *Nothing Is Impossible with God: Reflections on Weakness, Faith, and Power* (Greensboro, NC: New Growth Press, 2012), chap. 1, Kindle.

2. C. John Miller, *A Faith Worth Sharing: A Lifetime of Conversations about Christ* (Phillipsburg, NJ: P&R Publishing, 1999), 59. In his own account, Jack refers to Fisk using the pseudonym Thomas Trask.

3. Both the quote from Fisk and Jack's own paraphrase are from Miller, 60.

4. Miller, 60–61.

5. Miller, 62.

6. Miller, 62.

7. Miller, 62.

8. Miller, 63.

9. Miller, 63. The original quotation says, "Dr. Trask."

10. Miller, 64.

11. Miller, 68.

12. Jack Miller, letter to the editor, *The Presbyterian Guardian* 33, no. 7 (September 1964): 114.

13. D. Clair Davis, "The Significance of Westminster Theological Seminary Today," September 20, 2012, https://docs.google.com /document/d/1FZbqGq10PI2jQ2wMpG6XtL0hdDKLTkYk tvkxJlz-SBU/edit.

14. Edmund P. Clowney, "Moulded by the Gospel," *The Presbyterian Guardian* 38, no. 5 (May 1969): 55.

15. Clowney, 56.

16. Clowney, 57.

17. Cornelius Van Til, "Why Westminster Today," 1970, available online from Presuppositionalism 101 at https://presupp101.files .wordpress.com/2019/05/van-til-why-westminster-today.pdf.

18. Quoted in Mark R. Rushdoony, "Rousas John Rushdoony: A Brief History, Part VII—'He's on the Lord's Side,'" *Faith for All of Life*, January/February 2017, 3.

19. John M. Frame, "Machen's Warrior Children," The Works of John Frame & Vern Poythress, June 6, 2012, https://frame -poythress.org/machens-warrior-children/; taken from John M. Frame, "Machen's Warrior Children," in *Alister E. McGrath and Evangelical Theology: A Dynamic Engagement*, ed. Sung Wook Chung (Grand Rapids: Baker Academic, 2003), 113–46.

20. C. John Miller, *Evangelism and Your Church* (Phillipsburg, NJ: Presbyterian and Reformed Publishing Company, 1980), 5; quoting from George Redford and John Angell James, eds., *The Autobiography of William Jay* (1855; repr., London: The Banner of Truth Trust, 1974), 569, where this quotation first appeared.

21. Jay E. Adams, *Biblical Sonship: An Evaluation of the Sonship Discipleship Course* (Woodruff, SC: Timeless Texts, 1999), 6.

22. C. John Miller, *Outgrowing the Ingrown Church* (Grand Rapids: Zondervan, 1986), 21.

23. Miller, 20–21.

24. Miller, 21.

25. Miller, 21.

26. Both Lovelace quotations in this paragraph are from Richard F. Lovelace, *Dynamics of Spiritual Life: An Evangelical Theology of Renewal* (Downers Grove, IL: IVP Academic, 1979), 207; quoted in Miller, Outgrowing the Ingrown Church, 21.

27. Miller, *A Faith Worth Sharing*, 88.

28. Miller, *Outgrowing the Ingrown Church*, 21.

29. Miller, 21.

30. Miller, 21.

Chapter 3: Cheer Up! God's Spirit Works in Your Weakness

1. C. John Miller, "Prayer and Evangelism," in *The Pastor–Evangelist: Preacher, Model, and Mobilizer for Church Growth*, ed. Roger S. Greenway (Phillipsburg, NJ: Presbyterian and Reformed Publishing Company, 1987), 39.

2. C. John Miller, *Evangelism and Your Church* (Phillipsburg, NJ: Presbyterian and Reformed Publishing Company, 1980), 41.

3. Quoted in C. John Miller, *Powerful Evangelism for the Powerless* (Phillipsburg, NJ: P&R Publishing, 1997), 16.

4. Miller, 16.

5. Miller, 15.

6. Miller, *Evangelism and Your Church*, 40–41. Emphasis in original.

7. Miller, "Prayer and Evangelism," 40.

8. C. John Miller, *Repentance: A Daring Call to Real Surrender* (Fort Washington, PA: CLC Publications, 2009), chap. 4, Kindle.

9. Miller, chap. 7.

10. J. H. Bavinck, *An Introduction to the Science of Missions*, trans. David Hugh Freeman (1960; repr., Phillipsburg, NJ: P&R Publishing, 1992), 222.

11. Bavinck, 222.

12. Bavinck, 271–72.

13. Bavinck, 222.

14. Miller, *Repentance*, chap. 6.

15. Quoted in Miller, epilogue.

16. Miller, chap. 6.

17. Miller, "A Note to the Reader."

18. Miller, chap. 7.
19. Miller, *Outgrowing the Ingrown Church*, 32.
20. Miller, *Repentance*, chap. 7.
21. Miller, *Outgrowing the Ingrown Church*, 24.
22. Miller, 24.
23. C. John Miller, *A Faith Worth Sharing: A Lifetime of Conversations about Christ* (Phillipsburg, NJ: P&R Publishing, 1999), 90.
24. Miller, *Outgrowing the Ingrown Church*, 41.
25. Miller, 41–42.
26. Miller, *Repentance*, epilogue.
27. D. Martyn Lloyd-Jones, *Spiritual Depression: Its Causes and Its Cure* (Grand Rapids: Wm. B. Eerdmans, 1965), 21.
28. Miller, *Outgrowing the Ingrown Church*, 155.
29. Miller, 156.
30. Rose Marie Miller, *Nothing Is Impossible with God: Reflections on Weakness, Faith, and Power* (Greensboro, NC: New Growth Press, 2012), chap. 1, Kindle.
31. Miller, *Outgrowing the Ingrown Church*, 154–55.
32. Rose Marie Miller, *From Fear to Freedom: Living as Sons and Daughters of God* (Colorado Springs: Shaw Books, 1994), 66.
33. Miller, *Outgrowing the Ingrown Church*, 155.

Chapter 4: Cheer Up! Justification Is by Faith Alone, Even in the Twentieth Century

1. See A. Donald MacLeod, *W. Stanford Reid: An Evangelical Calvinist in the Academy* (Montreal: McGill–Queen's University Press, 2004), 259.
2. MacLeod, 259.
3. MacLeod, 259.
4. Geerhardus Vos, *The Pauline Eschatology* (1930; repr., Grand Rapids: Baker Book House, 1979), 149.
5. John Calvin, *Institutes of the Christian Religion*, trans. Henry Beveridge, vol. 2 (Edinburgh, 1845), 3.14.11.
6. Jack's version of a similar stretch of wording from Beveridge's translation of Calvin, *Institutes of the Christian Religion*, 3.14.13.

Chapter 5: Cheer Up! God's Kingdom Is More Wonderful Than You Ever Imagined

1. F. Kefa Sempangi with Jennifer Melvin, *From the Dust: A Sequel to* A Distant Grief (Eugene, OR: Wipf and Stock, 2008), 1.
2. F. Kefa Sempangi, *A Distant Grief: The Real Story Behind the Martyrdom of Christians in Uganda* (Ventura, CA: Regal Books, 1979; repr., Eugene, OR: Wipf and Stock, 2006), 179.
3. Rose Marie Miller, *Nothing Is Impossible with God: Reflections on Weakness, Faith, and Power* (Greensboro, NC: New Growth Press, 2012), chap. 9, Kindle.
4. Miller, chap. 9.
5. C. John Miller and Barbara Miller Juliani, *Come Back, Barbara*, 3rd ed. (Phillipsburg, NJ: P&R Publishing, 2020), 125.
6. Miller and Juliani, 125.
7. Miller and Juliani, 125.
8. Quoted in Miller and Juliani, 126.
9. Miller and Juliani, 126.
10. Miller and Juliani, xii.
11. Miller and Juliani, 51.
12. Rose Marie Miller, *From Fear to Freedom: Living as Sons and Daughters of God* (Colorado Springs: Shaw Books, 1994), 78.
13. Miller and Juliani, *Come Back, Barbara*, 101.
14. Miller and Juliani, 101.
15. Miller and Juliani, 113.
16. Miller and Juliani, 115.
17. Miller and Juliani, 115.
18. Miller and Juliani, 116.
19. Miller and Juliani, 116.
20. Miller and Juliani, 116.
21. Miller and Juliani, 116.
22. Miller and Juliani, 116–17.
23. All quotations in this paragraph are from Miller and Juliani, 126.
24. Both of the quotations in this paragraph are from Miller and Juliani, 127.

25. Miller and Juliani, 136.

26. C. John Miller, *A Faith Worth Sharing: A Lifetime of Conversations about Christ* (Phillipsburg, NJ: P&R Publishing, 1999), 134.

27. Quoted in Miller, 134.

28. Miller, 135.

29. Miller, 135.

30. All quotations in this paragraph are from C. John Miller, "Let Us Pray," *New Horizons* 9, no. 3 (March 1988): 4.

31. All quotations in this paragraph are from C. John Miller, letter to the editor, *The Philadelphia Inquirer*, July 2, 1988, 10.

Chapter 6: Cheer Up! Come On, Let's Die Together! It's a Great Way to Come to Life

1. C. John Miller, *Evangelism and Your Church* (Phillipsburg, NJ: Presbyterian and Reformed Publishing Company, 1980), 5–6.

2. Both of the quotes in this sentence are from Miller, 6.

3. Miller, 6.

4. Both of the quotes in this sentence are from Miller, 6.

5. C. John Miller, *The Heart of a Servant Leader: Letters from Jack Miller*, ed. Barbara Miller Juliani (Phillipsburg, NJ: P&R Publishing, 2004), 79.

Conclusion: Cheer Up! The Way Up Is the Way Down

1. "Unprecedented" is how Hunter describes such a figure. See James Davison Hunter, *To Change the World: The Irony, Tragedy, and Possibility of Christianity in the Late Modern World* (New York: Oxford University Press, 2010), 38. For more on the dynamics beind gospel-centered movements, see Timothy Keller, "Movement," in *Center Church: Doing Balanced, Gospel-Centered Ministry in Your City* (Grand Rapids: Zondervan, 2012), 249–380.

2. Jay E. Adams, *Biblical Sonship: An Evaluation of the Sonship Discipleship Course* (Woodruff, SC: Timeless Texts, 1999), 1.

3. See Tim J. R. Trumper, *When History Teaches Us Nothing: The*

Recent Reformed Sonship Debate in Context (Eugene, OR: Wipf and Stock, 2008), 54–55. See also 56–77.

4. Quoted in Trumper, 57n12.

5. Quoted in Trumper, 54.

6. See Collin Hansen, *Young, Restless, Reformed: A Journalist's Journey with the New Calvinists* (Wheaton, IL: Crossway, 2008), 29.

7. See David Van Biema, "10 Ideas Changing the World Right Now," *Time*, March 12, 2009, http://content.time.com/time/specials/packages/article/0,28804,1884779_1884782_1884760,00.html.

8. Mark Oppenheimer, "Evangelicals Find Themselves in the Midst of a Calvinist Revival," *The New York Times*, January 3, 2014, https://www.nytimes.com/2014/01/04/us/a-calvinist-revival-for-evangelicals.html?_r=0.

9. Trevin Wax, *Counterfeit Gospels: Rediscovering the Good News in a World of False Hope* (Chicago: Moody Publishers, 2011), 15–16. See also Dane Ortlund, "What's All This 'Gospel-Centered' Talk About?" The Gospel Coalition, September 16, 2014, https://www.thegospelcoalition.org/article/whats-all-this-gospel-centered-talk-about/.

10. *Time* magazine is particularly foreboding: "It will be interesting to see whether Calvin's latest legacy will be classic Protestant backbiting or whether, during these hard times, more Christians searching for security will submit their wills to the austerely demanding God of their country's infancy." Biema, "10 Ideas Changing the World Right Now."

11. C. John Miller, *A Faith Worth Sharing: A Lifetime of Conversations about Christ* (Phillipsburg, NJ: P&R Publishing, 1999), 141.

12. C. John Miller, *Evangelism and Your Church* (Phillipsburg, NJ: Presbyterian and Reformed Publishing Company, 1980), 101.

SELECTED BIBLIOGRAPHY

Key Sources

Adams, Jay E. *Biblical Sonship: An Evaluation of the Sonship Discipleship Course.* Woodruff, SC: Timeless Texts, 1999.

Bavinck, J. H. *An Introduction to the Science of Missions.* Translated by David Hugh Freeman. 1960. Reprint, Phillipsburg, NJ: P&R Publishing, 1992.

Clowney, Edmund P. "Moulded by the Gospel." *The Presbyterian Guardian* 38, no. 5 (May 1969): 55–58.

Davis, D. Clair. "The Significance of Westminster Theological Seminary Today." September 20, 2012. Available online at https://docs .google.com/document/d/1FZbqGq10PI2jQ2wMpG6XtL0hd DKLTkYktvkxJlz-SBU/edit.

Dooyeweerd, Herman. *A New Critique of Theoretical Thought.* Vol. 1, *The Necessary Presuppositions of Philosophy,* translated by David H. Freeman and William S. Young. Philadelphia: The Presbyterian and Reformed Publishing Company, 1953.

Frame, John M. "Machen's Warrior Children." The Works of John Frame & Vern Poythress. June 6, 2012. https://frame-poythress.org /machens-warrior-children/.

Hewitson, Ian A. *Trust and Obey: Norman Shepherd and the Justification Controversy at Westminster Theological Seminary.* Minneapolis: Next-Step Resources, 2011.

Kamiya, Gary. *Cool Gray City of Love: 49 Views of San Francisco.* 2013. Reprint, New York: Bloomsbury, 2014.

Keller, Timothy. *Center Church: Doing Balanced, Gospel-Centered Ministry in Your City.* Grand Rapids: Zondervan, 2012.

Luther, Martin. *Commentary on Romans.* Translated by J. Theodore Mueller. 1954. Reprint, Grand Rapids: Kregel Classics, 2003.

———. *Galatians.* The Crossway Classic Commentaries. Wheaton, IL: Crossway, 1998.

MacLeod, A. Donald. *W. Stanford Reid: An Evangelical Calvinist in the Academy.* Montreal: McGill–Queen's University Press, 2004.

McVicar, Michael J. "Aggressive Philanthropy: Progressivism, Conservatism, and the William Volker Charities Fund." *Missouri Historical Review* 105, no. 4 (July 2011): 191–212.

———. "Reconstructing America: Religion, American Conservatism, and the Political Theology of Rousas John Rushdoony." PhD diss., The Ohio State University, 2010. https://citeseerx.ist.psu.edu/view doc/download?doi=10.1.1.1033.5085&rep=rep1&type=pdf.

Miller, C. John. *A Faith Worth Sharing: A Lifetime of Conversations about Christ.* Phillipsburg, NJ: P&R Publishing, 1999.

———. *Evangelism and Your Church.* Phillipsburg, NJ: Presbyterian and Reformed Publishing Company, 1980.

———. *Outgrowing the Ingrown Church.* Grand Rapids: Zondervan, 1986.

———. *Powerful Evangelism for the Powerless.* Phillipsburg, NJ: P&R Publishing, 1997.

———. "Prayer and Evangelism." In *The Pastor-Evangelist: Preacher, Model, and Mobilizer for Church Growth*, 33–51. Edited by Roger S. Greenway. Phillipsburg, NJ: Presbyterian and Reformed Publishing Company, 1987.

———. *Repentance: A Daring Call to Real Surrender.* Fort Washington, PA: CLC Publications, 2009.

———. *The Heart of a Servant Leader: Letters from Jack Miller.* Edited by Barbara Miller Juliani. Phillipsburg, NJ: P&R Publishing, 2004.

Miller, C. John, and Barbara Miller Juliani. *Come Back, Barbara.* 3rd ed. Phillipsburg, NJ: P&R Publishing, 2020.

Miller, Rose Marie. *From Fear to Freedom: Living as Sons and Daughters of God.* Colorado Springs: Shaw Books, 1994.

———. *Nothing Is Impossible with God: Reflections on Weakness, Faith, and Power.* Greensboro, NC: New Growth Press, 2012. Kindle.

Robertson, O. Palmer. "The Current Justification Controversy." *The Trinity Review,* July/August 2003. http://www.trinityfoundation .org/PDF/The%20Trinity%20Review%200203a%20TheCurrent JustificationControversy.pdf.

———. *The Current Justification Controversy.* Unicoi, TN: The Trinity Foundation, 2003.

Rushdoony, Mark R. "Rousas John Rushdoony: A Brief History, Part VII—'He's on the Lord's Side.'" *Faith for All of Life,* January/February 2017.

Sempangi, F. Kefa. *A Distant Grief: The Real Story Behind the Martyrdom of Christians in Uganda.* Ventura, CA: Regal Books, 1979.

———. *From the Dust: A Sequel to* A Distant Grief. Eugene, OR: Wipf and Stock, 2008.

Serge. *Sonship.* 3rd ed. Greensboro, NC: New Growth Press, 2013.

Sponaugle, Ella Mae. *Iva.* Morrisville, NC: Lulu Press, 2013.

Trumper, Tim J. R. "An Historical Study of the Doctrine of Adoption in the Calvinistic Tradition." PhD diss., University of Edinburgh, 2001. https://www.era.lib.ed.ac.uk/bitstream/1842/6803/1/533896.pdf.

———. *When History Teaches Us Nothing: The Recent Reformed Sonship Debate in Context.* Eugene, OR: Wipf and Stock, 2008.

Van Til, Cornelius. "Why Westminster Today." 1970. Available online from Presuppositionalism 101 at https://presupp101.files.wordpress .com/2019/05/van-til-why-westminster-today.pdf.

Vos, Geerhardus. *The Teaching of Jesus concerning the Kingdom of God and the Church.* New York: American Tract Society, 1903.

———. *The Pauline Eschatology.* 1930. Reprint, Grand Rapids: Baker Book House, 1979.

Warfield, Benjamin B. "Are They Few That Be Saved?" 1918. Available online from Reformed Theology and Apologetics at https://reformed .org/eschaton/few_saved.pdf.

Manuscript Collections

Many of the unpublished sources—such as letters, journals, church newsletters, and session minutes—that contributed valuable information and quoted material to this book can be found within a few collections of works that relate to Jack Miller and Westminster Theological Seminary.

C. John Miller Oral History Interview Collection. Archives and Special Collections. Southeastern Baptist Theological Seminary Library, Wake Forest, North Carolina.

The C. John Miller Manuscript Collection. Presbyterian Church in America (PCA) Historical Center, St. Louis, Missouri.

Archives. The Montgomery Library of the Westminster Theological Seminary, Glenside, Pennsylvania.

Complete Online Bibliography

A full listing of the many sources that were consulted as part of the research for this book is available in a complete bibliography that may be accessed online.

Graham, Michael A. "Bibliography." Research. The Jack Miller Project. Accessed November 12, 2020. https://thejackmillerproject.com/research/.

Did you find this book helpful?
Consider leaving a review online.
The author appreciates your feedback!

Or write to P&R at editorial@prpbooks.com
with your comments. We'd love to hear from you.